FORD CONSUL, ZEPHYR AND ZODIAC

Other titles in the Crowood AutoClassic Series

FORD CONSUL, ZEPHYR AND ZODIAC

GRAHAM ROBSON

THE CROWOOD PRESS

First published in 2007 by
The Crowood Press Ltd
Ramsbury, Marlborough
Wiltshire SN8 2HR

www.crowood.com

British Library Cataloguing-in-Publication Data
A catalogue record for this book is available from the British Library.

ISBN 978 1 86126 9430

Designed and edited by Focus Publishing,
Sevenoaks, Kent

Printed and bound in India by Replika Press Pvt. Ltd. ·

Contents

Introduction

The family Consul was the very first new car I ever drove, the car in which I passed my driving test, and the car in which I competed in my very first rally, and because of this I suppose it was inevitable that, one day, I would want to write a book about the famous Consul-Zephyr-Zodiac model range. Perhaps I should be more discreet over the other 'first' – that it was also the car in which I enjoyed many a sweet romantic interlude as well.

That black Consul – LYG 131, registered in Yorkshire, and remaining in the family for more than ten years – arrived in 1953 when there was still a waiting list for all new motor cars. Not only was it the first car I ever drove, it was also the first new car my father had ever owned. He enjoyed it enough to go on local club rallies in Yorkshire, with me learning the co-driving trade alongside him – though we couldn't make much headway against the TR2s and MG TDs that also turned up. Although we both had to make allowances for the wallowy handling, for the slippery nature of the bench front seat, the rather infuriating steering-column gear change, and the poor traction on slippery surfaces, it was a car we both enjoyed because it served us so well, for so many years. As I recall, it never let us down: there was no MoT test in those days, but if there had been, I am sure it would have sailed through on every occasion.

Reliability, dependability, and sheer family usefulness: that, of course, was the hall-mark of this Ford family, for the company's engineers and managers had always meant it to be that way. In twenty-two years, over four generations, Ford sold Consuls, Zephyrs, Zodiacs and Executives as family and business machines, not as sports models – and did so in huge numbers. Maybe these cars no longer bring tears of nostalgia to many eyes, but as a business project they brought untold profits to the company – and that is what the automotive business is all about.

When I sat down to write this story, I knew it would be relatively easy to provide a blow-by-blow account covering types, sizes, power outputs and production figures, but I wanted to do a lot more than that. I wanted to flesh out the story with a study of personalities, company politics, and national conditions – and of course with the story behind the links with the parent company, Ford-USA. For instance, how important was an ex-GM engineer called Earle MacPherson to this story? Where and how did Ford-UK's long-term king-pin Sir Patrick Hennessy fit in? Who really styled the cars? And how much influence from Dearborn went into the shaping of each generation? What was the rationale that went into providing common parts – 'building blocks', as our generation now calls them – that were not only suitable for two or even three generations of Consul, Zephyr and Zodiac, but were also used in other Ford cars? In addition – and this was very important in marketing terms – how significant was it that the cars should be seen to be competitive in racing and rallying?

As ever, research turned up more and more answers to many of the questions I had never before seen answered, such as why did Ford-UK not build its own convertibles, why did it stay with three-speed gearboxes for so many years, and why did it choose a particular type of independent rear suspension for the Mark IVs? Over the years, the cars were moved gradually further up the social stage – so, was it wise to produce the Executive of the 1960s and 1970s?

This, in other words, was an ever-evolving history that I found absolutely fascinating to investigate, and I hope it gives the reader as much pleasure scanning its pages as it did for me to write it.

Graham Robson 2007

Acknowledgements

Rather than use pictures of restored cars taken in modern surroundings, I tried very hard to locate correct period images taken at the time when each of these models was current. This was not as easy as I had hoped, and I am therefore extremely grateful to two people in Ford's photographic archive, Dave Hill and Steve Roots, who went out of their way to help me when I trawled through their records of transparencies, negatives and computer images. Without them I know this book would contain far fewer illustrations; not only that, but by diligent delving they managed to unveil views, topics and photographs of events I didn't know even existed.

Another hero who shall at last be acknowledged is Philip Young, doyen of the classic rallying movement, who spent much time digging out some images of Mark IIs in rallying, and who encouraged me to search even further to fill in the gaps.

From my own archive, I retrieved many images that had been stored against just such a requirement – which reminds me that previous Ford archive incumbents (Sheila Knapman and Fran Chamberlain among them) have also indulged my search for 'Old Ford' illustrations on previous occasions: both are now happily retired, but I hope they will hear that I am still extremely grateful for their help.

John Mullins (a pseudonym) was also kind enough to let me quote from his extensive review of the Abbott of Farnham business, published in *Thoroughbred & Classic Cars* in the 1990s. And when I came to analyse the industrial story behind the convertible models, I also found Bill Munro's book, *Carbodies, The Complete Story* (published by The Crowood Press in 1998) to be invaluable. Bill is happy to know that this resourceful Coventry-based company is now receiving the attention it deserves.

Finally I want to thank Steve Cropley (editor-in-chief of *Autocar*) for allowing me to quote from that magazine's peerless collection of road tests and performance figures, and also from features and descriptive passages about these cars.

Consul/Zephyr/Zodiac Timeline

1947/1948	Concept design work began on the original Consul/Zephyr range, with direction, styling, and much of the engineering based at Ford-USA in Dearborn, USA.
June 1948	Launch of the first all-new post-war Ford-USA range. No technical link with any European Fords, but with styling that would directly affect the shape of Ford-UK's Consul/Zephyr models.
October 1950	Official preview of the original Consul/Zephyr saloons.
January 1951	Series production began at Dagenham, originally of Consuls, with Zephyrs following shortly afterwards. All cars with four-door saloon styles, bench front seats and steering-column gear changes.
October 1951	Prototypes of Consul/Zephyr convertible models first shown at the London Motor Show. All cars given revised facia/instrument package style.
Mid-1953	First deliveries of Consul and Zephyr convertibles.
October 1953	Launch of the Zephyr Zodiac (usually known as Zodiac) saloon.
October 1954	Launch of the factory-approved (though not manufactured) estate car, by E. D. Abbott of Farnham.
August 1955	Borg Warner overdrive transmission became optional.
February 1956	Original Mark I range replaced by new, larger, re-styled Mark II saloon range.
October 1956	Introduction of Abbott-converted Mark II estates.
February 1959	Introduction of new 'low line' versions of all Consul/Zephyr/Zodiac types.
Mid-1959	Completion of brand new PTA (paint, trim, assembly) building at Dagenham, vital to accommodate the company's expansion plans. Consul/Zephyr/Zodiac assembly was transferred to this new plant at once.
September 1960	Front-wheel disc brakes became optional extras.
May 1961	Front disc-brake installation standardized on all models.
April 1962	Introduction of the new style, Mark III range of Zephyr 4/Zephyr 6/Zodiac saloons, to replace the Mark II models. No convertible versions ever went on sale.
October 1962	Launch of Abbott of Farnham estate car conversion of Mark III types.
October 1963	Optional centre-floor gearchange now available.
January 1965	Introduction of Zodiac Executive, flagship version of the Zodiac.
April 1966	Launch of entirely new-generation Zephyr V4/V6 and Zodiac Mark IV saloons, with V4 and V6 engines.
October 1966	Introduction of Executive Zodiac saloon, and new Abbott-built Mark IV estate cars.
Autumn 1967	Power steering standardized on the Zodiac.
March 1972	Mark IV models finally discontinued, replaced by the new-generation Consul/Granada types. Except for their engines and transmissions, those were all-new cars.

1 Pilots and Prefects: the 1940s at Dagenham

No car is ever conceived in a vacuum, or designed without influence from its predecessors. That is why any book about cars such as the Consul and Zephyr must first of all relate what came before, why and when. In other words, although Ford's legendary Model T has no part in this story, the car itself, and the factories in which it and its successors were assembled, were all-important in setting the scene for the Consuls and Zephyrs.

The very first Ford cars were built in the USA in 1903, and the legendary Model T was originally launched in 1908. To tap the British potential of this car, Ford then set up an assembly plant at Trafford Park, near Manchester, and the Model T soon became a best seller. This, though, was in an old building (it was actually a redundant tramcar factory), and by the mid-1920s the company was looking to move on, from mere assembly to iron-ore-to-complete-cars manufacture.

A massive but marshy site was bought at the village of Dagenham in Essex in 1924, although actual construction of a new plant, on the bank of the River Thames, did not begin until 1929. The very first Dagenham-built product was a Ford Model AA 30cwt (1,500kg) truck, completed in October 1931; the 4-cylinder Model A car followed a few months later.

This is one of the last Model Ts, the world's best-selling car that dominated Ford's business until the late 1920s. Many of its features, including transverse leaf spring suspension and a separate chassis frame, were still being used on all British Fords in the late 1940s.

In the meantime, Ford-USA had conceived the car that would change the face of Ford in Europe: the all-new, tiny, but rugged little 8hp Model Y saloon. On sale from the end of 1932, the 8hp was soon joined by the 10hp, these cars eventually becoming Anglias and Prefects, and by the mid-1930s they had also been joined by an ever-changing family of V8s. Although these cars were almost perversely old-fashioned, that seemed to be of no consequence. It was no matter that they all had simple side-valve cylinder heads, three-speed transmissions, or beam-axle suspension with transverse leaf springs at front and rear: they were available in big numbers, they were reliable, and above all they sold at remarkably low prices.

When war came in September 1939, Ford-UK was already the third largest of Britain's car makers – Austin and Morris were market leaders – and

was already aiming higher. The six years of war that followed, from 1939 to 1945, did not change that resolve, although it caused all such schemes to be put away for 'the duration'. Not only that, but because Ford-UK had spent the war years making Rolls-Royce Merlin V12 aero engines, military trucks by the thousands, and an impressive array of tractors, bren-gun carriers and other military machinery, its factories had to be completely re-equipped when peace finally returned.

Situated on the Thames estuary, Ford-UK's principal factory at Dagenham in Essex was in full view of the enemy and quite impossible to camouflage, and had always been a prime target for the Luftwaffe. Although there was often some damage, heroic efforts always restored the still-modern factory to full production in a matter of days. Both Dagenham and the Briggs body-manufacturing plant alongside had received

The first new model to be built at the Dagenham factory was the 933cc-engined Model Y, which went on sale in 1932.

Briggs Motor Bodies

When Ford's Dagenham complex was developed in the 1930s, the company's principal body supplier, Briggs Motor Bodies, set up shop alongside, and would eventually be connected to the assembly lines by overhead conveyor.

Although Briggs was independently owned, and in theory could take on work for any car company in the business (it did, indeed, supply others), Ford soon made sure that they were inextricably linked with their own plant and their own needs. It was the same situation in the USA. By the time the Consul/Zephyr range came to be developed in the late 1940s, there was no doubt that they would be chosen as the suppliers of the new-fangled monocoque saloon shells.

Ford-UK first considered buying up Briggs in 1951 (at a time when it was still 62 per cent owned by its Detroit parent), for by this time Briggs was Britain's second-largest body-stampings business (Pressed Steel Co. of Cowley was the largest), but the decisive move was not finally made until 1953. The total cost was a mere £5.6 million (a bargain then, and what looks like an incredible bargain today).

Within two or three years Briggs had got rid of all its non-Ford business, which had included shell production for Jowett, and major pressings work for Austin and the Rootes Group. Every one of the Consul/Zephyr/Zodiac shells was produced at Dagenham. Although Ford eventually rechristened this the 'Body Plant', old hands called it 'Briggs' for decades to come – and Ford's fast-expanding styling studios were centred there until the entire operation was lifted, first to Aveley, then finally to the new Dunton technical centre in the 1970s.

Briggs was eventually integrated with the new PTA building (see page 192) as the Body Plant, and was linked to it by an overhead conveyor to take completed shells across a public road. Even after the PTA was closed in the early 2000s, the Body Plant continued in business.

---

direct hits, although none had been critical to the plants' survival. Not even the V1 (flying bomb) or V2 rockets could add to the destruction.

Peacetime Again

Immediately after the European war ended in May 1945 (victory over Japan would not follow until August), work began to re-convert Dagenham to the production of private cars and trucks again. For years, tens of thousands of tracked bren-gun carriers, four-wheel-drive trucks, tractors for military use, and myriad conversions of private car chassis, which included turning them into mobile canteens and mobile cinemas, had poured off the assembly lines. Now it was time to re-instate them, to build Anglias, Prefects and V8 models. It helped, of course, that the running gear and chassis of the smaller cars had been in production throughout the war. Even so, the turn-round from military to civilian assembly was achieved remarkably quickly. The very first post-war Ford car – an 8hp Anglia – was completed on 21 June 1945, and was soon joined by the four-door Prefect, though there was no attempt to revive a V8-engined 'big Ford' until the Pilot appeared in 1947.

Because this was a period in which there was a post-war (indeed long-lasting) shortage of sheet steel, the British government applied rigid rules regarding supply. The amount of steel to be made available for British market cars as opposed to cars for the export market, meant that the vast majority of new Fords would have to be sold overseas. The same situation arose for every other car maker, which partly explains why there was a short-lived boom in the sales of aluminium-bodied (though expensive) cars such as the Allards and Armstrong-Siddeleys of the industry. One consequence was that soon there was such a demand for all Ford cars that colossal, and quite irreconcilable, waiting lists built up, and no matter how hard Ford tried to produce more and more of the same old designs (which in normal conditions might not have sold anything like as well), they were unable to supply those orders. Even so, in the calendar year 1947, no fewer than 115,000 vehicles of all types (including trucks and tractors) poured out of Dagenham.

The author's father's case was a perfect example. Having bought his first second-hand car in 1948, he then decided to order a new Ford Prefect to replace it. He therefore went to his nearest Ford dealer, where he was told that it would

In 1947/1948, when Ford-UK started work on the new Consul/Zephyr programme, cars based on this 1930s-style Model Y were still being built at Dagenham in huge numbers.

In the late 1940s, all assembly at Dagenham was in the same building that had produced the first trucks and saloons in 1931/1932. The new Consul/Zephyr types would have to make the best they could of these facilities until the late 1950s. The photograph shows Prefects being built in the late 1940s.

be at least three or four years before a car would be ready. The dealership made clear that they did not really need his business, but as a concession would add his name to their lists. A new car would be ready 'in due course', he was told, probably not in the colour he wanted, and probably not even the same model as he had requested. And so it was: the Prefect ordered in 1948 eventually turned up in 1953, as a Consul – thus starting the author's interest in such machines, an interest that has never faded.

It should also be noted that even if a car was available to a private customer, his choice of Ford cars would be extremely limited for some years. By the end of 1945 a 'priority' customer (a doctor, say, or what today's politicians might even describe as a 'key worker') could only choose between a 23bhp/933cc Anglia with two passenger doors and a £293 price tag, or a 30bhp/1,172cc Prefect with

four passenger doors costing £352. No more and no less, for no other Ford car appeared in the lists.

The next car to be added, in the summer of 1947, was a massive, but nonetheless technically obsolete, saloon-badged Pilot, a modified version of a 1936-type V8-62, complete with an 85bhp/3622cc engine, a price of £748, and the sort of fuel consumption bound to make it unpopular in those days of strict fuel rationing. Like its smaller cousins, the Pilot had transverse leaf-spring suspension, a three-speed gearbox, and part mechanically operated brakes. Henry Ford himself might have been proud of such Stone Age fixtures and fittings in the 1930s, though the dealers and many customers were not. In the late 1940s they were quite appalled, and it was therefore only the facts of a supply crisis that kept these cars selling.

In fact by 1947, when the Pilot was launched,

When work on the Consul/Zephyr began in 1947/1948, this gargantuan V8-engined saloon, the Pilot, had just been announced by Ford-UK. It was expensive, old-fashioned and elephantine, and was really obsolete from the day it was born.

it was high time for Ford-UK to be planning its first real post-war cars, and to be filling out the range. All its rivals were well ahead in this process, and by 1949/1950 (for a really new model couldn't possibly be brought to market before then) it, too, could be well ahead.

Although Ford-UK was still under the financial thumb of its parent (Ford-USA), it was at least a highly profitable and productive subsidiary. Patrick Hennessy was its newly appointed general manager, and he had the ear of Henry Ford II; therefore it could at least fight successfully for its share of investment to fund the future. However, H.F.II's problem was that several other subsidiaries were also clamouring for funds at the same time: in France, Ford-France needed to re-invest and to repair the damage and sabotage caused by bomb damage and by German occupation from 1940 to 1944; while Ford-Germany had to repair all the damage caused by bomb damage, and by German shelling as the Wehrmacht retreated inside its own borders in 1945.

Applying a wise judgement of priorities, Ford himself first channelled funds into France, then into Britain, and only after that into Germany. The French inherited a small/medium car project that Ford-USA had originally schemed up for itself (this became the first post-war Vedette of 1949); while the Germans had first to rebuild, then survive with more mundane machinery, ending up two years behind Dagenham. For Patrick Hennessy there was news that work on a new British Ford – mainly to be carried out in the USA, but with a kernel of UK-based engineers – could begin in earnest in 1948. Although the style was to be worked up in Ford-USA's design studios at Dearborn, Michigan (just a few miles west of the centre of Detroit), and much of the engineering would be carried out in Dearborn too, a team of British engineers was hastily sent over to the USA to get involved at once.

Mr Ford had also discovered just how much the Ford-UK engineers were dependent on Ford-USA; that at that time they still had no dedicated

---

The Dearborn Connection

Although Ford had been assembling Model Ts in the UK – originally at Trafford Park, near Manchester – since 1911, there was precious little design and engineering input to British models, from British personnel, until the mid-1930s. Until that time, all major chassis, engine, drive-line and body engineering and development was centred at Ford-USA's Dearborn HQ, near Detroit; the world-famous Model Y, which evolved into the Anglia and Prefect, was totally conceived in the USA.

It was not until after World War II that Ford-USA began to grant its British subsidiary more independence, and more responsibility to British personalities. When the Consul/Zephyr family was conceived in 1947/1948, all the main project work was carried out at Dearborn, though a small team was sent out from Dagenham, not only to learn, but to influence the process as much as possible.

The fact is, though, that the styling of the new cars – the MacPherson strut front suspension, the general layout of the overhead valve engines, and that of the three-speed gearbox – was all conceived at Dearborn, and it was only as the 1950s progressed that more and more responsibility, and innovation, came back to Britain.

By the mid-1950s, the majority of new mechanical design was being carried out in Britain, first at Rainham (near Dagenham) and later at a newly built plant at South Ockendon; and although a styling studio was set up at Briggs Motor Bodies in the 1950s, for years to come it mainly took its orders on themes and trends from Dearborn. Although the shape of all four Marks of Zephyr was unique to Ford-UK, each and every one of them was heavily influenced by Dearborn, or by Dearborn personnel who had been seconded to the new studios.

It was not until smaller cars, such as the Anglia 105E and the Cortina, came along that a Ford-UK product really was an all-British enterprise.

It was the constant nagging from characters such as chairman Lord Perry, or from Patrick Hennessy, and even from Henry Ford II himself, that had made this possible. When H.F.II made his first ever visit to Ford-UK in February 1948, he confirmed impressions gained at his press conference. Stating that it was in engineering that Ford-UK had a weak point, he admitted that, 'A chief engineer is required, as well as a body and styling engineer …. Action is necessary!'

Post-war Anglias had this very rudimentary, 1930s-style facia in the late 1940s. Something quite revolutionary and different would be needed for the 1950s.

engineering block (although this would shortly be supplied, at Rainham, just a couple of miles east of the Dagenham complex); and that Ford-UK relied totally on Briggs Motor Bodies for its body supplies, something he hadn't realized until he visited Dagenham. Henry Ford also noted that Patrick Hennessy was, effectively, the future of Ford-UK: in his own diaries, which became public many years later, he wrote that Hennessy '… is the executive upon whom we hope to build the future Dagenham. He has all the potential qualities which the position of either managing director or board chairman demands.'

By this time, in fact, Ford-UK's plans were beginning to settle down. The newly instituted 'Dagenham Policy Committee' met for the first time in January 1948, and early in the year a team of engineers from Dagenham travelled to Dearborn to join their American colleagues in working

on a new British car. Luckily for them, their arrival was just months too late for an abandoned 'small' Ford-USA project to be imposed upon them – 'small', by the way, being by North American standards – for this V8-engined machine had already been allocated to Ford-France, where it would soon appear as the Vedette. Dagenham's delegation was headed by George Halford, with mechanical advice and expertise coming from a young Fred Hart (who would later become even more famous for his work on the Anglia 105E of the late 1950s, and on later big Fords), and body shell knowledge from Andy Cox of Briggs Motor Bodies.

Although there was still no 'Product Planning' department as such (a formal department would not be set up until the mid-1950s), Patrick Hennessy had consulted closely with his colleagues, his sales force, and with the most deep-thinking of his dealers, and had concluded that what Ford-UK needed was an all-new model to fill the yawning gap between the 30bhp Prefect and the 85bhp Pilot – one that had to look modern, be modern, and to behave like a modern car should. (Although consulting dealers was not always wise, as a later Ford-UK chairman, Sir Terence Beckett, once made clear: 'In my time, if the company had been successful, and you asked them what they wanted, they always wanted more of the same ....')

Originally, as we now know, Patrick Hennessy (and Henry Ford II) had wanted to get such a new Ford-UK product on to the market before the end of 1949, but such a schedule was never likely to be maintained, and the timing slipped by a full year before the new Consul/Zephyr types finally reached their public. Even then, they were only revealed in October, and series production did not begin until January 1951.

Deciding on the size and type of car to be developed was one of the easiest decisions Ford-UK ever had to make, for clearly it needed something in the 1.5 litre to 2-litre bracket, something which could go after the mass of sales already being snapped up by its rivals, and something whose engineering could take advantage of the latest taxation regulations just coming into force in the UK. It was also assumed that because every mechanical part – and I do indeed mean every part – of the new cars would be newly developed, they would cost a fortune in investment, and should be expected to live for at least two, if not three, full design generations.

Facing Up to the Opposition

By the end of 1948, when new-model engineering was well under way, Ford already knew that since 1945 they had slipped well behind all their British rivals, technically if not in cost control and production capability. Bearing in mind the

Although Ford dealers knew their cars were slipping behind the opposition, they were loyal to the brand. Jack Reece (right) and his brother Peter were Ford dealers from Liverpool who bravely drove cars like this underpowered Anglia in rallies such as the Tulip of 1950.

Until the Consul/Zephyr types arrived, Ford-UK's post-war cars were all 1930s-shape and 1930s-style models, neither modern-looking, economical, nor attractive to look at. Massive changes were needed.

antediluvian layout of the Anglia/Prefect/Pilot models, the following summarizes what other makers in Britain's 'Big Six' had already achieved, or were about to achieve in the class:

Austin: Had already launched newly styled A40 and A70 models, with overhead-valve engines and soft coil spring independent front suspension. Although these cars still used separate chassis frames they looked modern, and by British engineering standards were trendsetters in some ways.

Jowett: Maybe the Javelin was a little too costly (and therefore out of the Consul class), but it had been brand new in 1947, with appealing fastback styling on a Briggs-produced unit-construction body shell. The engine was an overhead-valve flat four, there was a four-speed gearbox, torsion bar independent front suspension, plus rack-and-pinion steering. Only the price – £819 – and a doubtful reliability record held it back.

Morris: Although Alec Issigonis's appealing little Minor had made all the headlines, the larger Oxford MO and Six MS types of 1948 were similar in so many ways, with rigid unit-construction body shells, and torsion bar independent front suspension. The Six had an overhead-camshaft engine, while the Oxford had rack-and-pinion steering gear.

Rootes Group: Two differently badged cars had to be faced: the 1.2-litre Hillman Minx and the 2.3-litre Humber Hawk, both of which were launched in 1948. Both types had modern styling and unit-construction body shells along with independent front suspension, but both were still afflicted with side-valve engines of a pre-war type.

Standard: The all-new Vanguard had been previewed in 1947, and was on sale from the summer of 1948. Although it still kept a separate chassis frame, it had independent front suspension. The body style was all new and (by the standards of the day) attractive, while the overhead-valve engine was eventually to establish itself as a near-unburstable power unit.

Vauxhall: Although Vauxhall was controlled by General Motors, at the time the largest car maker in the world, in 1948 its cars were still some way behind the times. Introduced in 1948, its L-Type Wyvern/Velox types were really no more than

Monte Carlo harbour in the rain, with a V8 Pilot followed by an Anglia; but that was about as glamorous as it got for Fords in the pre-Consul period.

heavily face-lifted H-Types, originally launched in 1937. That car, at least, had been the first British machine to boast a monocoque body/chassis unit, and had always used overhead-valve engines, but these were positively puny (55bhp from 2.3 litres!), and the chassis was lumbered with soft Dubonnet-type independent front suspension.

For Ford, therefore, it was important that their first-ever post-war car – and, to be brutally honest, their first mechanically new design since the early 1930s – should catch up with their opposition, and if possible should also take a full step ahead. This, of course, would need a complete and radical change in business philosophy. Up until that point there had been very little year-on-year investment in new products, and mechanics working on a 1948 Anglia, Prefect or Pilot could easily recognize the same components they had first encountered in the 8hp Model Y (1932) and the V8 models (1935).

Although engineers and, in particular, accountants love to wring the utmost from long-established designs, clearly the only old-car component that could be carried forwards was the famous blue oval Ford badge itself. Everything else would have to be – and deserved to be – new. Accordingly there would be novelties in every aspect of the car – whether mechanical, in the body, or in the styling – and the whole of Ford's

organization, from top management, to factory, and on to the dealerships, would have to come to terms with this.

Over and above all this was the fact that this had to be a profitable project, and not an indulgence for anyone. At Ford it could not be considered on its own, for it would eventually have to be joined by a replacement for the Anglia/Prefect models too, and both these ranges would have to contribute to on-going profits, and to positive cash flow, to allow Ford-UK to establish its own independence.

There was no question of letting the engineers get away with a 'thinking aloud' scheme; they would have to finalize a model range that had a future, which laid the foundations for more and more derivatives to follow, and which would be both customer and dealer friendly. Whether they liked it or not, Ford's all-powerful cost accountants would be looking over their shoulders at every turn, determined to shave cost out of everything from a body panel, to an engine block, or an electrical system.

Laying the Foundations

By the time that George Halford's British task force arrived in Dearborn in 1948, Ford-USA had already started work on the 'new British Ford'. I have deliberately used this phrase because as far as I can see (or, at least, Ford has not told us otherwise), no flamboyant project name was ever applied to it. Compared with Ford-USA's stagnant 'thirties, when few mechanical innovations were made to the cars, most of the personalities involved in this project were fresh to top level responsibility. Called back from the US Navy in May 1943 to rescue the company that his father's fast-developing senility was threatening to destroy, Henry Ford II had become Ford-USA's president in 1945. Ernest Breech (ex-Bendix division of General Motors) became his executive vice-president in 1946, effectively to run the business for him.

Engineering at Dearborn was then led by Harold T. Youngren (whose previous job had been as chief engineer of GM's Oldsmobile Division), but he already had the reputation of being a 'safety-first' engineer, who liked to use systems and layouts with which he was already familiar.

Ford, on the other hand, had just acquired the services of Earle S. MacPherson, who had recently led the GM effort to produce a new small car, the 'Chevrolet Cadet'. Like many such GM projects, before or later, the Cadet had been cancelled because it was too novel for the company's top management. One of those novel features was a totally different type of independent front suspension, apparently not protected by any GM trademark rights, which MacPherson would eventually make famous under his own name.

Then there was the styling department, which had recently been in turmoil following the influx of new blood from other companies. Before work could be finalized on the all-new post-war Fords, Bob Gregory had abruptly left the company, so styling work on the new-for-1949 Ford was carried out by George W. Walker, who was then an independent styling consultant. His influence was still all around the studios in Dearborn.

All this, and the existence of a brand new engineering building, meant that Ford-USA was finally able to look forward to producing new models that looked good, from modern premises with modern facilities. Compared with the stultifying days of the 1920s and 1930s, when Henry Ford (Senior) still seemed to treat almost all innovation with suspicion, these were great days.

The new range developed by the combined American/British team went on to be completely different from anything that had gone before. A study of the actual design details belongs to the next chapter, but the comparison chart below shows just how complete the revolution was to be.

By any standards, this was set to be a major design, development, investment and manufacturing programme, and because a start was not made until 1948, Ford-UK was already having to run hard to catch up with the competition. The next two or three years would be fascinating and tumultuous, and would be pivotal to the company's future.

Feature	Old-type Prefect/Pilot	New-type Consul/Zephyr
Structure	Separate frame and body shell	Unit-construction body shell
Style	Out-of-date 1930s type	Ultra-modern
Engines	4-cylinder or V8 Side valve	4-cylinder or straight 6-cylinder Overhead valve
Suspension	Beam axles/Transverse leaf	Independent front suspension/coil springs
Brakes	Mechanical	Hydraulic
Electrical system	6-volt	12-volt

2 Consul and Zephyr

In 1948, and even before detail work on the running gear of these new cars could be finalized, the first two major aspects that had to be settled were the style and the structure, the two being almost inextricably linked. At this time, incidentally, they carried project codes of EOTA (4-cylinder) and EOTTA (6-cylinder): Ford's days of giving new cars catchy project names such as Colt, Brenda or Archbishop, were a long way into the future. The story behind the timing of the growth of this

Sir Patrick Hennessy was Ford-UK's up-and-coming general manager before he became chairman and chief executive in the 1950s. By any measure, the Consul/Zephyr programme was his baby, for which he received full support from Henry Ford II in the USA.

project is crucial to the whole story. Every detail of the first true post-war Ford-USA cars – the 1949 model year cars – had been settled in 1947, and with the potential success of those cars in mind, Ford-USA thought they should 'read across' much of the same format to the British project.

Looking back at what was in those new domestic market Fords, which made their public debut in June 1948, we must be glad that this did not happen. Ford-USA, after all, had already part-developed a new 'small' car of their own, abandoned it, and handed it over to Ford-France, where it would become the Vedette. That car was not a success, and we may be fairly sure that a similarly 'transatlantic' Ford-UK car would have failed, too.

Often recalled in North America as the car that saved Ford-USA, the new post-war Ford of June 1948 was built up around a separate chassis frame with cruciform cross-bracing, with coil spring/wishbone independent front suspension, but with a choice of old-type straight 6-cylinder, or old-type V8 engines, both of them with side valves. That might sound 'old hat' to you, but Ford's thrusting new president, Ernie Breech, had made his thoughts to the policy committee crystal clear in 1947:

> I have a vision. We start from scratch. We spend no time or money phoneying up the old cars, because this organization will be judged by the market on the next Ford it produces, and it had better be a radically new one ….

It simply had to be. The American Fords made in large quantities after mid-1945 had been based

This was Ford-USA's first truly post-war model, announced in mid-1948. Anyone with an eye for line, proportion, and for what later became known as 'styling cues', can see that it strongly influenced the Consul/Zephyr that was to follow.

on those introduced in 1940/1941, and they had been face-lifted versions of pre-war models that had first appeared in 1938.

Headed by two important personalities who were new to Ford – Harold Youngren (engineering) and George W. Walker (design consultant) – the new American model looked completely and astonishingly different from any Ford that had gone before. Although the wheelbase stayed as before, the engines were moved 5in (12.7cm) forwards in the frame to allow a larger passenger compartment to be developed; and of course the coil spring/wishbone independent front end was a real novelty.

As far as the show-room browsers were concerned, though, it was the overall style which caused such a sensation – for this looked totally different from that of any previous Ford. Now, for the very first time on a Dearborn-styled car, the contour of the wings swept smoothly along the flanks, from headlamp to tail lamp, there was no longer a question of running boards being placed under the doors, and there was a startling front-end treatment, with the headlamps being carried high and wide, on either side of a boldly detailed grille. It was altogether typical of Ford's North American capabilities that it immediately offered

Ford Vedette – no relation

Over the years there have been suggestions that the Ford (France) Vedette of the 1940s and 1950s, which preceded the Consul/Zephyr range, was somehow related to the British cars – but this is absolutely not true.

Ford-France, whose factory at Poissy (west of Paris) had been badly hit by Allied bombing during World War II, was rejuvenated in the late 1940s (it actually got priority over Ford-UK). Introduced in October 1948 at the Paris Salon, the Vedette was actually a lineal development of a USA-designed 'compact' car, which had been abandoned in that nation after prototypes experienced a negative reaction from the dealers. Handed over to Ford-France, and finalized by Maurice Dollfus, it eventually went on sale in 1949. Because it had a fast-back body style, a separate chassis frame, coil spring/wishbone independent front suspension, and a side-valve 2.2-litre V8 engine, it was totally different from anything being planned by Ford-UK.

In fact, Ford-France was sold to Simca in late 1954, just after a new-generation Vedette had appeared, with many features that copied what Ford-UK had been using for four years. Many years later, Poissy had become one of the various Peugeot assembly plants scattered all round France, though no trace of Ford's heritage remained.

Ford's plant at Dagenham was alongside the River Thames to the east of London, and was completed in 1932. In the early years it was a fully integrated business that took in iron ore from ships, and manufactured almost the entire cars on the premises. The Briggs body-making plant is remote, and at the top of this shot. From the late 1950s it would be integrated into the operation.

this car as a two-door and four-door saloon, as a convertible and as a 'woody' estate car.

As far as Walker, Richard Caleal, and his associates Bob Bourke and Holden 'Bob' Koto were concerned, all the creative work on this new car had been completed, in essence if not in detail, by the end of 1946, and work on the face-lifted 1950 and 1951 models was also ready by the summer of 1948. Accordingly, when George Halford's Ford-UK task force arrived in Dearborn in 1948,

they found an American styling/design force ready and anxious to get on with what was to be the first of their next true post-war commissions. To anyone with an understanding of the way that styling designers work, there was no question that work they had just completed on the post-war Ford-USA models would strongly influence the shape of the British Fords.

Unit Construction – Ford's First Monocoque

For years in the late 1930s, engineering departments all around the world had been arguing about the advantages and drawbacks of the relatively new-fangled unit-construction structures that were already being adopted for aircraft. In essence, such structures combined the strength of the chassis with the body shell, and if the engineering was done properly, not only would the result be a more rigid structure than before, but it could be lighter, too.

By the time World War II caused a temporary halt to work on most automotive innovations, the debate had more or less been resolved. Those in favour of keeping separate chassis layouts had lost out to those who preferred chassisless layouts,

---

Unit-Construction Body Shells

Lanchester of England had been pioneers on a very small scale, with their hand-built cars, but the first concerted move to combine chassis frames with steel body shells came in the 1920s when the very first unit-construction 'monocoque' shells were built in Italy for the Lancia Lambda. Even so, like the Lanchester these were still open-top cars. It was not for another decade, in 1934, in a Budd-inspired project, that the very advanced front-wheel-drive Citroen traction avant saloon arrived, this having the world's first true unit-construction shell. In 1935 Briggs Motor Bodies supplied prototypes of such shells to Ford's subsidiary, Lincoln, over in North America, and a production car, badged the Zephyr, went on sale shortly after this.

There were many reasons why a unit-construction shell structure like this was desirable, for it promised to make structures much more rigid than ever before, careful packaging would allow increased space in the cabin, and it was likely that overall height and overall weight could be reduced. The major disadvantage for every manufacturer was that the capital tooling costs would be high, and therefore that production runs would really need to be increased.

As so often in the 1930s, Britain's car makers were slow to adopt the new technology. Britain's very first unit-construction production car was the H-Type Vauxhall Ten of 1937, and it was followed just one year later by the new-generation Morris Ten Series M. The unit-construction Hillman Minx Phase 1 appeared in September 1939 (just in time to be frozen out by the outbreak of World War II).

From 1945, all those three cars continued, but there would be no unit-construction Standards until 1949 (the Triumph Mayflower), and no unit-construction Austins until 1951 (the A30). After that, a flood of new models made monocoques the engineering of choice ....

because almost every business factor, particularly those of engineering integrity and of unit costs, was favourable. In Europe maybe this happened quickly and decisively, but in North America it was delayed for some time. Although both Ford and General Motors would soon welcome unit-construction cars into their European subsidiaries' ranges, they were not always ready to do the same thing in the USA where what was known as 'the annual styling change' was still expected, and where unit-construction shells made this more difficult (and more costly) to achieve.

So although Ford-USA had chosen to keep a separate chassis frame as the basis of its post-war North American market models, this explains why the company didn't seem to have spent much time in discussion about the structure to be chosen for the British Fords: almost from day one, it became clear that a unit-construction structure would be employed. Unit construction? Combined body/chassis unit? Monocoque? Several names were commonly used at this time (and still are, of course), but the principle was never in any doubt.

In the good old days – and let us not forget, many tens of millions of cars had been built in this way – a car came together by being based on a simply engineered, separate steel chassis frame, to which all the running gear could be mounted, and which would effectively provide a sturdy, self-supporting and movable assembly before the body was then added. Body shells were still separate entities, in small companies still constructed around wooden skeletons, but where sales volumes were high, more commonly built of all-pressed/welded steel. Such all-steel shells had progressively taken over in Detroit in the late 1920s, and in the UK in the 1930s.

Technically, the two problems had always been that such 'body-on-frame' assemblies had not been anything like as rigid as required (the overall torsional stiffness of the combined chassis-plus-body was only augmented, rather tenuously, through the mounting bolts that held body and chassis together), and their layout, almost by definition, meant that the passengers had to sit several inches higher than they would ideally want to do. It was only when far-thinking engineers were given just a little time to work out, step by step, what could and/or should be possible, that the idea of combining separate pieces of expensively tooled kit began to emerge; but because this was likely to involve a lot of expensive capi-

Sir Patrick's task with the new Consul/Zephyr range was to plug the big marketing gap between the Pilot, and small Fords such as this Anglia, pictured here in war-time guise complete with headlamp masks.

tal investment, only the mass-market car builders could consider it at first.

To lower the seats, and therefore to enable the cabin roof to be lowered too, it was of course necessary to lower the floor pan (at least where the seats were positioned), but to achieve this it usually meant that the main chassis side members had to be splayed out further than they had been conventionally positioned, and this reduced the torsional strength of the frame. It also meant that either the under-door body sills had to be moved further outboard, or they had to be made slimmer, or combined with the chassis frame members.

The first, and obvious, half-way move towards the ideal of a chassisless construction was originally to concentrate attention on the floor, and to provide a platform chassis. Way back in 1939, when Ford-UK was still using separate chassis frames with channel-section side members, to which Briggs-built steel body shells were bolted on the assembly lines, Austin had introduced new 8hp and 10hp models, both of which had platforms in which the floor panels were already an integral part of the engineering – and others would follow. In Germany, incidentally, Dr Ferdinand Porsche had chosen the same layout for what would eventually become the world's best-selling car of all time: the VW Beetle.

The Ford task force, however, was having none of this, for they had already seen the way that unit-construction body shells had been put on sale by several rivals in the 1930s. Though Ford-USA had been rather tardy in taking up the new type of construction (the biggest deterrent of all, of course, was the very high cost of tooling up for press tools and assembly jigs for such items), their engineers had not been locked away in a time warp, and they already knew just what had to be done.

Along with their development colleagues at Briggs, and with other body engineering specialists, a lot of deep thought had already gone into providing the best theoretical layout of a chassisless body shell. To deliver on all the various theoretical promises of its construction, it needed to provide a lowered floor pan, a more spacious cabin than before, to be stiffer and lighter than the conventional body-on-frame of old, and to be able to accept all the stresses and impacts from the

suspension and steering that would normally be absorbed by the chassis.

For those pioneers it was never going to be easy. However, by 1948 standards, either in Dearborn or in the UK, there was no longer anything new about chassisless bodies, and Ford could tap into its own data banks, and also look at what its rivals had already achieved. In the USA it was Ford's own Lincoln Zephyr (Ford had already owned Lincoln for some years) that was the mass-production pioneer, for this car had been launched with a Briggs Motor Bodies unit-construction design in 1935/1936. By 1948, therefore, these cars had already proved their structural point, but it had also become abundantly clear that it was always going to cost a great deal of money to change, face-lift or replace such an existing structure.

As far as the forthcoming Consul/Zephyr models are concerned, it was important to understand that the strength and the shock-bearing capabilities of a unit-construction body shell were developed in an entirely different manner than those of the old-style body-on-frame. One way to understand the merits of unit-construction shells is to consider the shell of a hen's egg, which is at once one of the lightest, best designed, and most elegant lightweight structures in the world. An egg, naturally, can immediately be demolished by crushing force, but can nevertheless develop astonishing resistance to steady pressure, or to twisting, before it does so. The same applies to the steel unit-construction body/chassis unit of a motor car.

In the old layout, all stresses were carried by the steel chassis itself, low down and under the separate body shell. Such frames were often adequately robust to resist bending stresses, but rather weak in withstanding torsion. Engineers who understood about stressed-skin construction (this technology had originated in the aviation business, and because of the links to unit-construction coachwork was spreading rapidly into motor-car building), and the still unrefined art of tracking stress paths in a complex assembly, realized that a unit-construction shell could improve dramatically on this.

By welding up several steel boxes – passenger cabin, engine-bay panels, and rear end panels sur-

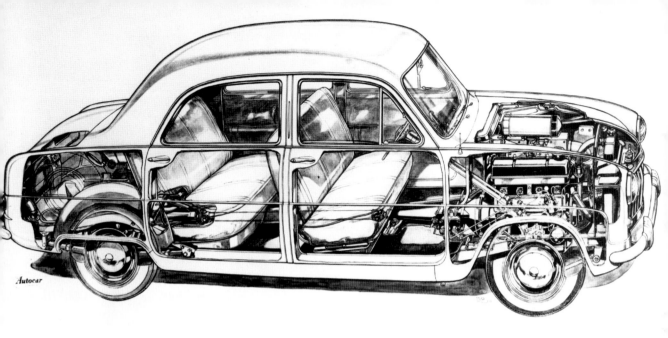

This was the layout of the Consul, as so lovingly detailed in Autocar's *cutaway drawing of 1950, and showing that this was Ford's first chassisless (unit construction) private car.*

rounding the luggage boot – they could make the entire body sides, the pillars, and the roof panel assemblies into load-bearing members. By utilizing what are known as 'stress paths' – through skin panels, and in parts of the shell which, in a separate body construction, were quite unstressed – it should always be possible to share the load around the structure much more than before. Accordingly, to withstand the same inputs, it ought to be possible to slim down some of the previous low-mounted sections – notably the main chassis rails, cross-members and suspension supports, though these would still be in the same traditional locations.

Evolving the Consul/Zephyr Layout

Because every facet of the post-war British Fords was set to be new – no old-type engines, transmissions, suspensions or chassis features, none of any nature, were to be retained – Ford was able to advertise these as 'Five Star' cars. Not only would they have unit-construction body/chassis, but overhead-valve engines, independent front suspension, and 12-volt electrical systems.

The entire layout relied on the new structure for its integrity, so the Ford-USA team and the British taskforce concentrated on this at first. Naturally, since Briggs Motor Bodies of Dagenham would build the finalized body, Andy Cox

had a big input into the feasibility and detail of the design. Right from the start, it seems, Ford acknowledged that there was a huge gap to be filled in its model range between the small 1172cc-engined Prefect and the large 3622cc-engined Pilot. As I have already noted in the first chapter, in Britain some of Ford's major competitors already had cars to sell in this market sector, so the company had no option but to try to fill it at a stroke. It therefore seems to have been decided straightaway that not one, but two models – what became the 'Consul' with a 4-cylinder engine, and the 'Zephyr' with a 6-cylinder – should be introduced at the same time. As far as possible the engines would stem from a single new design, while the body shell should be engineered to accommodate both the '4' and the '6'.

At this stage it is important to note that the four-door saloon shell was the only one envisaged. The same passenger cabin – in other words, the four-door assembly from the engine bulkhead backwards – would be common to every derivative, and the difference in length between the straight 4- and straight 6-cylinder engine would be accommodated in and around the engine bay, and by lengthening the wheelbase. In three-dimensional terms, and in relation to the main passenger cabin, the main gearbox, clutch

As this charming period study makes clear, the Consul had a shorter wheelbase than the Zephyr, but the cabin of both types was the same. The styling, strongly influenced by Ford-USA's new-for-1949 models (see page 21), was thoroughly up to the minute, and was a complete breakaway from anything Ford-UK had previously put on sale.

bell housing and clutch face would be common to all types, which meant that the 6-cylinder engine would 'grow' several inches further forwards than the '4'.

Because the layout and detail design of this new range clearly revolved around the engineering of the new unit-construction body shell, the former's main features should be described; and it should also be made clear that, because of the high position of its top mount, the MacPherson strut could only be used in a unit-construction shell, for it would have been technically unfeasible to 'grow' structural members up to that height from an old-style separate chassis frame.

More than any publication of the day, it was *Motor* magazine that listened most closely to the briefing it got from Ford, and printed one of the most perceptive analyses of the new shell:

Both cars are based upon fundamentally similar four-door saloon bodies of welded-up integral steel con-

struction, no separate chassis frame being used in either case. The base structure of floor and body side rails is reinforced by U-section pressings above the rear axle, and has box-section forward extensions which vary in length as between 4- and 6-cylinder cars: in either case, large side pressings forming the door frames, and another combining the windscreen frame and door panel, provide reinforcement which gives complete rigidity to the centre section of the car, whilst fixed panels alongside the ohv engines and a bulkhead encircling the radiator extend this reinforcement to the extreme front of the car. Without excessive weight, expensive complication, or obstructed access to vital mechanical parts, immense structural strength and rigidity have been attained …

Although it was probably for styling reasons (though it must undoubtedly have added to the structural strength of the rear quarters), the rear wheel-arch cutouts were much smaller than Ford had usually used in the past. This, and the fact that

13in road wheels were used – the smallest diameter wheels a Ford had ever employed – meant that the rear wings were almost, though not quite, flush-mounted over the wheels themselves.

An additional detail, which would be familiar to any structural engineer involved in modern motorsport saloon car shell stiffening, was that there were also substantial pressed panels linking the top of the suspension mounts and the bulkhead itself. (Although modern cars do not have such panels, whenever a roll cage is added for motor sport, tubes linking the same parts of the car are invariably fitted....)

A quick comparison between the shorter (Consul) and longer (Zephyr) body shells showed that the Zephyr's 4in (10cm) longer wheelbase allowed those struts (and therefore, in traditional terms, the line of the 'front axle') to be moved forwards. This was done to support the longer 6-cylinder engine and to balance the weight distribution as much as possible.

New MacPherson Front Suspension

Although the all-new Consul/Zephyr family could boast much innovation (for Ford, that is), in 1950 the family's truly unique feature was what became known as the MacPherson strut independent front suspension. It would have been enough, surely, to know that a British Ford finally had independent front suspension, but this particular layout, which was named after its inventor, Earle S. MacPherson, was totally new in its concept, layout and detailing.

This resourceful American engineer had worked up this layout with his previous employer (General Motors), before moving to Ford and bringing his invention with him. Amazingly GM appeared to have had no patent or trade mark rights to stop this happening – though you may be sure that Ford did not make the same mistake! It was not until Ford's master patents expired (or until resourceful race-car engineers such as Colin Chapman found ways of working around them) that MacPherson struts were taken up by the majority of the world's car makers, though the generic name has always survived.

First of all, what is meant by 'independent suspension' in automotive terms? Basically, it means that one suitably controlled and damped road wheel can move up and down without disturbing the geometry of the other wheels, or disturbing the stability of the car itself. The trick is always to ensure that this is done without

---

Earle S. MacPherson

If only General Motors had not been such a penny-pinching organization, Ford might never have used MacPherson strut suspension on its cars. It was only after General Motors decided not to invest in the new-type independent front suspension that MacPherson himself had designed for them, that he resigned, defected, and moved across town in Detroit to work for Ford instead.

Trained as an engineer, Earle MacPherson flew American fighter aircraft during World War I, then made his name in the engineering division of Chevrolet. Having led the Chevrolet Cadet small car product from 1945 (which was later cancelled), in 1947 he conceived the original strut suspension that bears his name. But at GM, one frustration after another led to him leaving, to join Ford in a senior engineering position. Taking his strut suspension schemes with him (there were, apparently, no hang-ups over any patent or trademark issues), he convinced his new bosses about the engineering, stress distribution and cost-saving merits of the new system – but not for domestic use – and saw them adopted on the Consul/Zephyr cars that would be introduced in October 1950.

Even so, the first post-war Ford-France cars (the 'Vedette', see page 15) used a conventional coil spring/wishbone layout, though these cars had been finalized well before MacPherson joined Ford. Nor was this system fitted to the first of the post-war German Fords, for the original Taunus 12M of 1952 featured a coil spring/wishbone system too. MacPherson struts would not be adopted on Ford-USA models until the late 1970s.

Earle S. MacPherson went on to become Ford's vice president of engineering before retiring in 1958. He died soon afterwards, in 1960.

disturbing the steering, or the dynamic stability of the structure.

In the 1940s, of course, there was nothing new about the concept of independently sprung wheels, front or rear, and many differing layouts were still being used. However, in almost every case, such suspensions were mounted either to separate chassis frames, or to substantial steel sub-frames that were themselves fitted to a unit-construction structure. What are now known as 'packaging engineers' (those hard-pressed people who have to squeeze a total technical package into a space which they are always convinced needs to be larger and more spacious!) knew that to provide the correct articulation of wishbone members, many proven independent systems intruded into the engine bay, making access to the engine and its add-on components more difficult.

Earle MacPherson had thought this through, and had started by blocking out the space within which 'his' new system should not encroach, and had moved everything in the suspension layout outside that. The result was a layout so elegant in

its simplicity that almost every rival immediately realized that, one day, he might have to follow suit.

Looked at from the front view, the new MacPherson system pushed a combined coil spring/damper pillar (always known as a strut) as far outboard as possible, combined it with the stub axle (or 'knuckle') casting close to the wheel, and saw it fixed at the top to a flexible mounting high up in the inner wheel arch. There was no top wishbone, and no need of one.

To locate the stub axle/knuckle at the base, it would have been enough to use a conventional lower wishbone and tie the anti-roll torsion bar to it, yet MacPherson simplified this even further, providing only what became known as a track control arm, with the arm of the anti-roll bar doubling duty as a drag link, or forward facing arm of that lower wishbone. In this original form,

The Consul/Zephyr range was the first in the world to use the innovative, efficient and space-saving MacPherson strut independent front suspension. As is clear from this diagram, the suspension was neatly wrapped around the engine bay, but did not intrude at any point.

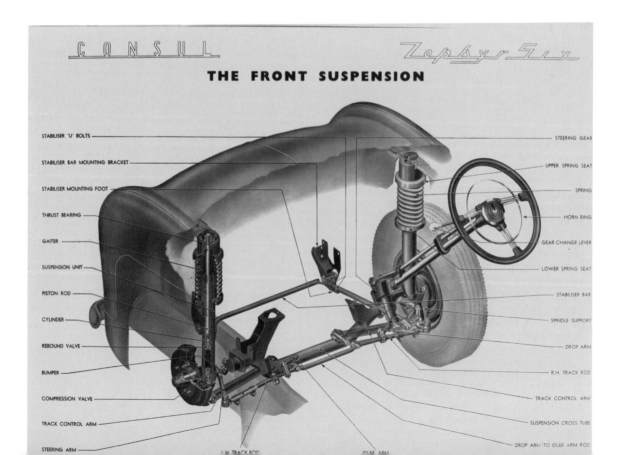

THE FRONT SUSPENSION

STABILISER "U" BOLTS

STABILISER BAR MOUNTING BRACKET

STABILISER MOUNTING FOOT

THRUST BEARING

GAITER

SUSPENSION UNIT

PISTON ROD

CYLINDER

REBOUND VALVE

BUMPER

COMPRESSION VALVE

TRACK CONTROL ARM

STEERING ARM

L.H. TRACK ROD

IDLER ARM

STEERING GEAR

UPPER SPRING SEAT

SPRING

HORN RING

GEAR CHANGE LEVER

LOWER SPRING SEAT

STABILISER BAR

SPINDLE SUPPORT

DROP ARM

R.H. TRACK ROD

TRACK CONTROL ARM

SUSPENSION CROSS TUBE

DROP ARM TO IDLER ARM ROD

and as refined over the years, this was a miracle of detailing, with just three major links: the spring/damper/strut, the track-control arm, and the drag-link/anti-roll bar. The truly remarkable fact, too, was that this assembly was seen to be draped around the engine bay without intruding at any point.

If there was any drawback, it was that the coil spring, mounted high on the strut itself, was rather bulky. It would, of course, have been possible to use slim and light longitudinal torsion bars, fixed to the inner pivot of the track control arm, instead – but as such bars were more expensive to manufacture than simple coil springs, Ford did not consider this alternative.

By comparison, of course, the rest of the chassis was conventional in the extreme – conventional, that is, by industry standards, but still decades ahead of what Ford-UK had been inflicting on their customers for so long. Hydraulically operated drum brakes, front and rear, were a real advance on the cable/mechanical variety used on old-type Fords, and the worm-and-peg steering was at least the same type as used by most of Ford's rivals. Unhappily the windscreen wipers were still of the suction-operated variety, that suction depending on the pressure inside the engine's inlet manifold, which meant that they tended to slow down when the throttle was fully open. On these cars, however, there was a vacuum booster pump incorporated in the base of the fuel pump, which helped alleviate the problem. Even so, what we might now call 'conventional' electrically operated wipers were still years into Ford's future.

New Engines, More Innovation

Ford was proud of the fact that the engines they launched for the Consul and Zephyr of 1950 – very closely related 4-cylinder and 6-cylinder power units – were the very first overhead-valve units to be fitted to a Ford, anywhere in the world. Although millions of Fords had previously been built in the USA, in the UK, and in Europe with side-valve engines (in North America these were known as L-head types) the com-

---

Overhead Valve Engines

Now that almost any modern car seems to have twin-overhead camshafts and 4 valves per cylinder, it is easy to forget that what we now think are old-fashioned, simple overhead valve engines, were still not universally used until the 1950s.

Right from the start, all Ford engines – whether American, British, French or German – used a simple side-valve layout. When post-war car assembly began again in 1945, Ford corporate engines were either side-valve '4s', side-valve straight-6s or side-valve V8s. History now tells us that Ford's very first overhead-valve engines were those used in the new Consul/Zephyr types (these were mainly designed in the USA, though development and evolution were handed over shortly after launch), for the first overhead-valve Ford-USA '6' was not revealed until late 1951.

Ford-UK's very last side-valve road car engine was the 1172cc power unit used in Ford 100E Populars in 1962.

---

pany had never felt it necessary to rush to change, even though their major rivals were all doing this ahead of them. (In fact, when the EOTA/EOTTA models came to be designed, Ford-USA engineers were already developing overhead-valve power units for domestic models, though such engines would not be offered on American Fords until the end of 1951, a year after the Consul/Zephyr types had been launched.)

Although the general layout of the new power units was straightforward enough, there was much innovative detail intended to make the engines easier and cheaper to manufacture, and to maintain in service. As already noted, to provide a span of capacities (and, please note, to allow for possible changes and enlargements in future years), the plan was to produce straight 4-cylinder and straight 6-cylinder engines, which would have their own unique cylinder block and head castings, and cast crankshafts, but would otherwise share many components such as pistons, connecting rods and valve gear.

The intention was that all these engines should be manufactured on the same machinery, from castings produced in Ford's own foundry. At Dagenham's engine plant, a completely new gen-

These were the inner secrets of the new Consul (4-cylinder) and Zephyr (6-cylinder) engines – this being a Consul power unit. Both engines were machined and assembled on the same facility at Dagenham, sharing the same bore, stroke, pistons, connecting rods, valve gear, camshaft drive arrangements, and many other details.

This was the compact 4-cylinder Consul engine, showing off the very rudimentary 'exhaust manifold' tube that Ford used on these engines …

… and the 6-cylinder Zephyr engine is clearly a very close relative indeed.

Above *This 'chassis layout', so typical of the simple way that Ford-UK showed off its wares in those days, shows how the MacPherson strut front suspension dominated the layout.*

Below *The lengthy 6-cylinder Zephyr engine almost completely filled the engine space of the original model, even though the wheelbase of the unit-construction shell was stretched to accommodate it.*

eration of machine tools and assembly facilities was laid down, this being brand new in 1950. At the time, for sure, Ford can have had no idea that this engine would still be in use fifteen years into the future.

The Effects of the Motor Tax

It is important to realize, too, that these were the first new Ford engines to be developed after Britain's motor taxation regime had been changed. Up until 1947, a car's annual registration licence fee was calculated under an archaic formula related to the piston area of the engine itself, this being known as the 'horsepower tax'. Engines with small bores and long strokes (the Ford Prefect being an ideal example) attracted a much lower annual licence fee than one with large pistons and much piston area (like the old Model T, for instance).

Unhappily this had led to the evolution of cars with small capacity and underpowered engines, which often made them very difficult to sell in overseas markets. Much lobbying from the industry over a period of years eventually convinced the government that if exports were to be encouraged, then the time had come to change. After an interim period in 1947, from 1 January 1948 the annual licence duty was changed to a flat fee of a mere £10.

The effect on new engine designs was immediate, and was nowhere more exemplified than with the new Consul/Zephyr engines. Instead of being tall and narrow with small cylinder bores and poor breathing, they could be altogether more sturdy – squat in layout, even – with more solid crankshafts, pistons and connecting roads, with wider cylinder bores, shorter strokes, and the inherent ability to rev higher when needed. Thus for the first time on a British Ford, the new engines were designed with what became known as 'over-square dimensions', in that the cylinder bore was larger than the stroke. These dimensions – shared between 4- and 6-cylinder engines – were 79.37mm × 76.2mm, which sounds exotic and exact, but in prosaic Imperial measure was 3⅛in × 3in!

Although Ford breathed a sigh of relief when it beat Vauxhall in the modernization race, there were only months in it – for Vauxhall would launch this new Wyvern/Velox range in 1951, when it was a direct competitor to the Consul/Zephyr.

Interestingly enough, Ford-UK's big British rival, Vauxhall, was also designing its own new family of engines in the same post-war period, and when these were finally revealed in 1952 they were seen to have exactly the same bore and stroke dimensions. Although this was probably a coincidence – design of the Vauxhall engine would certainly have been finalized before the Ford engines were revealed – it was a case of 'great minds thinking alike' ....

Although the major change to an over-square layout was radical enough, much of the rest of the engine was conventional, at least by Ford's standards. The cylinder block and head were in cast iron, the short-stroke crankshafts (three-bearing for the '4', four-bearing for the '6') were in cast steel, and the valve gear was conventional, with pushrod valves operating in simple wedge-profile combustion chambers.

The final innovation (though hardly a praiseworthy one) was in the way the exhaust manifolds were arranged. Quite simply, Ford arranged for square exhaust ports to exit via semi-circular machined recesses in the head casting, the 'manifold' being no more than a long metal pipe with suitable perforations on one side, clamped up to the cylinder head, and which fed directly into the exhaust downpipe. It was, of course, totally primitive (indeed, the author has never seen anything quite as primitive on any other automotive engine), but Ford's cost accountants must have been delighted by its simplicity.

And this arrangement delivered exactly what the planners had required – 47bhp for the Consul and 68bhp for the 6-cylinder Zephyr – with ample mid-range torque, the result being cars that were always able to keep up with their rivals; indeed the Zephyr soon proved to be a very sturdy competition car. Moreover this crude set-up, and the use of simple down-draught Zenith carburettors, did not seem to stifle the engine too much; to give a comparison, the new 2.2-litre Zephyr, rated at 68bhp, produced 30bhp/litre, whereas the old Pilot V8 had produced just 23.5bhp/litre.

A Brand New Three-Speed Gearbox

So much attention was given to the new engines that the introduction of a brand new three-speed gearbox was almost totally ignored. Unlike the Prefect three-speeder (too small, too flimsy, with a central gear change by a rather willowy lever) and the Pilot three-speeder (too old-fashioned), Ford concluded that they needed a totally fresh design.

As with the engines, therefore, major investment was made in a new gearbox line at Dagenham, for at the time Ford envisaged using the same new gearbox behind the new engines, no matter how long the life of that assembly might be. Because it was fashionable at the time (and, as I have already mentioned, to make sure that the centre floor ahead of the front bench seat was uncluttered), a steering-column change was fitted as standard, there being no provision for a centre-floor change at that time. As conceived, there was no synchromesh on first gear (nor would that feature be added in the next decade and more), though at the time such an omission was normal.

Years of experiences of the family Consul lead me to recall that a well maintained example of this steering-column change could be a remarkably sturdy and precise installation – much better, for

---

Steering-Column Gear Changes

Cynics would say that there was never any such thing as a good steering-column gear change. With a gearbox on the floor, between the passenger footwells, and the lever itself on the column, about six feet of cabling, rods and levers away, it was almost impossible for an engineer to devise a positive change.

So why did it happen? It was more or less forced into existence after World War II, when most British manufacturers sought to make their cars more attractive to export customers, and to provide more space and leg room in the front seats. Although Ford's three-speed transmissions originally made it easier to devise a suitable linkage than if four speeds had been provided, over time and mileage – and like every other system – these eventually developed slop and imprecision. On any car, Ford or non-Ford, once centre-floor alternatives became available they were instantly popular, and steering-column change linkages gradually faded away. But not on the big Zephyrs and Zodiacs ....

instance, than the awful change found on certain Austin, Rootes Group or Standard-Triumph models of the same period. To use North American parlance, in the Ford's case, 'three on the tree' was at least as acceptable as 'four on the floor'.

A Style for the British Market

Although the style of the original Consuls and Zephyrs was conceived, influenced and essentially settled in Dearborn, it is important to realize that in the end this was an entirely British car. Unlike later Fords of the 1960s and 1970s, there was no immediate intention to have it assembled on more than one site – in this case Dagenham – and there were no plans for a different version to be evolved under another name, in another nation. The style of the original saloons, therefore, was intended to appeal to the British market (which it most assuredly did), and to Ford-UK's traditional markets (in particular the old 'Empire' territories in Africa and Australasia). These were conventional-looking cars by the standards of 1950, and considering that this was Ford-UK's and Briggs's first attempt at building a unit-construction machine, very neatly detailed, too.

Four big passenger doors all had full steel presswork all around the glass, and there were swivelling front quarter lights in the front doors; all those doors were hinged at the front. Although the front wings, inner panels and 'chassis legs' of the Zephyr were several inches longer than those of the Consul (as explained, this was done to allow the front wheels to be moved forwards, so that a balance under and around the 6-cylinder engine could be maintained), the shape of the front-end sheet metal presswork was essentially the same. Although the plain circular headlamps were in the same shared position, there was, of course, a very obvious difference in front grilles: that of the Zephyr was a full-width type with a horizontal motif, while that of the Consul was smaller, slightly recessed and with vertical grille bars.

Inside the cabins, though, the two cars were very similar – and frankly, were at once too transatlantic, and had facia layouts that were altogether too plain. Like many other new British cars of this period, they were developed with an eye to export sales which, British marketing 'experts' seemed to agree, meant they had to have bench seats at front and rear (hopefully to allow three-abreast seating, even if the body shells were not truly wide enough), and the already mentioned steering-column gear-change lever.

The author can clearly recall that when the family took delivery of its new Consul in 1953,

If the original Consul/Zephyr style had a failing, it was that the facia/instrument panel was really too plain. An update was sorely needed, but this original 'flat-dash' display would have to suffice until mid-1952.

he was appalled by the slippery and quite uncontoured nature of the front seat, and the fact that there was no centre arm-rest. On corners it was all too easy for the driver to find himself sliding from one side to the other (there were, of course, no safety belts in those days), and having to hang on tightly to the steering wheel; to attempt to change gear while all this was happening meant that he had only one hand in contact with the plastic-rimmed wheel....

Other authors have described the original facia layout as a 'simply styled flat dashboard' – which is really to damn it with faint praise. Except that Ford-UK had clearly made provision for right-hand-drive and left-hand-drive layouts (which meant that the glove box lid had the same profile as the instrument cluster on the opposite side of the panel), the style, as such, was almost non-existent.

Ahead of the driver's eyes, in a very plain full-width panel, was a speedometer whose needle moved in an arc, not round a circular dial, this being flanked by an ammeter and a fuel contents gauge, along with warning lights for low engine oil pressure and an ignition warning. There was no way that an overheating engine could be detected – not, that is, until the steam began billowing out of the bonnet ahead of the driver!

The steering-column-mounted gear-change lever was to the left of the column on right-hand-drive cars, and on these 1951 model year machines there was absolutely no cover – metal or plastic – to match the steering column itself, or the gear change column either. Customers who wanted a fresh air heater/demister could order one to be added to the car when it was being assembled (it could be done later in the car's life, but was not as simple or easy to install at that point), and there was provision for a radio, though naturally this was also an optional extra.

The dashboard was practical and up to a point informative, but it was by no means attractive – certainly not the sort that would cause a new front-seat passenger to sit back, look around, and say 'Wow!'. Although it undoubtedly did the job and certainly met Ford's cost targets, it would be the first feature to be ditched, within a year, when the updating process began.

Launch of the New Fords

Because the media was very kind to British manufacturers in those days and rarely broke any embargoes, the general public knew nothing about the new Fords until the very day – in mid-October 1950 – they were introduced. As far as the specialist press was concerned, Ford was helped because there was a printing dispute that kept *Autocar* and *Motor* off the streets for a short but crucial period in the days leading up to opening day at Earls Court itself.

Ford, in fact, was taking a very big gamble with these cars, and their presence at Earls Court was high profile, and they were surrounded by rivals. Occupying one of the largest stands of all inside that cavernous building, they found themselves only two stands away from Morris (from whom the Morris Oxford and Six were the obvious competition) and perhaps one hundred yards from Austin (whose A40 and A70 models were less advanced, but nevertheless modern). *Motor's* gushing welcome to the new cars was typical of press reaction:

> One of the rarest and most important of motoring events, the announcement of a new Ford range is an event which alone would ensure the success of the 1950 Motor Show. Those who have waited will not be disappointed by either the merit or the technical originality of the two new additions to the range of Dagenham-built cars....

Autocar made the same remarks in only a slightly different way:

> The long-awaited new models from the great Ford works at Dagenham are at last revealed and prove to be two new cars which should fully maintain the Ford reputation for performance and economy. They are extraordinarily interesting technically, with many new ideas to cut costs, save weight and simplify maintenance....

Although none of the specialist press made much of it at first, it also emerged that both cars – the Zephyr in particular – had a weight distribution that was heavily biased towards the front. Once again, to quote *Autocar*:

> Weight is a little more heavily concentrated on the front wheels on the six, despite the extra length of wheelbase, the figures being 59 per cent total weight at the front for the Zephyr, and about 55 per cent for the Consul.

But once the cars went into service in 1951, it wasn't long before the gloom merchants began to criticize this weight distribution, pointing out that it would promote heavy understeer, and that it would mean that there was less rear-wheel grip than was ideal. Unhappily this was true, and Ford didn't help their case by always specifying tyres that had little technical merit. Even so, there were customers who seemed not to mind wasting fuel by carrying around a bag of cement in the capacious boot at all times, while claiming that this solved the problem.

For Ford, in fairness, this was the very first time that such complaints had ever been raised about one of their private cars, since previous models of

the 'sit-up-and-beg' variety had a much more even balance. Nevertheless it was a situation that would persist with these cars for years to come.

Prices (including Purchase Tax) published at this time for the Consul and Zephyr were £531 and £608, but before sales began early in 1951 these were both eased slightly upwards. Ford, as always – before and since – had its finances tightly under control and scrutiny, and presumably saw the way that its costs were edging upwards during the winter.

Below *Perhaps the 1.3-litre Hillman Minx was slightly too small to be a direct competitor to the Consul, but from late 1948 it showed the way with neat styling and a unit-construction body shell.*

Opposite top *The Rootes Group had introduced the new postwar Humber Hawk in 1948, when it had a 2-litre engine, and immediately made the Ford Pilot look old-fashioned. With more powerful engines and slight styling changes, this was an obvious contender for the Zephyr market.*

Opposite bottom *Where the Pilot had failed, cars such as the Standard Vanguard of 1948 succeeded. Looking more modern than the Pilot, with a 2.1-litre overhead valve engine, it was a more attractive prospect in export markets. Even so, when the Zephyr came on the scene, it immediately made a big impression.*

Not a disguised prototype, but the pack of pressings and other components that comprised a CKD ('completely knocked down') pack of parts, which were exported for assembly overseas. Australia was the largest of Ford's CKD plants at this time.

Series Production

When Ford previewed the new Consul and Zephyr at the London Motor Show in October 1950, they were careful not to claim that it could go on sale straightaway – because at that point it could not. In fact, the assembly lines at Dagenham had still not started rolling, but as Ford needed to make an impact with their new car (there had been no show-time innovations of any nature in previous years), they went ahead with the launch anyway. Naturally the national press was quite ecstatic about this new model, and of course Ford's own display adverts made the most of their opportunities.

Preparations for series production were finally ready just before the end of 1950, so after a short Christmas break, on 1 January 1951 the very first of the 4-cylinder Consuls was driven off the line by Ford-UK chairman Sir Rowland Smith; the first of the 6-cylinder Zephyrs (which seemed to get somewhat less attention in the early stages) followed on 12 February.

These were the days (which persisted until the 1990s) when the British government imposed a considerable amount of extra taxation on the basic price of a new car. Even in the first five post-war years, this rate (which was applied to the wholesale price, as paid by the dealer) fluctuated according to the whim of the Treasury, or the need to raise more money. When the new Fords went on sale it was levied at the rate of 33⅓ per cent, which was a considerable disincentive to hard-pressed private buyers.

Early in 1951 therefore, the first time that these cars were listed in the UK, the Consul was retailed at £425, or £543.81 with British Purchase Tax added on, while the Zephyr 6 was priced at £487, or £623.03 with Purchase Tax. One of the extras, leather upholstery (in place of plastic seat covering), added £15 (19.65 with tax), while the fresh-air heater cost £12 plus tax.

An immediate comparison with all the current rivals (see the panel on page 140) showed that Ford seemed to have got it right, and in the still-fevered market for new car purchase, demand soon exceeded supply. Now, though, and looking back more than half a century, one questions Ford's reason for concentrating so much on Consul assembly at the expense of Zephyr assembly in the first model year, as export market demand was certainly in favour of the larger-engined car.

The waiting, therefore, was now over, and the management team that had worked on little else for the previous three years had to see what the marketplace made of their new machines. In January 1951, when the first deliveries were made, they would find out.

3 First Variations – and a New Zodiac

Although production built up slowly at first, there was no lack of demand, for in their style, engineering and performance the new Consul/Zephyr types were immediately seen to be decades ahead of the Pilot – and of course they instantly catered for a place in the market that Ford had not previously been covering.

For the first few months the assembly lines at Dagenham concentrated on building 4-cylinder Consuls rather than 6-cylinder Zephyrs. This was not because the Zephyr was not yet ready for sale – the engine and running gear, after all, were

After spending years building out-dated cars, Ford startled the world of motoring with its new Consuls and Zephyrs, whose shape, by any standards, was an entire generation ahead of what had gone before. All original Consuls were four-door saloons.

being machined on the same tools as the 4-cylinder equipment, and the body shell had much in common with the Consul shell – it was presumably because Ford's marketing staffs felt that they had to start satisfying the '1.5-litre' market (where they had never previously been represented) before they needed to start serving the larger car sector where the last of the slow-selling Pilots had still to be cleared from the showrooms.

Although these would eventually be dwarfed by the achievements of the mid- and late 1950s, Ford was no doubt delighted to see that 35,667 Consuls were produced in calendar year 1951. The production of Zephyrs did not begin until mid-February 1951, and then went ahead at a much slower rate, with only 3,463 cars being

In the early 1950s, tradition and so-called middle-class appeal was everything, which explains why this Consul study is set in the British countryside, and the model elegantly dressed for a day out.

Original Consul and Competitors

When the Consul was introduced, it faced direct competition in the British small/medium family car class from Austin, Morris, Vauxhall and Hillman; because the Standard Vanguard had a 2.1-litre engine, it was really too large to compete.

A new-generation Vauxhall (the Wyvern E–Type) would be launched in August 1951. This is a brief comparison of the five 1950/1951 types:

Model	Length (in/mm)	Engine (bhp/cc)	UK retail price (1951) including purchase tax	Comment
Ford Consul	166/4,216	47/1508	£544	Newly launched
Austin A40 Devon	153/3,886	40/1200	£537	Separate chassis. New model due in 1952
Morris Oxford MO	166/4,216	41/1476	£546	Side–valve engine
Hillman Minx	157/3988	35/1185	£544	Side–valve engine
Vauxhall Wyvern	165/4,191	35/1442	£531	Obsolete (L–Type) style, based on 1937 platform

Original Zephyr and Competitors

As with the Consul, in 1951 the new Zephyr faced considerable competition from other British car makers in the 'Big Six'. As Zephyr assembly began rather slowly (only 3,463 cars were built in the first year, 1951), this comparison table covers the early 1952 period, when Dagenham was finally able to satisfy all its orders:

Model	Length (in/mm)	Engine (bhp/cc)	UK retail price (1952) including purchase tax	Comment
Ford Zephyr	172/4,369	68/2262	£817	Launched in October 1950
Austin A70 Hereford	168/4,267	68/2199	£977	Separate chassis, 4-cyl engine. Launched in October 1950
Humber Hawk Mark IV	174/4,420	58/2267	£1,129	Side-valve, 4-cyl engine
Morris Six	177/4,496	70/2215	£997	Launched in October 1948
Standard Vanguard	164/4,166	68/2088	£919	Launched in mid-1948 4-cyl engine
Vauxhall Velox (E-Type)	173/4,394	54/3500 (64/4000 from mid-1952)	£834	Launched in August 1951, with new engine from mid-1952

produced before the end of 1951. Interestingly enough, once things settled down, and once the demands of export markets became known, Zephyr production rose to match that of the Consul, and would remain on a par for the next decade.

As a schoolboy, I can still remember going along to the local Ford dealership in rural Yorkshire when my father heard that the very first Consuls were being delivered in 1951. Having ordered his Prefect in 1948, he was told that the waiting list was 'at least five years', and so could do no more than admire this ultra-modern machine for all that time.

Not that there were any cars in the showroom, for a showroom was unnecessary at any British car dealership at that time: no sooner did a car arrive from Dagenham than the next customer on the waiting list would be informed, the car would go through its PDI (pre-delivery inspection), and it would be made ready for collection. For the lucky dealers this was, of course, a sellers' market: trade-in allowances were not generous, and neither was their attitude. If a customer complained that he had asked for, say, a green car, and it was a black car which arrived and was offered to him, he would be told there was no choice and asked 'Do you want this one, or not?'

Incidentally, in my father's case, after a wait of more than four years, the Prefect he had ordered

There was ample stowage accommodation in the new Consul and Zephyr models, though the spare wheel mounting tended to get in the way. Shame the suitcases aren't very smart!

had not turned up, so when he received an unexpected phone call early in 1953 to tell him abruptly that a brand-new black Consul was available, he snapped it up at once – and would keep it for the next nine years. Furthermore, as a fully paid-up Yorkshire business man, he listened to the trade-in offer for his older used car, turned it down, sold it privately, and never regretted that decision, either.

That Consul, incidentally, was the one in which I passed my driving test, took out my first serious girl friend, and competed in my first rally; no wonder I have fond memories of it. And what eventually happened to it? Years later, Father decided to trade it in, but at a different Ford dealership, and took delivery of a new Cortina 1200 instead ….

Motoring Press Opinion

Even though this was, indeed, a sellers' market where almost any car, however old-fashioned, would continue to sell in the early 1950s, what mattered in the long term was what you, Mr Public, thought about the product. It was also important to know that the establishment motoring press was 'on side' from the very beginning.

Although in those days there were really only two important weekly motoring magazines, *Autocar* and *Motor* – neither of which wrote truly penetrating reports on the cars that passed through their hands – Ford waited rather impatiently to read their opinion of the new Consul.

Autocar finally laid its hands on an early example – SHK 857, one of Ford's modest press fleet – in March 1951, and published its findings on 13 April 1951. Priced at £425 (basic), or £543.81 with British purchase tax imposed, it was in utterly standard condition, except that the optional fresh air heater (£12 plus British purchase tax), and a radio (price not given) had been fitted to the slot available to it in the 'flat dash' facia. The testers recorded a top speed of just 75mph (120km/h) – also 49mph (79km/h) in second gear, and 28mph (45km/h) in first gear, by the way – with 0–60mph in a pedestrian 31.1 seconds, and with overall fuel economy quoted as being between 24–28mpg (12–10km/h).

As already noted, in the 1950s it was a rather fruitless exercise to search for outright criticism in a road test report, while praise was much more obvious. In three rather breathless pages, *Autocar* commented:

First impressions…are that the engine is smooth and lively and satisfactorily quiet, and that the car is of an overall size handy in city traffic and on narrow and crowded roads; has light, accurate steering, and hydraulic brakes that give plenty of power, and that it has good stability. It is one of the outstanding cars produced since the war – that was, after all, six years earlier – in the popular class, and has handling qualities that would be acceptable on a car of any price.

A comfortable speed to maintain when in a hurry

is a genuine 55mph [88km/h]…users of the Consul in a hurry on business will find that there is plenty of reserve performance, and that average speeds of the order of 40mph [64km/h] are within its easy reach….

And of the handling:

The suspension permits very little roll unless extreme methods, outside ordinary reckoning, are adopted, and the ride is level on average surfaces, whilst severe shock is absorbed most efficiently ….Without being of that pattern, the steering gives the impression of possessing advantages associated with rack-and-pinion steering, in being finger-light, yet definite …

For the driver, perhaps a more vertical back rest of the one-piece front seat would give better support, its angle of rearward inclination not being particularly liked …

Series production of Consuls and Zephyrs got under way in 1951, and soon filled up the assembly lines at Dagenham. In earlier days, the same lines had seen Pilots and other Ford models being built, but this was a new generation of Ford, and all the more welcome for that.

By contemporary standards, this was scathing criticism of the seating layout of this car. The seat covering, incidentally, was very slippery indeed, as I found to my surprise when I first started driving Father's new car in 1953. And if the quoted performance sounds very sluggish, it should be noted that for 1951 it was perfectly acceptable. At the time, for instance, the Austin A40 Devon and the Hillman Minx could only reach 67mph (108km/h), and the (re-engined) Vauxhall Wyvern 72mph (116km/h). Even the Standard Vanguard, which had a 2.1-litre engine, could only just beat the Consul, at 77mph (124km/h).

Predictably, the same magazine's test of the Zephyr (when it came in November 1951) was more enthusiastic, for this was a much quicker car, with a top speed of 81mph (130km/h), 0–60mph in a spritely 21.1 seconds, though with a fuel consumption range quoted as only 23–25mpg.

This particular Zephyr had the revised facia/instrument display (described later in this chapter), the optional radio (£35.78), fresh air

Above *Not every Ford was black! This was the early 1950s Zephyr, showing that the lengthy engine had to be hidden inside a larger engine bay than the Consul, the wheelbase being stretched to suit. Even so, Consul, Zephyr and (later) Zodiac models all shared the same cabin and rear-end bodywork.*

Below *Not only did the original Zephyr have a longer wheelbase than the Consul, but it had a full-width radiator grille style, plus the badge words 'Zephyr' and 'Six' applied to the front of the bonnet.*

Style, class, wealth, British heritage – you can see what Ford's publicists were aiming at when they posed this Zephyr in front of an early de Havilland Comet. This particular shot originated in South Africa in 1952, which explains the unfamiliar type of registration number.

heater (£18.67) and – luxury of luxuries – leather upholstery (£25.67). Mechanically, of course, it was totally standard, and provoked the same carefully phrased praise and comment as had the Consul. Allowing for the careful way in which criticism was made in those days, it was interesting to note that:

> Although the gear change mechanism follows current fashion in that it is mounted on the steering column, the lever is much shorter than usual and very positive in operation; it is in some ways reminiscent of the remote control unit fitted on some sports cars ....

This inferred that other cars were not nearly as good – the Austins of the period were particularly awful examples. In addition, 'The slight but definite amount of inherent understeer quickly inspires confidence...' told us that there really

was a lot of understeer – owners like my own family later confirmed this with our own experiences. Ford, however, must have been pleased with the end-of-test summary which stated that:

> Judged both on performance and on value for money, the Zephyr is a very satisfactory car. It is quiet but lively, roomy without being cumbersome, and it has a very smart modern line without the vulgarity often produced by the addition of excess ornamentation. It goes and stops and handles well ....

The Effects of Purchase Tax

Although the new range had got off to a good start, in April British sales prospects were not helped by the government's decision to double the purchase tax on new cars, from 33⅓ per cent to no less than 66⅔ per cent. The author has already written in another book:

> Although politicians assured everyone who would listen that this impost was meant to be 'temporary', no one believed them. Instead, people gritted their teeth,

realized that motoring was still much more of an expensive toil than a pleasure, and carried on saving hard…

Doubling the purchase tax had a serious, if not crippling blow on the retail cost of a new Ford (and we must remember, of course, that in Britain there was still so much of a sellers' market that there was never any question of discounts being granted). Amazingly, demand for the new Fords did not seem to be affected, even though this was the immediate effect:

Car	Old price (to April 1951)	New price (after April 1951)
Consul	£544	£663
Zephyr	£623	£759

By today's standards, perhaps, this does not sound too bad, but please recall that the average working man's annual wage was probably less than £500. To get a feel for today's equivalent, multiply, perhaps, by 25 – which would have made a 1951 Consul cost £13,600 when it went on sale, or a whopping £16,575 after the rise in purchase tax.

Described by more than one source as a shattering blow, and as a real insult to the British motor industry (*Motor*'s editorial called it 'Dangerous Folly'), it was a self-defeating policy, for it helped to make the existing (Labour-controlled) government even less popular. Within months that government was swept out of office in a general election, a new Conservative administration took its place, and a gradual liberalization of British life began.

Even so, Ford-UK found that demand for its new cars remained buoyant, and the waiting lists remained – although they were slowly but inexorably getting shorter. It wasn't long before the dedicated assembly line at Dagenham was producing up to 800 cars every week; this doesn't sound many by the frenetic level of the early 2000s, but was no less than the directors had been expecting.

The Birth of the Convertible

In the meantime, one change was urgently pushed through, for it seemed the public did not like the plain, flat dash layout of the original cars. Even though a great deal of humble pie would have to be eaten (and there was a considerable amount of unplanned investment in new tooling), this had to be amended as soon as possible.

Accordingly, just one year after the two saloons had originally been launched (and while production of the still-rare Zephyr was still only starting to build up), Ford put on a big display at the 1951 London Motor Show. On a large stand placed in the very centre of the Earls Court hall (and faced across the aisle by the equally large Morris display) there were Prefects, Consuls and Zephyrs in profusion, though the Pilot had finally dropped out of production, along with the torquey but ancient V8 engine that had always powered it.

Altogether this was a rather disjointed display, for modern Consuls and Zephyrs were surrounded by old-type (1930s-style) Anglias and Prefects. On the other hand, there were two notable newcomers: drop-head coupé versions of both the Consul and the Zephyr. Although Ford admitted nothing at the time, to show these cars was distinctly premature, as they were not remotely ready for series production.

More significant was that, even though the Consuls and Zephyrs had only been in production for a matter of months, Ford's top management had taken heed of press and dealer criticism about the plain facia style of the first cars, and had ditched it in favour of a new layout. This time there was a separate instrument binnacle, and a smart moulded cover over the steering column and the gear lever linkage, the dash panel being reshaped.

Underneath all this was a full-width parcel shelf – and suddenly the facia layout not only looked better, but was much more practical and passenger-useful than it had originally been. Unhappily, though, the handbrake lever was still that anachronism, the awkward 'umbrella-handle' variety, tucked away under the parcel shelf where it was all too easy for the driver's left knee to come into contact with it. As ever, the full-width bench front seat was at once slippery, no more comfortable, nor any more supportive, than ever before. All these changes, incidentally, were not made at once, so there may be a number of nominally 1952 cars still in existence with the original type of flat dash.

The story of the birth of the convertibles (and the premature display at the Motor Show to tens of thousands of people) confirms, yet again, that even in the 1950s the arrival of new cars was not always a long and carefully considered process. Although Ford had made a variety of drop-top cars in the 1930s – mainly on the 8bhp/10bhp/Anglia/Prefect base – there had been no convertibles in their range since 1945. Not only that, but as far as Briggs Motor Bodies was concerned, the technology of converting monocoque saloons into convertibles was not well known.

Carbodies and the Soft Top

It is for this reason that a Coventry-based concern, Carbodies, joins the story at this point. Still an independent engineering business at this time, Carbodies had been producing body shells since 1921, and latterly had picked up prestigious business from companies such as Alvis, Austin, Hillman, MG and Rover. For Carbodies, however, the big post-war breakthrough came in 1948, when Rootes invited them to develop a drop-top version of the new-generation Hillman Minx model, where the saloon had a four-door saloon monocoque structure. Carbodies drew on all their experience and know-how by evolving a convertible with the same styling lines and proportions, but with a two-door style allied to a fold-back soft top. Although chopping off the roof destroyed much of the torsional rigidity, which meant that this product was by no means the stiffest of shells, as far as Rootes were concerned Carbodies had done a great job, and they were soon producing this style in big numbers.

Although Ford had never before done business with Carbodies on production coachwork, from time to time prototype work had been commissioned on cars such as the post-war Anglias and Prefects. Then in 1951, Ford-UK's boss, Patrick Hennessy, contacted the Coventry firm. His marketing colleagues had told him there was a market for soft-top derivatives – not enough, for sure, to make it worthwhile Briggs laying down all the

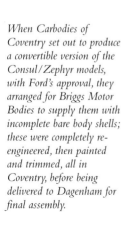
When Carbodies of Coventry set out to produce a convertible version of the Consul/Zephyr models, with Ford's approval, they arranged for Briggs Motor Bodies to supply them with incomplete bare body shells; these were completely re-engineered, then painted and trimmed, all in Coventry, before being delivered to Dagenham for final assembly.

Carbodies

When Ford decided to market a drop-head version of the Consul/Zephyr range, it had to look around for help. Briggs, the supplier of its saloons, was not able to make such bodies, so Ford eventually put out the job to Carbodies of Coventry.

Originally set up as a small body-building business by Robert 'Bobby' Jones, the business settled in Holyhead Road, Coventry in 1928, mushroomed during World War II, and evolved a method of converting unit-construction saloons into drop-head coupés in 1946. It was in the same period that Carbodies began manufacturing London-type 'black cabs' on behalf of Austin.

Carbodies' first series-production drop-head on the basis of a unit-construction hull was the Hillman Minx Phase 1 of 1946; this was followed by the new-generation Minx Mark I of 1948. It was following the obvious success of such machines that Ford made contact, placing a contract to build Consul and Zephyr droptops in 1951. The Jones family sold their business to BSA in 1954, after which Carbodies moved steadily closer to the BSA-owned Daimler business.

Although there was no further Ford business for Carbodies after the Mark II models were dropped in 1962, the firm continued to prosper for many years, and into the new century. Further major contracts included the building of the Triumph 2000/2500/2.5PI estate cars, and the continuing development of the London taxi theme. However, when the entire BSA Group hit financial trouble in 1973, Carbodies was sold off to the Manganese Bronze concern.

Thirty years on, the company has taken over all intellectual and manufacturing rights of the taxi cab from what had become British Leyland, and the parent company's name had become London Taxis International. No trace of any previous involvement with Ford remained.

facilities in Dagenham, but certainly enough to consider engaging a contract company such as Carbodies to do the job for him.

But this all came together at high speed. According to Carbodies' own archive, Ford made their first contact in the summer of 1951, asking them to build two prototype convertibles – a Consul and a Zephyr – within six weeks, for both had to be ready to go on show at Earls Court in October. This was a very demanding schedule, particularly as Ford also wanted to have the soft top of the Zephyr power-operated.

Although there was the likelihood of good business to be gained, for Carbodies this was 'deep breath' time. Three of its engineers – Jack Orr, Jake Donaldson and Ben Johnson – were told to drop everything else and get the job done. It was not as straightforward as it first seemed, however. Chopping off the roof was one thing, and could be done; converting the remainder of the shell to two passenger doors instead of four was another thing, and could be done; stiffening up the under-frame/platform to compensate for the loss of stiffness when the roof was chopped off was another task, and could also be done: but the big problem was in providing power operation for the soft top.

This was the first time that Carbodies had ever attempted such an installation. Devising the soft-top framework, and the hydraulic rams and pipework to operate it, was straightforward enough, but how to provide motive power? After a great deal of thought, power came from Lucas 12-volt engine starter motors (heavy but effective), which were never meant for such a task, but did the job.

Public reaction at the Motor Show was so positive that Ford immediately urged Carbodies to get the new style ready for production by using Briggs shells and making whatever changes were necessary, which they did, but not without a great deal of development trauma. It didn't help that Ford, in their wisdom, tried to second-guess Carbodies in what they were doing. I am grateful for having Bill Munro's permission to quote from his authoritative book on Carbodies (published by Crowood in 1998) for what happened:

> Ford in their wisdom decided to query Carbodies' expertise in the building of drop-head coupés: after some months of production, they asked why the gap at the top of the door-shut was wider than at the bottom. Certainly it is noticeable, but this widening gap was necessary, because no matter how much strengthening is put into an open car's floor, its body when loaded will sag very slightly….
>
> Ford wanted it changed, and would stand for no

Above Carbodies of Coventry did such a superb job in developing the convertible version of the Mark I cars that it was difficult to see it was actually a conversion. The two passenger doors were longer than the front doors of the saloons, and a different type of door handle was fitted. The soft top of the 6-cylinder cars was power-operated.

Below Even with its soft top erect (it was manually operated in the Consul application), the Mark I convertible was neatly detailed. Carbodies of Coventry carried out the body shell conversion, but otherwise there were no mechanical changes compared with the saloons.

Ford Consul/Zephyr/Zodiac Series I (1950–1956)

Layout

Unit-construction steel body/chassis structure. Front engine/rear drive, sold as four-door five-seater saloon and estate car, or as two-door five-seater convertible.

Consuls had 4-cylinder engines, and 100in wheelbases, Zephyrs and Zodiacs 6 cylinders and 104in wheelbases. Consuls and Zephyrs were built from early 1951, Zodiacs from late 1953.

Engine

Type	In-line 4-cylinder (6-cylinder)
Block material	Cast iron
Head material	Cast iron
Cylinders	4, in-line (6, in-line)
Cooling	Water
Bore and stroke	79.37 x 76.2mm
Capacity	1508cc (2262cc)
Main bearings	Three (four)
Valves	Two per cylinder, overhead, operated by pushrods and rockers from camshaft mounted in side of cylinder block
Compression ratio	6.8:1 (7.5:1 on Zodiac)
Fuel supply	One downdraught Zenith carburettor
Max. power	47bhp @ 4,400rpm (Zephyr 68bhp @ 4,000rpm, Zodiac 71bhp at 4,200rpm)
Max. torque	72lbft @ 2,400rpm (Zephyr 108lbft at 2,000rpm, Zodiac 112lb ft at 2,000rpm)

Transmission

Manual transmission: Steering column change. Three-speed, synchromesh on top and second gear. Optional Borg Warner overdrive on 6-cylinder models from August 1955.

Internal gearbox ratios:

Top	1.000:1
2nd	1.643:1 ★★
1st	2.842:1 ★★
Reverse	3.861:1

Final drive ratio	4.625:1 at first, 4.556:1 from late 1952 (4.375:1 at first, 4.444:1 from late 1952)

★★ Limited numbers of cars were produced with different ratios from November 1952 to April 1953.

Optional Borg Warner overdrive (0.70:1 ratio) on 6-cylinder models from August 1955.

Suspension and steering

Front	Independent, coil springs, MacPherson struts, anti-roll bar, telescopic dampers
Rear	Live (beam) axle, half-elliptic leaf springs, lever-arm hydraulic dampers
Steering	Worm-and-peg
Tyres	5.90-13in, cross-ply (6.40-13in, cross-ply)
Wheels	Pressed-steel disc, bolt-on
Rim width	4.0in

Brakes

Type	Drum brakes at front and rear, with no servo assistance
Size	9.0in diameter front drums, 9.0in diameter rear drums

Ford Consul/Zephyr/Zodiac Series I (1950–1956) *continued*

Dimensions (in/mm)

Track	
Front	50/1,270
Rear	49/1,245
Wheelbase	100/2,540 (104/2,642)
Overall length	162.5/4,128 (171.75/4,362)
Overall width	64/1,626
Overall height	60.75/1,543
Unladen weight	Consul 2,436lb/1,105kg; Zephyr 2,604lb/1,181kg; Zodiac 2,660lb/1,206kg

counter arguments from Carbodies. To satisfy Dagenham's orders, a Ford convertible was built with the door-shuts set as they wanted. Four rather large gentlemen then came to test the car, and took it for a drive. Things seemed fine until they tried to get out, and couldn't – neither of the doors would open!....

Carbodies had therefore proved that they knew what they were talking about, and the Ford remained in production until 1956 as originally engineered ....

Because of development problems – it took a very long while to settle on the form and scope of the under-platform cross-brace stiffening that would restore stiffness to the topless body, and still not cost too much – and the time it took to set up the production facilities in Coventry, the first deliveries of convertibles did not take place until 1953. As happened so often with projects like this, a balance had to be struck between production efficiency, the proper use of materials, and how much new capital was needed to set up the press tooling and jigging required in order to make the cars in quantity. It was not the most cost-efficient job that Ford would have liked to tackle, particularly as the Carbodies plant was at least 100 miles (160km) from Dagenham, in Coventry – and there were no motorways, and no M25 ring road around London, in those days – which meant that a lot of truck transport was involved.

In the case of the Consul and Zephyr convertibles, Briggs Motor Bodies provided bare but complete shells from Dagenham; these were trucked up the old A5 trunk road to Coventry,

eight at a time (four on the main truck, and four on the trailer it towed), after which Carbodies would cut, carve, weld, reinforce, paint and trim the new shells before sending them back down the A5 to Dagenham once again. Once the system was working properly there was no empty truck mileage involved, because the same trucks that conveyed bare shells from Essex returned with modified shells. Because of all the shell reinforcement, also the extra plumbing for power-operated Zephyr Six types, and the need to keep the doors in the correct alignment, this was never going to be a cheap operation; but Carbodies were expert at their craft, and Ford seemed to be pleased with the results.

The feature of power operation for the soft top on the Zephyrs was much appreciated; even more so was the fact that the top could be folded to just half way back, to a position that followers of the carriage trade used to call the 'coupe de ville'. To Ford customers (and Ford dealers for that matter), this type of soft-top layout and operation was a real advance on what they had ever been offered before; but Carbodies had already done this sort of thing, so for them it was just a routine job (they had already engineered the same sort of feature on conversions for makers such as Alvis and Daimler).

These cars would remain in production from mid-1953 until the end of Consul/Zephyr Mark I assembly in the winter of 1955/1956. Although by Ford standards this was a limited edition model, Carbodies treated it as one of their most important (and, one presumes, profitable) projects. In the end nearly 8,000 shells made the double journey to and from Coventry: 3,749 Consuls and 4,048 Zephyrs. Ford were so pleased with this model, and Carbodies so happy with the job it did, that both agreed they would follow it up with a Mark II version in 1956.

The New Zodiac – Widening the Range

At the risk of sounding romantic, during and after the coronation of H.M. the Queen the economic atmosphere here at home became distinctly more optimistic. Jingoist newspapers talked about a 'new Elizabethan age', but there were many other factors: economically, it seemed, the nation was feeling more confident, the drabness and the rationing of post-war life was gradually being swept away, and much of the 'make-do-and-mend' of those dreary post-war years seemed to be over. Two fuel-related events had already happened and made motorists feel a lot happier: petrol rationing had finally been abandoned on 26 May 1950 (just before the Consul/Zephyr range was previewed), and branded petrols, with a higher octane rating, had been reintroduced from February 1953.

This generally acceptable trend was reflected in the British motor industry and its fortunes. In 1952 the government was finally convinced that it must release more cars on to the home market. Early in the year the Chancellor stated that he would only allow 60,000 cars to be sold in the UK, but that figure was doubled in midsummer, and the restriction was effectively abandoned before the end of the year. Between 1952 and 1953 UK car production boomed, with figures rising from 448,000 to 595,000; as ever, the majority of such products went to overseas markets. More significantly, in one year UK car sales were allowed to soar from 141,037 (1952) to no less than 301,354 (1953). As a consequence, waiting lists began to crumble rapidly, and by the mid-1950s had disappeared completely.

These trends were reflected at Dagenham where, by 1953, Ford was building more than 90,000 Consul/Zephyr models every year –

more than 2,000 cars in a good week – and was already looking for ways to improve on those figures. Ford's bosses could see there was still an almost unlimited demand for their cars, that more and more people seemed to have good disposable money to spend, and that they were looking for a bit more luxury in their lives. Ford dealers, too, noticed just how much a new car owner was willing to spend on his car by dressing it up: radio, heater, leather upholstery (all factory options), then wing mirrors, extra spot lamps, sun visors and (in some cases) engine conversions. It was clear, the dealers thought, that there was a demand for a more luxurious (and therefore more highly priced) Ford in the range.

Ford, therefore, moved quickly to give it to them, in the shape of a model called the Zephyr Zodiac: no more and no less than a Zephyr Six with all the bells, buzzers and toys that the marketing department could provide. The new car was launched as an Earls Court Motor Show surprise, and as *Autocar* wrote:

> …The Zodiac has all the special fittings that the fonder owner loves, only the radio being a true extra. Two interesting items are a screen washer and white-wall tyres.…

All in all, the equipment of the Zodiac was such that the customer might already have been tempted to fit them for himself. The most notable improvement to the running gear was that the Zodiac had been given a higher compression ratio engine (to take advantage of the highest rating of the branded fuels now available), these now being rated at 71bhp instead of 68bhp. A heavy duty battery up front, and a padded toolbox in the boot, all added to the feeling that Ford had tried to think of everything. But it was the visual appeal of the new Zodiac – so obviously based on the Zephyr, but so different in so many luxurious little ways – that made all the difference. Perhaps it was with this car, rather than with the Cortina of the 1960s, or with the sporting models which followed on, that Ford established its long-held reputation for alert marketing and sales techniques.

1953 and the launch of the first-ever Ford Zephyr Zodiac, the days when one still dressed up for a night out! White-wall tyres, wing mirrors, extra driving lamps, extra brightwork, a duo-tone colour scheme and gold 'Zodiac' badges, were all part of the upgrade from Zephyr to Zodiac.

Externally the Zodiac differed from the Zephyr by having a duo-tone colour scheme – the junction between the two colours being logically placed on the crease along the body sides, this being emphasized by a chrome flash at that crease – by the use of white-wall tyres, extra decoration on the wheel trims, front and rear bumper over-riders, extra driving lamps, reversing lamps, wing mirrors and a chromed lockable fuel filler cap. Inside the car leather upholstery was, of course, standard equipment; this and the re-styled door trims were both in duo-tone, in colour schemes intended to match the exterior paintwork. Little things such as a cigar lighter (nowadays, in this politically correct age, we would no doubt call the socket an 'auxiliary 12-volt power supply'!), a vanity mirror in the sun visor on the passenger's side, and an electric clock, were all standard items.

All this was made available for an extra £96 (£851 instead of £755 – a price rise of 11 per cent) and clearly, from the demand that immediately built up for this additional model, the enhanced specification was going to be very popular.

All in all, this 'dress-up' makeover operation was a low-investment gamble that paid off, and one which Ford would repeat several times in the future. As an example, there would eventually be an 'Executive' version of the Mark IV Zodiac, which also hit the right spot, while the addition

of a Cortina '1600E' to the range of Cortina Mark IIs was a real money-spinner. As far as the original Zodiac was concerned, it eventually sold 22,634 copies – about one in five of all 6-cylinder cars built in the two-and-a-half years during which the Mark I Zodiac was available.

At the time, what was interesting to other marketeers was that Ford's big rivals, Vauxhall, could make no immediate attempt to get back on terms, though they tried hard enough – the Cresta version of the Velox would follow in a year's time. BMC, on the other hand, did not upgrade their ageing models, for they had an all-new saloon, the A90 Westminster, coming along in 1954.

For 1954, therefore, Ford's product range was more up-to-the-minute than ever before. A new range of Anglia 100Es and Prefect 100Es had just been launched, and with the addition of the Zodiac to the range, and the availability of Carbodies-built convertibles, the Consul/Zephyr/Zodiac range looked like this:

Model	UK Retail Price
Consul saloon	£667
Consul Convertible	£809
Zephyr Six saloon	£755
Zephyr Six Convertible	£960
Zodiac saloon	£851

Although this is the very same car – OLE 550 – as seen on page 53 outside a glossy London location, this time the Zodiac has been posed alongside a gypsy caravan. Why? Your guess is as good as mine – all I know is that it shows off the Zodiac's fittings perfectly.

The Estate Car Conversion

In the meantime, there was still no sign of an estate car in Ford's range. In fairness, neither did there seem to be much of a demand, nor were such cars catered for by Ford's rivals – at least, not in big numbers. In these days of the twenty-first century, when estate cars, 'people movers', high-roof SUVs ('sport utility vehicles') and vast multi-purpose machines with four-wheel-drive seem to be everywhere, it is difficult to appreciate why there was such a restricted demand in the last half century. Yet the fact is, that when the very first 'square-back' Consuls and Zephyrs appeared (and even these were not actually factory-produced products), the British estate car/station wagon market was still in its infancy. For once, however, Ford would not be a pioneer in changing all this, for some of the other 'Big Six' manufacturers had already started to take notice.

A look through British price lists for September 1954, the traditional run-up period to the opening of the London (Earls Court) Motor Show, showed that there were Austin A30, A40 and A70 Countryman types, a Hillman Minx estate car, a Morris Minor Traveller and a Standard Vanguard estate car. Ford-UK, as happened so often, had still not broken any new ground, but was looking carefully at any trend that might develop.

E.D. Abbott Ltd, Coachbuilders

It is at this point that a respected and long-established independent coach-building concern, E.D. Abbott Ltd, of Farnham, in Surrey, joins the ever-developing story of these medium-sized Fords. Abbott (see the panel opposite) already had an established reputation for producing fine and interesting specialized coachwork, but had previously built rather expensive shells, and had not tried to break into the series production business.

Earlier in 1954, however, Abbott's bosses had looked around, and had confirmed their gut feeling that the traditional type of coach-building business was in steady and seemingly unstoppable decline. To bolster its business and to look into the future, the company had finally decided to investigate what we may now call the 'mass market'. What happened next was to change the face of Abbott, and Ford. When interviewed for *Classic & Sportscar* by John Mullins in the 1980s, Abbott's previous sales director, Trevor Lloyd, had this to say:

Abbott's of Farnham

The business that became Abbott's of Farnham started in 1909, when Thomas Warren set up a 'garden shed' coach-building operation in his own grounds at Wrecclesham, near Farnham. By the 1920s the business was larger and better established, and it then set up in more permanent premises closer to the town; after a series of transmutations it became Page & Hunt, although this operation went into liquidation in 1929. At this point E.D. Abbott (who had been working in P. & H., on the sales side) took over the redundant premises, and began the fight back.

By the end of the 1930s the company was known for building fine bespoke coachwork on expensive Rolls-Royce and Daimler chassis; it had survived a serious fire along the way; and it greeted World War II by building many aircraft parts, including much Spitfire bodywork for Vickers.

By the 1950s there were Abbott bodies on Healeys, Morgans, Bentleys, Rolls-Royces and Bristols; the first Ford estate car business came in 1954, when Abbott's set up their own private enterprise making conversions, with Ford allowing them access to the dealer network. It was not long before such work, which became 'official' in the late 1950s, took over completely at Farnham. Abbott's would eventually supply more than 13,000 estate car conversions, the vast majority of these to Ford-UK. Ford-UK did not start building its own estate cars until the 1960s, and then only on smaller models; but they made it clear that they would eventually take over 'big Ford' work from Abbott as well.

Having built the last Mark IV estate cars for Ford in 1972, there was no more work for Abbott's, so the business closed down, with the buildings then standing empty for some years. The Farnham site has now been completely redeveloped.

One day in 1954 Peter Woodgate [Abbott's senior stylist] came to see me after he'd been doodling on a Ford Zephyr catalogue. He had drawn an estate car back on it, and thought it might be worth our trying a conversion....

This, as far as I can see, was the first time that Abbott had even considered a 'conversion' of any other style, for it was a company that would rather tackle the entire body construction job itself. 'Ford did not want to buy the idea from us, which was our intention. However, they were quite happy for us to approach their dealer network, which we did.'

Once given the nod of approval, Abbott moved very fast, and had the first example of the proposed new type on show, on its coachbuilders' stand, at the Earls Court (London) Motor Show of October 1954.

In one of its Motor Show special issues, *Motor* was clearly taken with Abbott's enterprise, and under the stand description of the coachbuilders'

Mechanically, the Zephyr Zodiac of 1953–1956 was almost identical with the Zephyr Six on which it was based, its main selling point being the mass of extra equipment – 'fixtures and fittings' is how an estate agent would describe it – which was standard. In this view, the duo-tone colour scheme and the white-wall tyres are obvious.

display, surveyed the Ford Zephyr body conversion like this:

> The latter is designed to increase the luggage capacity of the standard Zephyr or Consul to almost shooting brake proportions, with no change in the seating arrangements, and a minimum of alterations to the body. Yet although the changes are slight, the effect is entirely different, the Abbott modification giving a very light interior, and an appearance of greater length.
>
> Study of the illustration will show how these things are brought about. The Ford boot-lid is discarded, and the rear quarters cut away above the waistline, to be replaced by generously lighted steel panels, welded to the normal wings, and to an extension panel in the roof giving a slightly stepped effect ….' [The stepped effect was actually to slightly reduce the height where the new panel was fixed to that of the Ford/Briggs roof pressing.]
>
> This is deliberate: it retains the strength of the existing roof dome, while providing a conveniently low luggage rack. Inside the space thus formed is a platform for luggage or goods measuring 32½ inches [81cm] long, by 47½ inches [119cm] wide, by 37½ inches [94cm] high, with access from the rear by a door hinged on the right-hand side, and containing the normal Ford rear window. Still greater capacity can be had by removing the detachable rear seat.
>
> This conversion costs £145 including all retrimming, etc, and no purchase tax is payable provided the vehicle has already been registered for use on the road ….

Looking back from the twenty-first century, that £145 price tag does not look frightening – but I must never forget to compare it with the price of new cars, and general price levels of the day. At the end of 1954, the retail price of a Ford Consul Mark I was £667 (£470 plus purchase tax), and that of the Zephyr was £755 (£532 before tax). To convert a saloon to the Abbott estate car state therefore added 22 per cent to the cost of a just-registered Consul, or 19 per cent to that of a new Zephyr. This cost increase was going to be a considerable marketing hurdle for Abbott to overcome.

Not only that, but to make sure that no purchase tax was payable on the conversion, the conversion work had to be done on a car that had already been bought, paid for, and registered as a saloon. Theoretically, at least (though I am sure that much smoke-screen manoeuvring went on), Joe Q. Customer had to order his new saloon car

Originally as a private enterprise, but soon with the approval of Ford-UK, Abbott of Farnham produced a neat estate car conversion on the Consul/Zephyr saloon base. This is a Mk II of 1956.

Estate Car Production

As is made clear in the main text, the production of the Ford estate cars was always carried out as a very professionally detailed conversion by Abbott's of Farnham. Fortunately, records have been kept of the rate of increase of the Mark II estate car production, this being as follows:

Calendar year	1956	1957	1958	1959	1960	1961	1962
Number	119	870	898	1,204	1,475	1,039	38
Grand total	5,643						

This shows that, by comparison with the saloons, the sale and production of estate cars was still a very restricted operation; even at its peak in 1959 and 1960, production rarely exceeded thirty conversions a week.

---

from a dealer, take delivery of it, have it registered, then have it returned to E.D. Abbott Ltd at their workshops at Wrecclesham, near Farnham, for the cutting, carving, rebuilding and retrimming to be completed. This was inconvenient enough even if the dealer was in the Home Counties or the south-east of England, but an expensive nuisance if the customer lived anywhere further north – and particularly in the north of England, Scotland or Ireland.

All this would take several weeks, and for all the financial reasons quoted above, at that price there was officially no question of a customer ever going along to Farnham, and picking up an already-converted machine that he had never before seen. It was possible, on the other hand, to arrange for Abbott to convert a not-complete new car, and deliver it on to the chosen dealer – but an extra £60 in purchase tax was extracted for that service.

Because of price implications like this (and the fact that most potential customers wanted to make up their minds, and take delivery there and then), initial demand for Abbott-converted Consuls and Zephyrs was slow, but as word gradually began to get around, slow and steady sales progress was made. Even so, and in spite of the fact that other estate car prototypes were built at Dagenham in the next few years, Ford itself was not tempted to follow suit. By 1955, therefore, the Consul/Zephyr range had finally reached its initial maturity, with surprisingly few mechanical

changes, or problems to report, along the way. Late in 1952 (not with performance enhancement in mind, but more likely to make the cars cheaper, more reliable and more refined to build), back axle ratios had been marginally changed from 4.625:1 (Consul) and 4.375:1 (Zephyr) to 4.556:1 and 4.444:1 respectively. This was simply done, inside the same back axle casing, by a change of tooth numbers.

That change, once made, was permanent, but internal changes to the gear ratios in the gearbox itself were first introduced in November 1952, and dropped in April 1953. For Ford, which was not normally known for a tendency to fiddle (BMC was better known for that sort of thing!), this was very odd, and would not be repeated in the future.

Shortcomings

In the meantime, both the cars began to be criticized for their rather limited engine power outputs, allied to heavy fuel consumption; but Ford was in no hurry to make changes, as its rivals (Vauxhall and BMC's Austin-Morris models) were always the most important competition, since few cars were yet being imported from European countries. And in spite of its growing success record in motor sport, the Zephyr also began to get a reputation as a tail-happy car that could be regularly persuaded to throw its tail out of line on sharp corners, particularly in the wet.

Cynics suggested that it was always wise to carry a load of sand in the boot to help 'hold down the wheels', which to this writer always looked like a good way of making the fuel consumption and the acceleration worse than before, when the real reason for this problem was in the very poor quality of the 13in tyres that Ford insisted in specifying for its cars. It was *Autosport's* exuberant (and, frankly, eccentric) John Bolster who perhaps summed up this habit perfectly:

On dry roads the car corners well: on wet and slippery surfaces, however, one becomes conscious that the rear wheels are relatively lightly loaded – wheelspin occurs if one accelerates violently in first or second gear, but the resulting tail slides are always easily controllable.

Laurence H. Pomeroy of *Motor* had similar remarks to make, stating that it was:

… possible to promote ready wheelspin and a quick breakaway at the back. But due to the direct and positive steering, such slides can be quickly ended, or accurately controlled, according to choice, and although the Zephyr can present problems to the novice, it is a safe and pleasing car for the experienced man.

This experience came, of course, some years before new-fangled radial-ply tyres became available in large quantities, and at the appropriate price, for at the time the lack of grip was mainly caused by the abysmal quality of the tyres with which Ford equipped their cars when new. At this time, cost control at Ford seemed to be more important than providing good rubber. Not for nothing did a wag describe the tread as being an amalgam of 'camel dung and wet, used tram tickets …'.

Ford, therefore, saw little need to boost the performance of their engines, for these were in the appropriate mainstream area. The Consul's 1508cc engine, after all, produced 47bhp at a time when the Vauxhall Wyvern produced only 40bhp, and the latest A50/Morris Oxford churned out 50bhp, while the Zephyr's 68bhp compared with 64bhp from the Vauxhall Velox and 85bhp from the Austin A90 Westminster. It was not that the latest Ford engines were incapable of producing more power, but that Ford was not interested in putting such power units on to the market. They were quite heavy, for sure – with cast-iron cylinder blocks and heads they could surely not be otherwise – and had heavy, solid and workaday pistons, connecting rods and crankshafts; but with the standard engines the main problem was in their breathing.

Boosting the Performance

As already described, Ford's production engineers had arrived at the cheapest possible way of matching the exhaust ports to an 'exhaust manifold', by making that manifold no more and no less that a tube with appropriate cutouts to match up with the ports themselves. This, and the fact that both engines used one of the simplest downdraught carburettors in the world – the downdraught Zenith – meant that power outputs, and revving capabilities, were strictly limited.

It was not that the engine was incapable of producing more power, or that Ford's engineers were totally ignorant of techniques (neither of those statements was true), it was merely that Ford-UK could see no need to develop the engines in such ways. The fact that neither engine fell neatly within any of the sporting capacity class limits didn't help, either; the Consul, for instance, measured 1508cc, but as the nearest capacity limit was 1500cc, it could not be used therein: the Zephyr, at 2262cc, was stuck in limbo, half way up from 2000cc to 2500cc, and therefore at a big disadvantage.

As far as the keener and more sporting motorists were concerned, there seemed to be a small, but perceptible demand to do something about it. Companies such as Lotus (for the Six model) and Allard (for the Palm Beach sports car) chose these engines on the grounds of cost and availability, so Britain's fledgling tuning industry set about satisfying this. Much of the work was concentrated on the 6-cylinder Zephyr and Zodiac engines, though some of the gains could easily be applied to the 4-cylinder Consul engine, too.

Some conversions were no more complex than the substitution of the cheap-and-cheerful Ford 'manifold' by a more seemly tubular system (mating these to the semi-circular machined recess in the head castings themselves was quite a challenge), while others were more ambitious. Even though the art and science of engine tuning was still, relatively speaking, in its infancy, it seemed to be agreed that the best could not be gained without big changes to the inlet side, too.

Over the years, it was the Raymond Mays and Partners company (based at Bourne, in Lincolnshire) that carried out the most ambitious work on both the Consul and Zephyr engines, not only by developing twin or triple-carburettor installations with (eventually) tubular exhaust manifolds, but by evolving high-lift camshafts and (eventually) entirely different cylinder-head castings.

Much of the development work involved was carried out on Mays' own road car, which he used for more than 30,000 miles (48,300km) in chasing across Europe in the (often fruitless) task of seeing the BRM Grand Prix cars gradually become competitive. Not for nothing did Mays (a commercial animal and sponsorship-seeker to his immaculately manicured fingertips, with an eye for business and freebies which was the envy of his peers) make sure that he started running Zephyrs as personal cars in the early 1950s, but he also made sure that he wrote about them in the motoring magazines too!

It was not until September 1953 that *Autocar* described both these engines, the feature showing that the two conversions were obviously closely related, for both used horizontal 1.5in H4 SU carburettors without air cleaners. To quote the text relating to the Zephyr conversion:

The Mays conversion includes the use of three SU carburettors of the H4 type fitted to the cylinder head after it has been skimmed to increase the compression ratio from 6.8 to 7.6:1 ....

[Once again I must remind the reader that the octane rating of premium petrol in the 1950s was by no means as high as it would become in the 1970s and 1980s, so although 7.6:1 sounds low, it was close to the limit of what that very ordinary cylinder head would accept.]

Other work on the cylinder head includes enlarging and improving the shape of the ports and giving them a polished finish. The combustion chambers are also polished. Additional valve springs are used so that the engine revs can be increased without the valve bounce stage being reached. The exhaust manifolding is not changed ....

Personally, I found the last comment of all quite astonishing – though in later years I note that Raymond Mays added a different manifold to his kits. I note, also, that no mention was made to camshaft profile changes, at least not at this point.

Even with such a simple conversion, *Autocar* recorded a top speed of more than 90mph (145km/h), and noted that 0–70mph acceleration took only 23.3 seconds, compared with 32.1 seconds on the standard car. At the time, in 1953, the conversion cost was £75 (plus labour costs for fitting), which was just 10 per cent of the Zephyr's normal retail price at this time. Cheap? Think again, for in modern terms, 10 per cent of a modern equivalent which might retail at £15,000 would be £1,500 – and would you have paid so much?

In the next few years, several other concerns made haste to offer tune-up kits for both the engines, the names of Aquaplane, Servais, Sports Autos, Derrington and Laystall all fighting with Raymond Mays for a slice of this still restricted market. Although we must all learn to treat their horsepower claims with a pinch of salt, it seems that it was certainly possible to bump up the Consul's output from 47bhp to 70bhp and more, while the 6-cylinder Zephyr (68bhp as standard) could be power-tuned to produced more than 100bhp. Such tuning, of course, did nothing for the fuel consumption, or for the refinement of the installation, though it certainly transformed the straight line performance. In the meantime, the 'works' Zephyrs demonstrated just how effective such engines could be on rallies, their crown-

Success in rallying, with cars on display, was one sure way of getting the public into Ford showrooms in the 1950s. This was February 1953, the location was central London, and that is the legendary Zephyr, VHK 194, which Maurice Gatsonides and Peter Worledge had just driven to victory in the Monte Carlo rally.

ing glory being on the 1953 Monte Carlo rally, where Maurice Gatsonides and Peter Worledge won outright against the cream of European competitors.

One Stage Further

In 1954, incidentally, Raymond Mays and Partners progressed one stage further than they had done in 1953, offering a kit that featured a more free-flowing exhaust system, where two cast-iron manifolds fed into twin downpipes, along twin semi-downdraught SU carburettors, and also their aluminium cylinder head. By any standards, this was a costly and all-embracing conversion, for which the initial price was £100, but only £5 was charged for fitting (which could be accomplished in a day), and a completely new exhaust system (usually with Burgess silencers) was included in that kit. The bulk of the installation, incidentally, was such that the battery had to be removed from the engine bay to a new place in the boot. This must have been beneficial to the grip and roadholding of the rear wheels, by the way – and reminds us of what Ford also did with twin-cam-engined Cortinas and Escorts in the 1960s !

This kit was the basis of that fitted to the fastest and most powerful Zephyrs of all in the next few years (Jeff Uren's British Saloon Car Championship-winning engines would be based on it, for instance), and it included all those desirable features that Ford's own engineers could never have specified on the standard cars, not only on the grounds of cost, but of complication and the difficulty of service.

The aluminium head itself was not only manufactured from aluminium (Rubery Owen, BRM's parent company, provided the casting from their specialist foundries in the West Midlands), but had six individual and steeply angled inlet ports (the standard iron head had siamesed ports), and ran a compression ratio of 8.2:1, which was stirring stuff indeed by the standards of 1954.

For what would prove to be a very effective piece of kit, RM charged £100, but delivered 106bhp, and claimed that a Zephyr could not exceed 100mph (160km/h) for the very first time. When the time came for the performance to be verified, RM lent the same car to *Autocar*, and also to John Bolster of *Autosport*, this being a machine in which a Laycock overdrive had also been installed – such a fitting also becoming available as a performance extra, but not yet from the factory.

It was typical of the cautious *Autocar* testers that no actual top speed was quoted as there was not time to achieve and measure this: '....The highest speed achieved during the test was 95mph ....at this speed the car was still accelerating, if only slightly, and it is very likely that it could top 100mph in favourable conditions.' Bolster, for his part, had no doubts, and quoted a 'two-way average of 102mph', though it is now known that the flamboyantly moustached JVB often used manufacturers' own claims to pad out his own impressions ....

Autocar's figures, meticulously recorded with an accurate fifth wheel speedometer, quoted 0–60mph in 13.2 seconds (compared with 21.1sec for the standard car), whereas Bolster claimed 13.6sec. All in all, *Autocar* had every justification in headlining its piece (26 November 1954, by the way ….) 'Fastest Zephyr Yet', and pointing out that 'The attraction of the conversion lies in the vastly improved power where it is most useful – in the 30mph to 80mph range.'

Preparing for Change

By 1955, when all such conversions and add-ons had been introduced to the standard cars, Ford was looking ahead to its next-generation Consul/Zephyr range, so few important technical changes were made in the final seasons.

There was, however, one important addition to the extras list, which was introduced in August 1955: that of the semi-automatic Borg Warner overdrive. Hindsight now tells us that this, effectively, was being done to test out the installation before it also featured on the options list of the Mark II models – but of course we did not know that at the time.

Although there was nothing new about 'overdrive' as such (this had appeared, for instance, on cars as diverse as the Rileys, and the 4¼-litre Bentleys of the 1930s), the idea of having a separate, bolt-on piece of kit to add to a main gearbox was a post-World War II invention. The Laycock de Normanville overdrive, as fitted to Standard-Triumph Vanguards and Renowns from 1950, then to a whole variety of cars which followed soon afterwards, was the market leader, and a rival system called the Handa also appeared in the 1950s. Both these were adapted to private enterprise conversions offered on Consuls and Zephyrs – but it was the Borg Warner installation which got the nod at Ford, and incidentally, at BMC too.

Perhaps it would be too cynical to remind ourselves that Ford-UK was an American-controlled business, and that Borg Warner was also an American concern, but the fact is that this was also a cheaper piece of kit than the Laycock installation,

and was not nearly as complex or bulky. In the Zephyrs and Zodiacs, it was available for £42.50 (fitted), or £60.11 when purchase tax had been added.

Although it was not as mechanically elegant as the Laycock overdrive, this Borg Warner installation was simpler, and apparently equally as robust. Used as an intriguing extra gearbox, which bolted on behind the main transmission, it could be operated in any gear (which effectively made the car into a six-speeder!), and above approximately 30mph (50km/h) would cut in by operating a facia switch at the same time as the throttle pedal was released for a second or two, and could be automatically disengaged by a kick-down operation (of pushing the throttle pedal to the floorboards in an over-taking manoeuvre). Not only that, but there was a 30 per cent reaction in engine revs when it was engaged, and clutchless gear changes could be made when the overdrive was in operation. If overdrive was left engaged, below about 30mph (50km/h) there was a freewheel action which operated smoothly and in a rather ghostly fashion until the car had almost come to a halt.

In some ways, though, this was much ado about nothing, for although the announcement came six months before the end of Mark I assembly, very few such units were ever fitted, as Ford dealers were cautious about specifying them unless they were specifically ordered by their customers.

Although the Mark I was still at the peak of its popularity – more than 106,000 cars were produced in calendar year 1955 – Ford had long since decided that the time had come to make a change. If only in its style, but also in the rather cramped interior package which it now seemed to offer (by comparison with some newly launched rivals) it was coming to look old-fashioned, so assembly, in fact, came to end on 22 February 1956. At this point a total of 406,792 cars of all types had been produced, which made it an extremely profitable venture for what, after all, was a business – and much hard work would be needed to ensure that the next generation models did even better.

4 The Mark II Cars

By 1953/1954, even before the Zodiac had really gone into series production, and when the original Abbott estate car conversion was only a gleam in Peter Woodgate's eye, Ford had started to look ahead, to develop a successor to the first generation Consuls, Zephyrs and Zodiacs. In the meantime, the line-up of private cars being assembled at Dagenham had changed a lot, the product range was looking much more modern, and yet more change was planned. The last of the massive V8-engined Pilots had been built in May 1951, the only surviving relic of the ancient Anglia/Prefect range (whose design roots were in 1932) was to be stripped out and called 'Popular' from October 1953, while a range of new small Fords, the unit-construction Anglia/Prefect models, was about to enter series production in October 1953. Ford considered they needed all the space at Dagenham for modern car production, so plans were already being laid to transfer 'Popular' assembly to an ex-Briggs factory at Doncaster: this would happen in mid-1955. Furthermore, in the next few years, tractor assembly was destined to move to a brand-new plant at Basildon (just a few miles east of Dagenham itself), and truck assembly would be transferred to Langley (to an ex-Hurricane fighter aircraft factory just to the north of London's Heathrow airport).

Not only that, but Ford-UK was already planning to expand further, by opening up a brand new PTA (paint, trim and assembly) building on the Dagenham estate, closer than before to the Briggs Motor Bodies body plant, and very close indeed to the main A13, which would allow many more vehicles to be produced. This, in fact, was eventually completed in 1959. Before long, it seemed, Dagenham's facilities would be able to concentrate on just two private car model lines, those of the new-type Anglia/Prefect, and a replacement for the successful Consul/Zephyr/Zodiac range.

Building on Success

Even by 1954, and two years before it was due to be replaced, there was no doubt that the original Consul/Zephyr/Zodiac line had been a huge success; compared with the bulbous old Pilot (only 22,155 cars of this type were built in four years) it had sold extraordinarily well. Later calculations would show that, at peak, more than 106,000 saloons of all types – well over 2,000 every working week – were being produced. This meant that every facility – both at the Ford plant, and in the nearby Briggs body plant – was working flat out (and very profitably, too) at all times. Even so, Sir Patrick Hennessy's management team had significantly bigger ideas for the future. Convinced that they could sell every car that could be produced, planning went ahead on a new generation of Consuls, Zephyrs and Zodiacs, with a capacity target of 130,000/150,000 units a year. By any previous Ford-UK standards, this was a remarkable and aggressive target.

Not that it was unreasonable. Once the bomb damage inflicted on factories and facilities had been repaired, car makers and components suppliers had settled down to reducing the waiting lists for new cars. And once the hiatus caused by re-armament to re-equip Britain's armed forces (and to reflect the Korean war) had been satisfied, British car output forged ahead. In 1951, the year in which the original Consul/Zephyr went on sale, 475,919 cars had been built; four years later, in 1955, that figure had been eclipsed by an output of 897,560 – and if Ford's planners had only been able to see into the future, they would have known that the first 'million-plus' year would follow in 1958.

No sooner had work been completed on the new small Fords – the unit-construction Anglia/Prefect 100E range – than Ford-UK's ever-growing band of engineers started work on the second-generation Consul-Zephyr-Zodiac cars, which would take over from the original variety. Their 'brief' from management was simple enough – as Sir Terence Beckett once told me on another occasion, if a car had been successful, Ford dealers would inevitably be clamouring for 'more of the same' – so the engineering team set out to do just that.

Economic realities meant that the new cars would have to use the same basic running gear, and the same basic mechanical layout on the

Carefully lined up in 1956 to emphasize the close family connection between all the Mark II models: Consul (closest to the camera), Zephyr (centre) and Zodiac.

Mark IIs as on the original models, though Ford made every attempt to improve the front/rear weight distribution compared with those of the originals. All the jibes about a lack of rear-wheel traction had clearly struck home, though without completely re-jigging the platform it was never going to be possible to make massive changes.

Along the way, though (as was the tendency in those days, just as it seems to have been ever since), the team also decided to make every aspect of the new cars bigger and better in all respects. This meant that they would inevitably be larger and heavier too – how many of us can remember an occasion when this was not so?

When the time came to launch the new range of models, although the sales staff would have liked to boast about an entirely new model, there had been neither the time, investment capital, facilities, nor a large enough engineering team to deliver that. The new car, when ready, would certainly be allowed to look all new, though much of what was hidden away would be an evolution of the original. Ford hoped that the buying public would neither know nor care about this. This was true except for the shell itself, and for the

style, though the actual 'chassis' platform was a modified version of what had gone before. What no one could have forecast at the time was that this modified platform would also be carried on in the next generation – the Mark III cars – and would therefore have a life of at least a decade.

Externally most of the panels were new. Computers were not then available to help speed up the process, nor was the technique of what is now known as 'simultaneous engineering' yet known, so as the launch dates were provisionally targeted for the first months of 1956, the new style and in particular the expensive and complex panels – the floor-pan, and the door inner panels were amongst the most complicated of all – had to be finalized, and released for tooling, as early as possible in 1954.

General layout

Although the style of the new car was totally different from what it replaced – crisp and angular, rather than rounded, more 'American' than before, and altogether larger than the original – there could be little doubt that one type was related to the other. Even if the two cars had been stripped of all badging and other identification, rival engineers, blindfolded until they were

shown the two generations of car side by side, would surely have recognized the carryover features – engine, transmission, MacPherson strut front suspension – that effectively formed the skeleton of each type.

There was much solid, automotive-engineering logic behind this. Although Ford-UK had concluded that they needed to replace the styling and packaging of the original cars before they became totally obsolete, they also realized that they had neither the manpower nor the financial resources to change everything and start over again. Accordingly, and in a way that would become familiar at Ford and increasingly familiar in some rivals' products, they elected to make almost all the visual pieces different and more modern, while leaving the basic core of the old models alone.

There was never much doubt, too, that the new model was going to be larger than the old. Although marketing staffs would later reiterate all manner of sociological data to justify this – 'people are getting larger .... they need to be able to stow more people and more belongings' – cars have usually tended to grow slightly from one generation to the next because status-conscious customers seemed to like it that way. Certainly it was always going to be difficult to replace one

Over in North America in 1954, Ford-USA introduced this new body style for its 1955 Model Year range. Most of the styling 'cues' from that car would be carried forward to influence what Ford-UK was planning for the Mk II Consul/Zephyr types.

Ford settled the style of the second-series Consul/Zephyr/Zodiac in 1954, with help and influence from Dearborn. This was one of the very first Zodiacs, on display in the Briggs Motor Bodies studio in Dagenham.

product by another that offered less, either in size or status: unless the new project was totally different and more technically advanced (the arrival of the BMC Mini in 1959 was a perfect example), that was a recipe for commercial suicide.

Accordingly, almost every dimension – external and internal – of the new Mark II models would be larger than before, which meant that the unladen weight of the cars would also increase, and this, almost by definition, meant that the engines would have to be larger and more powerful than before. Because this car was strongly influenced by its North American parents, it went without saying that the boot was to be considerably larger than before, the claimed volume being no less than 20cu ft, even though

The date is 1956, and the new car is the Consul Mark II, which puts the girls' fashions in context – but I can't think why they ever agreed to pose like that!

Way back in the 1950s it was fashionable to take one's cars across the English Channel in a car-carrying Bristol 170 aircraft. This airfield was at Lydd, the car is a Zephyr Mark II Convertible, and truly that was an available colour at the time.

the spare wheel and the 12gal (60ltr) fuel tank were both mounted to the floor of that compartment.

As before, too, the new family took shape around a unit-construction body shell (whose platform, in fact, was developed from that of the original Consul/Zephyr/Zodiac), and there would be a shared four-door passenger cabin, with all types using the same doors, glass, style and general packaging, but with different front end structures, and different rear wing/tail lamp treatments. As with the original cars, and once again for the mid-1950s, Zephyrs and Zodiacs would need longer wheelbases so that the longer, 6-cylinder engines could be accommodated in longer engine bays. Although it made economic sense to settle on a single body shell that could accommodate both engines (4-cylinder or 6-cylinder), such a move would not be made until the next generation of Consul/Zephyr/

Zodiacs came along in 1962.

This simple table shows the way the cars grew from Mark I to Mark II format:

Feature [All dimensions, except weight, in inches]	Mark I	Mark II
Wheelbase (Consul)	100.0	104.5
Wheelbase (Zephyr)	104.0	107.0
Overall length (Consul)	166.0	172.0
Overall length (Zephyr)	171.7	178.5
Overall width	64.0	69.0
Front track	50.0	53.0
Rear track	49.0	52.0
Unladen weight (Consul)	2,436lb	2,492lb
Unladen weight (Zephyr 6)	2,604lb	2,688lb

Interestingly enough, although the new car was substantially larger than the original, it only weighed between 56lb (25kg) and 84lb (38kg) more than before (which merely proves that fresh air weighs very little …). Much of that size increase, in fact, went into enlarging the passenger cabin (more detail about this later in the chapter).

Style

By this time Briggs Motor Bodies had been absorbed by Ford (see the panel on page 11), so there were no problems in persuading this body-making facility to make Ford its priority customer, and in the meantime the styling department had already been expanded to take on more and more ambitious work. Even so, although Terry Beckett became styling manager at this time, the actual artistic influences – both exterior and interior – were still heavily influenced by the latest fashions emanating from Dearborn. To quote Sir Terence on this period in his life: 'It was

very exciting to see these designs for weeks, and to go out into the street and think "This is very dull" – for we had always been looking into the future....'

As has already been made very clear, the original Consuls and Zephyrs were shaped in Dearborn and took their themes from the new-for-1949 Ford-USA models – and it happened again in the early 1950s. When the time came to shape the British Mark II models, much inspiration was drawn from new-type Fords and Mercury types from North America, which would appear in the autumn of 1954. Except that they used wrap-around windscreens (which were currently all the rage in the USA, though not yet adopted here), these cars introduced many of the obvious styling cues that would appear in the Consul/Zephyr/Zodiac Mark II cars, too.

Stylists will no doubt protest that they were never instructed to copy what their colleagues in Dearborn had already developed, and they are probably right to do so, but it is an artistic truism that if they were being regularly exposed – by

This was truly Mark II Consul country – a modern housing development somewhere in the Home Counties.

example, in conversation, and by a discussion of developing themes – to what Dearborn was doing, a striking likeness was almost inevitable. Ford, for sure, wanted to develop and keep a 'family resemblance' across the USA and Europe (there would also be similar 'coincidences' at Ford of Germany and even, for a short time, at Ford-France), which helps to explain the likeness.

Once again, a study of the dates is important. The shaping of the 1955MY Ford-USA cars (to be launched in September 1954) was finalized in the spring of 1953, only months before work began on the shaping of the Ford-UK Mark II Consul/Zephyr/Zodiac types – which was just enough time for the Briggs/Ford-UK design/styling house to study styling trends very carefully.

At the time, Ford made great play of their use of 'Oscar', a flexible robot figure 5ft 10.5in (1.8m) tall and weighing 165lb (75kg), to enable them to make the cabin, or 'greenhouse' as comfortable as possible. 'Oscar' was not the largest possible passenger, but was a very typical size, shape and bulk for the period (note, however, that the average British human being has grown by several inches and pounds in the most recent fifty years!), and would be adopted as normal size by several other competitors in the years that followed.

Once again, the brief handed down to chief

One of the features of the Mark II range was the panoramic windscreen – though Ford-UK never made the mistake of wrapping it completely round and ruining the strength of the front screen pillar and door post.

stylist Colin Neale and his team was purely to evolve new four-door saloons, and to make no allowance for other types. The convertible that would follow could be styled and engineered by Carbodies in Coventry, while the limited-production estate-car type could once again be evolved by the 'knife-and-fork' expertise and construction methods of Abbott's, down in Farnham.

Compared with the earlier type, the new model range (which Ford-UK decided to advertise as the 'Three Graces') was not only larger, it also had crisper lines that carried rather more chrome than before. And instead of having simple headlamp surrounds, there were slight but obvious hoods over the headlamps, while at the rear there were sharp-edged rear winds ending in vertically themed tail lamps. Naturally the Zodiac had a duo-tone colour scheme, and on this new body shell there were obvious crease and emphasis lines to make it look more natural than it had done on the 1953 to 1956 variety.

Grille designs, as expected, were themed to a particular model, so on the original cars the consul had a rather simple mesh grille, the fast-selling Zephyr an 'egg-crate' grille (which bore some similarities to the Aston Martin DB3 and DB3S racing sports cars of the period – something about which Ford did not mind being reminded), while the Zodiac's grille had more of a horizontal theme, with extra decorative detail on the front edge of the bonnet.

Although Ford-UK always insisted that the style of the 'Three Graces' had been carried out entirely in this country, there was no doubt that the interior style, shape and location of the fixtures and fittings all had a strong transatlantic flavour. Instruments were grouped under a semicircular cowl on the facia, and dished two-spoke steering wheels were used at first, with a complete horn ring. The full-width facia panel included a glove box ahead of the passenger's seat, the three-speed gearbox had its change-speed lever on the steering column, and (on a right-hand-drive car) the umbrella-handle handbrake was in its usual awkward place ahead of the driver's left knee.

Above *This was the rear aspect of the Zephyr Mark II, subtly emphasizing the width of the body shell, and that it could accommodate three adults in the rear seat.*

Right *In 1956, original Zephyr Mark IIs had this type of 'egg-crate' radiator grille, which would be modified later in that car's very successful career. Note that by this time the badging stated 'Zephyr' rather than 'Zephyr Six'.*

Below *Neat, informative, and well thought out – this was the original instrument panel display of the Mark II models. It would be supplanted by another style for the 'Low Line' models of 1959.*

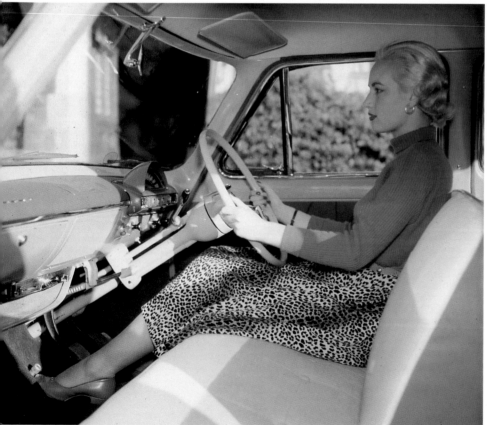

Above *In 1956 the Zodiac Mark II made its appearance at the same time as the latest Consul and Zephyr models; its duo-tone coachwork and now a unique radiator grille are good recognition points.*

Left *This was the facia/instrument panel layout of the original phase of Mark II cars, as built from 1956 to 1959. In those days, of course, there was little attempt to hide the steering column gear-change linkage behind plastic mouldings. On those cars, a bench seat and an 'umbrella handle' handbrake lever were standard, and the headlamp dip switch was a button on the floor.*

As ever, Ford also specified bench front seats, though subjectively these seemed to be better shaped and less slippery than before. It would still be years before separate front seats ever put in an appearance, and there was never a question of fitting a centre-floor gear-change lever, either.

Structure

Except that it was a slightly enlarged platform, both with a longer wheelbase and wider wheel tracks, the stress-bearing structure of the Mark II was engineered in the same way as that of the Mark I. As before, the passenger 'box' and the rear end of all the cars was shared (though clever styling decoration made them look different), and the 4-cylinder-engined Consul had quite a short bonnet and nose, whereas the 6-cylinder-engined cars (Zephyr and Zodiac) had a longer wheelbase and longer bonnet, all of which was to accommodate the more bulky engine. The distance from the centre line of the rear axle to the rear face of the engine flywheel was identical on all models, as was the profile of the floor, prop-shaft tunnel and surrounding presswork.

Although the layout of the new (Mark II) car was very much like that of the old (Mark I), Ford had somehow rejigged enough to make marked improvements to the weight distribution. On the Mark II Consul the weight distribution (unladen) was 53 per cent front/47 per cent rear, and when the car was running fully laden the weight distribution was almost completely equal, front to rear. On the new Zephyr the (unladen) distribution was 55 per cent (front), 45 per cent rear, this comparing with 60 per cent/40 per cent on the original Zephyr of 1950–1956.

The all-steel body shell itself was claimed to be just 12 per cent more rigid, both in beam and torsion loadings, and had been detailed so that more automation (in the form of spotweld guns) could be applied at the ex-Briggs factory. Not that there were any welding robots, of course – they were still at least twenty years or more into the future.

The three main transverse structural sections, whose profile and complex pressed shapes added considerably to the rigidity, were the rear seat pan structure (behind the squab), the dash/engine bulkhead panel, and the forward transverse bulkhead which surrounded the cooling radiator, and supported the headlamps. As on the Mark I, what we may call the inner wheel-arch/engine-bay valance panels were securely welded both to the dash/bulkhead, and to the front bulkhead, and as

Black over plum (damson, dark red – you choose) was an unusual duo-tone combination available on the Mark II Zodiac.

before were provided with stoutly detailed diagonal pressings linking the top turrets that held the suspension struts to the dash/bulkhead structure itself.

As before, Ford contracted Carbodies of Coventry to engineer, tool and manufacture two-door convertibles of the Consul and Zephyr types. There would be no Zodiac derivative at first, though that would follow. At the same time, and in the same rather informal way, Ford gave the nod to Abbotts of Farnham to produce estate car conversions. For the new estate car conversion, incidentally, Abbotts retained the Mark I Consul/Zephyr rear window glass, for since the Mark II had a fully wrap-around rear window it would have been impossible to use the new car's rear end.

As to the convertible, Ford and Carbodies soon got together to delineate each version from the other, not only by the running gear, but by the 'fixtures and fittings'. As expected, the Consul had a manually operated soft top, the Zephyr a power-operated soft top, and the Zodiac (which appeared in October 1956, some months after the original derivatives) not only had the power-operated roof, but a duo-tone colour scheme was available, and leather trim and upholstery as standard.

For these cars, during development Carbodies had more time to stiffen up the roofless body shell than they had enjoyed with the Mark Is. With more underbody strengthening, and some substantial flitch plates to add beam and torsional rigidity, the Mark II convertible shells only

The Abbott's of Farnham estate car conversion was available on all varieties of Mark II Ford, this being a Consul. Compared with the original Mark I variety, the Mark II was an altogether more integrated style – and very practical, too.

Above *Because the police needed to carry a mountain of gear in their patrol cars, an estate car was essential. Even so, only two officers could be carried, and all the loading space in this Abbott-converted Mark II would have been totally full.*

Right *This is how Abbott's of Farnham arranged for the rear loading door of the Mark II estate car to operate. The spare wheel was left in its normal saloon car location.*

Above By royal command: this special-bodied Zephyr estate car was built for H.M. the Queen to use in the late 1950s. We're not sure about the 'woody' styling, but the raised roof line was clearly very practical for ceremonial purposes.

Left This was the back end of the special-bodied Zephyr II estate supplied to the royal household in the late 1950s. It is registered KUV 1 – interesting to speculate if the number survives to this day.

Mark II Zodiacs came in a wide variety of duo-tone colour schemes, and for the first time the Zodiac trim was also made available on the convertible body style by Carbodies of Coventry. The location? Italianate maybe, but almost certainly Portmeirion, in North Wales.

Mark II convertibles – this is a Mark II – had bodies built by Carbodies in Coventry, the soft top of which folded away completely when the weather permitted.

A Zephyr Mark II convertible on the sands of Portmeirion. Lots of salt corrosion was sure to follow after such an excursion, but that didn't matter to the publicists, who wanted to make this smart car look as desirable and upmarket as possible.

Zodiac Mark IIs of 1956–1959 (pre-Low Line, that is) had front compartment/facia/instrument panels like this, with rather ornate seat and door trims, a full horn ring on the steering wheel, and a drop-down arm rest in the centre of the bench seat.

needed one catch per door (the Mark Is had needed two catches for each one). Once again, to quote Bill Munro's definitive book on Carbodies' products:

> As with the Mark I Fords, Carbodies was to bring in complete body shells [from Briggs/Ford], then remove the roof and doors, and press new doors and rear wings. They would then paint and trim the bodies and ship them back to Dagenham for wiring and the fitting of the mechanical components ....

As with the Mark Is, this was still a complex business, but selling prices were loaded accordingly, for by all accounts this was a profitable and (by Ford standards) relatively small operation.

Engines

To no one's surprise, the original type Consul/Zephyr/Zodiac engines were carried forward for use in the new models, but because the new cars promised to be heavier, and because the marketing staffs requested more performance than before, both of them were enlarged.

Although this enlargement – both the cylinder

bore and stroke of both models were increased by a prosaic ⅛in (or 3.18mm) – sounds simple enough to achieve, it was not quite so. For manufacturing reasons, the machined height of the cylinder blocks (between the cylinder head joint face and the sump joint face) had to remain the same, as had the cylinder bore centres, and this was only achieved after the always cautious Ford engineers had concluded that recast cylinder blocks, still with water surrounding each bore, were still up to the job.

As before, the 4-cylinder (Consul) and 6-cylinder (Zephyr/Zodiac) engines shared the same bore and stroke, and the table opposite shows how the new compared with the old.

Interestingly enough, although this engine would be employed until the very end of Mark III production in 1966, there were no further enlargements, though peak power outputs were pushed up considerably in the later years.

Transmissions

There were no immediate changes from the basic transmission layout of the later Mark I cars, in that all manual transmission cars had a three-speed

Engine	Bore (mm)	Stroke (mm)	Capacity (cc)	Peak power (bhp/rpm)
Consul Mark I	79.37	76.2	1508	47/4,400
Consul Mark II	82.55	79.5	1703	59/4400
Zephyr Mark I	79.37	76.2	2262	68/4,000
Zodiac Mark I	79.37	76.2	2262	71/4,200
Zephyr/Zodiac Mark II	82.55	79.5	2553	85/4,400

gearbox, with a change speed lever mounted on the steering column, and with semi-automatic Borg Warner overdrive available as an optional extra; however, the rear axle ratios had been raised to provide higher ('longer') overall gearing.

On the new cars, the Consul was given a 4.1:1 rear axle, and the Zephyr/Zodiac types a 3.90:1 ratio, which compared with 4.556:1 (Consul) and 4.444:1 (Zephyr/Zodiac). The same tyre sizes as before were retained, so overall gearing was therefore increased. On the Zodiac, for instance, the new cars had gearing of 18.5mph/1,000rpm (with Borg Warner overdrive, 26.42), which compared with 16.15 (23.0) on the earlier types.

As already mentioned in the previous chapter, just before the end of Mark I production, semi-automatic Borg Warner overdrive became an optional extra on these cars, though as the installation was new, production and availability were very slow to build up. It was a different story on the Mark II, however, where this overdrive was prominent in the options list right from the start.

In fact there was more to come. Eight months after launch (actually in October 1956) Ford was finally ready to announce the option of automatic transmission for the 6-cylinder cars, although it did this in a surprisingly modest manner. On the eve of the London Motor Show, and at the same time as the Zodiac convertible made its bow, the automatic transmission option was also mentioned. This, in fact, was a Borg Warner DG three-speed-plus-torque-converter type, an American-designed transmission now being built at Letchworth and normally fitted to big V8-engined cars from Detroit; in fact it was already

being fitted to bigger, more powerful and much more expensive cars such as the Jaguar Mark VIII (and, soon, the XK and Mark I saloon types, too). When this was introduced, Ford pointed out that, outside North America, the Zephyr would be the cheapest car in the world for which automatic transmission was available.

Although this were true, there were several good reasons why this should be so. At that time, the state of the art with automatic transmissions meant that their torque converters still suffered very significant losses, both in power transmission, and therefore in fuel efficiency. When such transmissions were matched to very powerful engines in expensive cars (Jaguar's XK power units, and Rolls-Royce/Bentley engines were perfect examples) this could be shrugged off, but with less powerful cars it could not.

Frankly, when Ford-UK set about choosing an automatic transmission, it did not have many options, for no medium-capacity transmission was yet available – though the American company, Borg Warner, was expanding its new factory at Letchworth, in Hertfordshire, with precisely that in mind. In the end, and almost by default, Ford chose the bulky Borg Warner DG, which added more than 160lb (72.5kg) to the weight of the car, knowing that although it would do little for its performance, it would, at least, gave reliable two-pedal motoring, and would have a very easy time in these 2.5-litre cars.

Was such an automatic transmission worth having? Here was a difficult case for Ford to argue, for the penalties of offering two-pedal motoring were a distinct lack of acceleration (a Zephyr took nearly 32sec to reach 70mph (113km/h), which was 6sec longer than normal), it could record only 23.1mpg (12.25ltr/100km), but cost £187 (this being on top of the normal retail price of £871, and therefore a lofty 21 per cent impost).

So was anyone really surprised that, when impressions of the car's less lively performance got around, sales were extremely limited? Ford, in truth, did not really have much choice, for if they were to offer an automatic transmission, this would have to be it. A more suitable automatic transmission, and more efficient for medium-sized cars (the Borg Warner Type 35), would not be available for another five years – and even then, it was years before more than one in ten British motorists could be persuaded to buy them in their new cars. (Ford, in any case, thought they had sprung a march on their main competition, for there would be no automatic transmission Vauxhall Velox/Cresta until 1960; BMC's big 6-cylinder cars used the same automatic as Ford; while the Humber Hawk/Super Snipe range never offered automatic of any type.)

Chassis

Any engineer looking under the skin of the Mark II cars would see obvious, and technically very close similarities to the 'chassis' of the Mark Is.

However, not only were the wheel tracks significantly wider than before, but Ford claimed that the rear axle was of a completely new type, and more robust, with a larger size of differential and beefed-up axle shafts – they did not say, nor did they need to, that the same axle would also be used under their medium-capacity vans, being developed for manufacture on a parallel assembly line at Dagenham.

Although the same size 13in steel road wheels, and their matching tyres, were retained, the front wheels hid wider front brake drums, for on Mark I Zephyrs their performance had sometimes been found marginal. Even at this stage, too, Ford was beginning to consider the idea of fitting front-wheel disc brakes (Girling discs would be standardized on the Triumph TR3 from late 1956, only months after the Mark IIs were launched), but – and this was so typical of the Ford approach to engineering – it was not about to adopt such advanced engineering until another company had experienced all the teething troubles!

Testing and Launch

Looking back, as we do, from a period when no new model can be brought to market in less than three years, after millions of miles of testing,

The Mark II Convertibles looked good with the hood down, and if the Zodiac derivative was chosen, it provided fast open-air motoring.

This is a perfect angle to show that the convertible version of the Mark II still left ample space for two rear-seat passengers. To ease their access, the split-bench front seats were arranged to have fold-forward backrests.

multiple crash tests, styling clinics, and the building of a fleet of prototype cars, the speed and simplicity with which this programme went from 'good idea' to the market place is positively uplifting. At the still-compact Engineering Department at Rainham, we now know that the project moved smoothly from 'good idea' in 1953/1954, to the running of the very first prototype (a Zephyr 6) in December 1954, with the next two cars – logically enough a Consul and a Zodiac – following in January 1955.

Only a handful more prototypes would be built, and tested, in 1955, because time was short, and 'Job One' (which was, and still is, Ford-speak for the building of the very first car on the assembly lines) was scheduled for January/February 1956. It goes without saying that Sir Patrick Hennessy and his colleagues had already bravely ordered the costly body-press tools as soon as the lines had been agreed in the styling studios, but well before on-the-road testing had actually begun!

It helped, of course, that except for the myriad number of details, and of course for the enlarged and more powerful engines, the general layout and running gear of the Mark II was much the same as that of the last of the Mark Is. Testing did not merely take place in the UK, but also in continental Europe (especially on high-speed German autobahns, which were still the ideal location of roads where sustained high speeds could be attained, and maintained), in the snows of Scandinavia, and in the heat and dust of East Africa (where the original Mark Is had already covered themselves in glory in the Coronation Safari rally).

Following the lasting success of the original Mark I types, Ford was, of course, brimming with confidence in its new range. Although the old-type cars did not disappear at once, the new type soon became established. Not only had that peculiarly British post-war disease, the waiting list, virtually disappeared, but the new cars were immediately available in a complete range, which lined up like this:

Consul saloon	£781.35
Consul Convertible	£946.35
Zephyr	£871.35
Zephyr Convertible	£1,036.35
Zodiac	£968.85

If you look at this side-on view of a Mark II Convertible, you would be forgiven for guessing that the body shell was no longer very stiff. It was, in fact, much more rigid than expected, for Carbodies had added a great deal of extra stiffening under the floor pan.

In addition, before the end of the year, Abbott was able to launch its Ford-approved estate car conversion on Mark II models, this being available at a built-up cost of £1,028, £1,118 and £1,223, while Ford would also round out the range with (for the first time) a convertible version of the Zephyr, for what at the time seemed to be the exorbitantly high price of £1,253 85p.

Even though the British economic climate was not quite as healthy as industrialists would have liked, demand for the 'Three Graces' took off like a rocket, and once the range had filled out to incorporate nine derivatives – three saloons, three convertibles and (though at arm's length) three estate cars – sales surged ahead. In the Mark I's last full year, more than 106,000 cars had been built at Dagenham, either completely finished, or shipped overseas, in particular for assembly at Geelong, near Melbourne, in Australia. By 1957, 104,000 Mark IIs were built, and – looking ahead – in 1959 no fewer than 132,000 cars flowed off the track at Dagenham.

In 1957, however, Ford's marketing experts spotted another niche that they considered

should be filled, so from October the £871 Consul de Luxe went on sale, this car being mechanically the same as all other Consuls, but with a much higher standard of trim and equipment (equal to that of the Zephyr in every respect) – though amazingly enough, a fresh-air heater was still an optional extra, which in fact was fitted to the majority of all cars built for the home market.

Out in the open market the performance-improvement kits developed for the Mark Is were still available on Mark IIs, for all the thrusting little companies in this business found it easy enough to adapt their offerings to the new engines. Although the engines had been enlarged internally, they all retained the same castings and fixing points, so with a bit of judicious redevelopment a new tuning kit could soon be finalized.

Although Consul tune-up kits were on offer, these had only limited appeal. It was for the Zephyrs, where club racing and rallying at up to international level might be attempted, that there was a real demand. The Raymond Mays' installations still seemed to produce the best results – it helped that enthusiasts seemed to know that it was to Mays that the Lincoln Cars-based 'works' team turned when they had the opportunity of running non-standard cars in motor sport; and what was good enough for the 'works' was surely good enough for them! When fully tuned by Raymond Mays' engineers, the 2.6-litre Zephyr engine produced well over 100bhp, and a top speed of more than 100mph (160km/h) – so the aerodynamic qualities of the 'transatlantic' styling could not have been quite as craggy as they looked.

Mid-Life Facelift: the 'Low-Line' Conversion

When Ford revealed what became known as the 'low-line' Mark IIs in February 1959, this came as a real surprise to their rivals. Although all British car makers were beginning to embrace the transatlantic tendency to apply face-lift retouching from time to time, only the Rootes Group had yet gone so far as to change things (if only cosmetically) at yearly intervals. Even so, Ford had to react to innovations from its competitors, who were all busy in the late 1950s:

When Ford introduced the 'Low Line' models in 1959, the principal style change was to flatten the roof panel to reduce the overall height of the car, while at the same time this revised type of instrument display was included.

BMC introduced the new Farina-styled Austin A55 Cambridge and Morris Oxford Series V cars; Vauxhall was about to sanitize the styling of the original 'ugly duckling' Victors; Standard's Vanguard became 'Vignale' in 1958; Humber had launched a new unit-construction Hawk; while the Hillman Minx was known to have a larger engine and styling changes on the way.

Nevertheless, although Ford certainly took

In the late 1950s/early 1960s, one of Ford-UK's most important Zephyr/Zodiac competitors was the Humber Super Snipe; Ford benefited by selling at lower prices, and having much the better dealer and service network.

Above *Announced in 1957, the Humber Hawk had a 4-cylinder engine, and was a direct competitor, though it was significantly more expensive.*

Below *If Standard's Vanguard had not been such an agricultural design with an old-fashioned 4-cylinder engine, it could have been bigger competition for the Ford Zephyr Mark II, for it was aiming at the same sort of clientèle. This was the 'Vignale' version of 1959.*

Although Ford's designers had bowed to style pressure from Dearborn and Ford-USA, they made a very integrated job of the Mark II cars, which would be built, little changed, from 1956 to 1962. Forget the 'number plate' for a moment – but the gold bonnet badge and the unique grille make this Zodiac version totally distinctive.

lessons from its North American parent (and saw the way that clever cosmetic changes could produce what looked like new models every season), it left the Mark IIs severely alone from early 1956 (launch-time) until early 1959, when the 'low-line' cars were launched.

There was, in fact, much less change at this point than the publicity suggested, for nothing was done to the drive lines, and almost every exterior body panel was left alone. In fact the only significant change to the structure of the cars was that a new, and flatter, roof panel pressing was provided, welded on to the existing steel metalwork around the screen, rear window and door frames, this saving about 1.5in (3.7cm) in overall height. Because Abbott of Farnham continued to produce estate cars on a conversion basis, they had to make minor changes to their own tooling and assembly facilities to accommodate this change; but as with the saloons, it was an alteration that one had to search for, to notice.

Anticipating the criticisms that would surely follow, Ford pointed out that the reduction in height did not mean that there was much less passenger headroom than before, because they had made adjustments to the position and structure of the seats themselves. At the same time – and this was certainly only for cosmetic effect – the headlamp surrounds (bezels) were made of

stainless steel, there was extra stainless-steel brightwork surrounding the roof gutter and around the glass, and there were new tail-lamp designs to suit.

All this was matched by a rethink of the interior and facia/instrument panel styling and equipment, which was just as 'transatlantic' in its looks as ever before. On all derivatives the speedometer was now a rectangular shape under a suitably profiled cowl (the earlier type had been semi-circular), the main control switches had been repositioned, and the facia panel itself seemed to be more shock-absorbent than before.

The handbrake lever was still of the 'umbrella handle' variety (Ford called it a 'twist to release' control lever), positioned in the centre of the main facia panel itself. There was a new type of steering column shroud, which of course also held the column-mounted gear-lever control, the steering wheel itself had been restyled, and there was now a half horn ring (or D-ring) control instead of the full ring of earlier types. All this was allied to a range of new trim materials, and such American-inspired features as door arm-rests adjustable for the height of the Zodiac, and a heater that was now standard on the Zodiac while an optional extra on other models, and it showed that improvements in the visual package were considered enough, for at this time there were no upgrades in the mechanical running gear.

Sunny day, pretty girl, attractive surroundings, perhaps Henley-on-Thames: an ideal setting to show off the Zodiac Mark II.

Certainly the public seemed to like what it was being offered, for Consul/Zephyr/Zodiac sales continued to rise. In 1959, the year in which the 'low-line' cars were revealed, total production rose yet again, this time to 132,492 cars, a new record for the range and one that would never again be approached. So not only did Ford seem to have its products and its specifications right, but at this stage, the sales and marketing staffs always seemed to know what the public wanted, and what it did not particularly like. This surely explains why the manual transmission cars were only ever available with three forward speeds, and with the gearchange on the steering column. Ford could see very well what its opposition was up to, and already had prototype four-on-the-floor installations on test, but it was not about to introduce them before they were needed.

New Assembly Plant

It is surprising that some other observers and historians have ignored one of Dagenham's most startling innovations at this time, namely the building, commissioning and opening up of a brand new final assembly building, sandwiched between the main A13 road and the London–Tilbury railway line. This, in Ford-speak, became the new PTA building (where 'PTA' stands for paint, trim and assembly).

This new plant was a mile north of the original 1920s/1930s factory, and was closer than the original to what the older generation still called the Briggs body plant, the two buildings being connected by a 725ft (220m) long overhead conveyor over a public road called Kent Avenue. The plant could build many more cars in ideal modern conditions, and was intended to look after Ford's ambitious plans for the future. In 1958/1959, Consul/Zephyr/Zodiac final assembly was moved from one plant to the other, and with surprisingly little disruption – 1959, in fact, being the year in which record production of these cars was achieved. The last Zephyr of all was assembled in the old plant in April 1959.

Way back in 1954, Ford-UK had laid plans to totally modernize its rambling estate at Dagenham, because the original buildings close by the Thames had reached the limit of their capacity.

Costing £10 million (a colossal investment by the standards of the day), it operated on two storeys – bare bodies were painted on the upper floor, with final assembly taking place at ground level – it occupied no less than 250,000sq ft (23,225sq m), and was a gargantuan 1,215ft (370m) long.

Ford made much of the fact that this new building could handle up to a thousand bodies at any one time, and that the systems had been installed to support no fewer than six different model lines: and so it was. This was the plant that initially assembled Anglia 105Es and Consul/ Zephyr/Zodiac types, but the Classic joined these during 1961, and the sensationally successful Cortina was added in 1962. In the next three decades, models would come and go, but each and every one of the later types of Consul, Zephyr and Zodiac would be assembled there.

The plant's last task was to build front-wheel-drive Fiestas, after which the PTA was finally emptied and closed down in 2002. This building was then progressively torn down, while on another part of the Dagenham estate a colossal new diesel engine manufacturing plant took its place. Ford, it seems, believed in acknowledging its traditions, but not becoming stuck in a rut.

The Introduction of Disc Brakes

These days, of course, even the smallest and most humble family cars tend to have front-wheel disc brakes with ABS anti-skid control (which is, indeed, compulsory on new European cars) and all manner of sophistication. It is something of a surprise, therefore, to realize that disc front brakes were not even made available (optional extras only, at first) on the Consul/Zephyr/Zodiac range until September 1960.

A quick look at authoritative Buyers' Guide tables published at the end of 1959 show that disc brakes were still something of a novelty on British family cars, for at this time they were usually confined to expensive cars, or sports cars. For the record, as the British motor industry approached the end of the 1950s, front-wheel discs had become standard on more than fifteen production cars, but the only such cars in Ford Zephyr/Zodiac marketing territory were the new Austin A99 Westminster family and the Humber Super Snipe. Ford therefore made great haste to keep up with trends, and finally made Girling discs optional within the year.

The engineers, however, had not been rushing things, as prototype cars had been out on test for some years. Where sporting regulations would

On 25 April 1959, Ford built the 489,460th and last car on the original assembly line in the ageing Dagenham assembly plant close to the Thames. The car chosen for this honour was a Low Line Zodiac Mark II. Henceforth, final assembly would be in the brand-new PTA (paint/trim and assembly) plant built close to the ex-Briggs Body Plant and the A13 trunk road.

allow it, the 'works' Zephyr rally cars had been using disc brake installations since mid-1958 (see Chapter 6), these having been provided by Engineering, though with manager Jeff Uren adding his own preparation touches. It was typical of Ford-UK's marketing specialists that at first they introduced a disc brake installation as an optional extra, and not as standard – not only so that they could make extra profit for a time, but because they could gradually, but surely, build up experience ahead of the day when discs needed to become standard.

When the disc brake kit was launched it featured 9.75in front discs with Girling calipers, and cost just £29.75p, which was something of a bargain when its price was compared with overdrive (£60.21p) or even a fresh air heater (£15.58p). But although the installation looked novel at the time, it would soon become run-of-the-mill to all Ford users. Pads were of the quick-change variety, with automatic adjustment, and vacuum servo assistance was inclusive.

It may help to know that a very similar Girling installation had been used on all Triumph TR3s built from the end of 1956, along with another similar, but heavier duty Girling set up on the Humber Super Snipe since the autumn of 1959. Ford, incidentally, advertised the new feature by pointing out that a disc brake-

equipped Consul cost £803, which was '£180 less than any other disc-equipped British family car'.

Technically, of course, there were two important advances, one being that disc brakes were inherently more powerful, and much more fade-resistant than even the best of drums; and the effective brake swept area was increased from 240sq in (all drum brakes) to 299sq in (front disc/rear drums). Cautious and pragmatic as always, Ford-UK had made sure that disc brakes had been tried out by other companies (particularly the Super Snipe) before they committed them to their own cars.

Predictably, in the very week that the option of disc brakes was made available, Ford provided *Autocar* with a road-test car to get their opinion, and the result was all they could have wished for. Not only was this overdrive-equipped machine very lively – its top speed was 91mph (144km/h), and it could sprint from 0–60mph in 16.5sec – but the disc brake installation clearly worked well:

All who drove the car had unreserved praise for the brakes. Although disc brakes are fitted to the front only, the whole system is linked to a vacuum servo, and pedal effort is comparable with that of previous Zephyrs ....The action is very smooth and

Given the right set of regulations, a Mark II Zephyr could be a surprisingly competitive saloon car racer. DBH 250 was owned and driven by David Haynes, of Haynes of Maidstone (who are still Ford dealers to this day). David clearly recalls driving his race car to and from the circuits, and sometimes raced with the radio playing ....

Handling tests being carried out at the MIRA proving grounds near Nuneaton in Warwickshire. The '00' registration of this Low Line car is a sure sign of a 'works'-owned car.

progressive, and when applied hard at high speeds the brakes slowed the car squarely, there being no tendency for it to wander ....As is usually the case with disc brakes, their effectiveness was slightly reduced during the first application or two before they became warmed. This is noticed only after driving away in the morning, or after a spell of motorway driving. Heavy rain did not affect their efficiency, and squeal was noticed only on occasions during light application at low speeds.

A large vacuum reservoir under the bonnet ensures that assisted braking is available even with a dead engine, and six successive applications were made without losing vacuum ....

Not only that, but the clientèle flocked to order their new cars with disc brakes installed, and before long the majority of all Mark IIs being assembled at Dagenham were equipped with disc brakes. Ford, clearly, was enthusiastic about this new feature, for in a real technical departure it also arranged for its UK dealers to offer existing Mark II owners a disc brake conversion kit, for which the dealer charge was just £32, plus fitting charges.

At no point was such a conversion offered on Mark I models (the front suspension layout of the two cars was similar, if not the same), nor would Ford have approved its fitment – but no doubt some such installations were made. So if any such

---

Disc Brakes

Although disc brakes were used in some military aircraft during World War II, and made their British motor-racing debut in 'works' C-Type Jaguars in 1952, they were not made ready for production cars until the mid-1950s.

Announced in October 1955, the new Citroen DS19 was the first series-production car to use disc brakes, while discs were added to two British cars (the Jensen 541R in very limited numbers, and the Triumph TR3) in October 1956. For production cars, discs were expensive at first, and by no means easy to service, so they tended to be fitted to costly high performance cars (Jaguar XK150s and Aston Martin DB4s were ideal examples) before they began to filter down the price range. By the 1960s Dunlop, then Girling and finally Lockheed, all got discs into large-scale production, which meant that mass-production cars such as Ford's Cortina GT of 1963 were given disc brakes from the outset.

Except on cheap cars, and then only on lightly loaded rear wheels, drum brakes are now rarely seen.

---

car appears in the new century, do not suppose that a priceless heirloom has been unearthed, because it hasn't; but at least be impressed by some previous owner's enterprise.

Ford's next new range of passenger cars was the smaller but still medium-sized Classic, which had front-wheel disc brakes as standard; when it was launched in May 1961, it was entirely predictable, therefore, that these would also be standardized on the Mark IIs. Naturally there had to be a slight increase in the list price of every model, and this was £25.50, no matter whether it was a Consul or a Zephyr convertible; but it was, in fact, cheaper than the optional extra on-cost quoted in previous months.

Final Year

Although few people knew it at the time, by 1961 the Mark II range was entering the last full year of its production life, so few significant technical changes, and almost no styling modifications, were made thereafter. Although total production was significantly down on the peak of 1961, this was not all the fault of the Ford (which was approaching its fifth birthday), but of general UK sales conditions. A few statistics will make this clear: 84,286 Mark IIs were built in 1961, compared with that amazing 132,492 in 1959; while in the same period, UK production slumped from 1,189,943 to 1,003,967 and – worse – exports fell from 568,971 to a miserable 370,744. It's worth noting, too, that at the modern Dagenham PTA (Paint, Trim and Assembly plant) there was some disruption and congestion caused by the introduction of the new Classic and Classic Capri models.

Perhaps the most significant change was not an engineering initiative, but a marketing one, in which Ford decided to realign their model naming policies. Although everyone liked the 'Consul' title, Ford decided it would keep that name for the new, smaller Fords, and would eventually phase it out of the larger car range. However, in 1961 and 1962 (until the Mark III arrived) the existing Consul Mark II would become 'Consul 375'; but this title was short-lived, and has been completely forgotten except for the few classic Ford enthusiasts who are still running one.

By this time, in any case, this range of big Fords was over-familiar, the sort of car that always seemed to have been around, that was likely to give good, reliable motoring without excitement, but which rarely caused a stir. As *Motor's*

technical editor, Joe Lowrey, commented in his twelve-month round-up of road-test cars in October 1961:

> Nowadays the Ford Consul 375 is the sort of car one takes for granted – which is not at all the same thing as saying that familiarity breeds any contempt for it. A good-sized car which gets there pretty briskly, the latest smartened-up version of this family saloon got treated rather like a sports car by younger colleagues, and thrived upon such treatment....

His comments about the latest 6-cylinder-engined car, on the other hand, were much more enthusiastic:

> Almost without competitors as quite a big and rapid car which can become a completely open tourer, the Ford Zephyr Convertible gave me some enjoyable miles, especially as I happen to like the optional semi-automatic overdrive on this model, which some colleagues virtually refuse to use.
>
> Like almost any convertible, this one shakes and rattles when the corresponding saloon would be quiet, but if this were the only extra cost of having an openable car, I think our roads would swarm with drop-head cars ....

By this time, in any case, the career of these Mark II cars was coming to an end. Although Ford would have liked to bring in a replacement before the end of 1955, it had to wait until the first few weeks of 1956. The last Mark IIs were built a few weeks after the replacement Mark III had been launched (this was done, they say, to fulfil overseas commitments, especially of CKD packs).

Like the Mark I, the Mark II was a big commercial success, given that more than 650,000 of these 'Three Graces' had been built, of which about 80,000 were Zodiacs, and about 12,000 convertibles of one type or another, though there were only 5,643 estate cars. And as sold in Australia, the pick-up/'Ute/station wagon programme totalled just over 25,000. If the new Mark III were to do better than this, a massive effort would be needed.

Here's a version you may not have seen before – unless, of course, you lived in Australia where the Mk II 'Ute' (Utility, or pick-up) was marketed. It was never officially sold in the UK.

Ford Consul/Zephyr/Zodiac Series II (1956–1962

Layout

Unit-construction steel body/chassis structure. Front engine/rear drive, sold as four-door five-seater saloon and estate car, or as two-door five-seater convertible.

Consuls had a 4-cylinder engine, and a 104.5in wheelbase, Zephyrs and Zodiacs a 6-cylinder engine and 107in wheelbase.

Engine

Type	In-line 4-cylinder (6-cylinder)
Block material	Cast iron
Head material	Cast iron
Cylinders	4, in-line (6, in-line)
Cooling	Water
Bore and stroke	82.55 x 79.5mm
Capacity	1703cc (2553cc)
Main bearings	Three (four)
Valves	Two per cylinder, overhead, operated by pushrods and rockers from camshaft mounted in side of cylinder block
Compression ratio	7.8:1 (6.9:1 optional)
Fuel supply	One downdraught Zenith carburettor
Max. power	59bhp @ 4,400rpm (Zephyr/Zodiac 85bhp @ 4,000rpm) with low compression, 55bhp and 81bhp respectively)
Max. torque	91lb ft @ 2,300rpm (Zephyr/Zodiac 133lb ft at 2,000rpm) with low compression, 87 and 127lb ft respectively)

continued overleaf

Ford Consul/Zephyr/Zodiac Series II (1956–1962) *continued*

Transmission
Manual transmission: Steering column change. Three-speed, synchromesh on top and second gear. Optional Borg Warner overdrive on 6-cylinder models. Optional Borg Warner automatic on 6-cylinder models from October 1956.

Internal gearbox ratios:
Top   1.000:1
2nd   1.643:1
1st   2.842:1
Reverse   3.861:1

Final drive ratio: 4.11:1 (3.90:1)
Optional Borg Warner overdrive (0.70:1 ratio) on 6-cylinder models
Optional automatic transmission (6-cylinder cars only)

Internal gear ratios:
Top   1.00:1
Intermediate   1.435:1
Low   2.30:1
Reverse   2.01:1

Suspension and steering
Front   Independent, coil springs, MacPherson struts, anti-roll bar, telescopic dampers
Rear   Live (beam) axle, half-elliptic leaf springs, lever-arm hydraulic dampers
Steering   Worm-and-peg
Tyres   5.90-13in, cross-ply (6.40-13in, cross-ply)
Wheels   Pressed-steel disc, bolt-on

Brakes
Type   Drum brakes at front and rear, with no servo assistance.
               Servo-assisted front wheel discs became optional from September 1960,
               and were standardized in May 1961
Size   9.0in diameter front drums, 9.0in diameter rear drums
               (9.75in front discs from September 1960)

Dimensions (in/mm)
[1956 to February 1959]
Track
   Front   53/1,346
   Rear   52/1,321
Wheelbase   104.5/2,654 (107/2,718)
Overall length 172/4,369 (Zephyr 178.5/4,362, Zodiac 180.5/4,585)
Overall width 69/1,753
Overall height 62/1,575
Unladen weight Consul 2,492lb/1,130kg, Zephyr 2,688lb/1,219kg, Zodiac 2,744lb/1,244kg

★★ From February 1959, when the Low Line facelift was introduced, these were the changes:
Overall length (Consul) 174.5/4,432
Overall height 60.5/1,537

5 Third Generation Success

Six years after the Mark II had gone on sale, it was finally replaced by a new and far more 'transatlantic' model – the Mark III. By any standards this was larger, flashier, and altogether less European in its outlook than any previous Consul or Zephyr type. Even so, it was destined for a relatively short life, for the Mark IV would take over after a mere four years.

Although the new type looked novel – and in most details it was novel – the running gear hidden away under the dramatic new style was very familiar to most Ford watchers. Not only were the 4-cylinder and 6-cylinder engines closely related to what had gone before, but the general 'chassis' layout – complete with MacPherson strut front suspension, and simple leaf spring

location of the back axle – was the same as before. Even the body shell's platform – what we might have called the 'chassis' in earlier times – was merely a lightly modified version of the established Mark II assembly. As *Motor*'s description so diplomatically put it: 'Thus although the hull is totally different in appearance, it is the most changed part of the whole car; it can be regarded as a development of the Mark II chassis ….'

But not the style: when the new range was launched in April 1962 it was seen to look even more 'transatlantic' than the Mark II had ever been – and considering that the newly appointed design chief was Canadian-born Roy Brown whose recent work had been carried out at Dearborn, this was almost inevitable. By any standards,

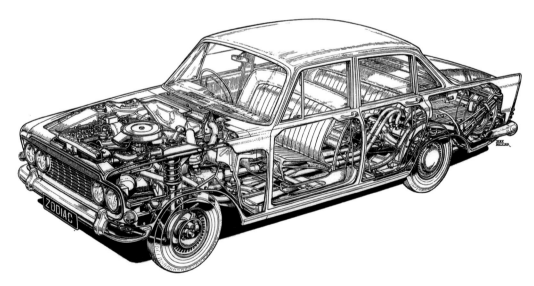

This was the anatomy of the new Mark III range, revealed in the spring of 1962. Although the platform and running gear were directly related to the Mark II's platform, the style and superstructure were entirely fresh. MacPherson strut front suspension was now an integral part of all Ford passenger cars.

This was the thriving Dagenham factory complex in the 1960s, as modernized to assemble models such as the Anglia 105E, the Cortina – and the Zephyr / Zodiac Mark III. This view is taken pointing east, with the new PTA (paint, trim and assembly) building centre left, linked to the Body Plant (ex-Briggs) factory by overhead conveyor. Trailing smoke are the chimneys attached to the original 1930s-generation factory by the side of the Thames.

Commissioned in 1959, Dagenham's all-new PTA (paint, trim and assembly plant) was located close to the A13 trunk road. The overhead conveyor in the bottom left of the shot allowed shells to be transferred from the (ex-Briggs) Body Plant. The total floor area of the new PTA building was a massive 1.4 million square feet / 130,310 square metres.

Dated 1959/1960, this was the final mock-up of the new Zodiac Mark III style, showing the four-headlamp style that would be standard on this type. Look carefully, and you will see that the grille is definitely false. Those were the days when all new Ford products carried such an 'E' project code.

the Mark III stood on its own in the history of Ford-UK design, for it bore no visual resemblance to the Mark II it replaced, nor to the medium-sized Consul Classic that would arrive on the market in 1961, or to the Cortina at the end of 1962.

Market Forces

By the late 1950s, Ford-UK was at its most confident. Not only had the existing Mark II Consul/Zephyr/Zodiac types become commercial successes by any standards, but it also looked as if the all-new Anglia 105E types would become the fastest-selling small cars the company had ever made. In Britain and all around the world, the demand for new cars seemed to be insatiable, and (for those with long political memories) this was also the period in which British politicians were boasting that we had 'never had it so good!'.

Sir Patrick Hennessy's team knew full well that they would need a new-generation Zephyr/Zodiac range in the 1960s, if only to match the flood of competitors that had been launched in an attempt to match the Mark IIs. Launched in 1956, that range had been so successful that it is worth recalling just how the opposition had reacted. BMC (still British market leaders at this point in history) had commissioned Pininfarina to style new four-door saloons that would carry

Austin, Princess and Wolseley badges: these appeared in 1959. In the meantime, the Rootes Group had introduced a pair of new monocoque models, the Hawk and Super Snipe in 1957 and 1958; while Vauxhall (whom Ford feared more than any other rivals) launched a smart pair of Type PA Velox and Crestas at the end of 1957. Even Standard, still struggling to sell Vanguards, was known to have a new 6-cylinder engine on the way.

At this time, because Ford-USA was firmly locked into the process of making every year's new cars bigger, better, more powerful and visually smarter than the ones they replaced, there was no doubt that any replacement for the existing Mark IIs would follow the same philosophy. But it was all going to take time. Although first thoughts came as early as 1957 (well before the 'Low Line' Mark IIs went on sale), the new model would not actually go into production until 1962.

For practical and economic reasons, incidentally, the Mark III would be the very first of this long-running family of 'Big Fords' to run on a commonized (in this case a 107in/2,718mm) wheelbase, which was the same as the 6-cylinder Mark IIs had been using since 1956. This meant that the 4-cylinder-engined cars could enjoy a positively spacious engine bay (which was engineered to take the length of the 2.6-litre 'Six'),

Although the Mark III was built on a lightly modified version of the Mark II's platform, the style looked, and was, startlingly more modern. On the Zodiac version (but not on Zephyr derivatives) the extra window behind the rear door glass seemed to make all the difference.

Viewed from any angle, the Mark III was clearly inspired by transatlantic design trends, but was nevertheless a handsome machine.

and that the manufacturing engineers only had to allow for one basic platform and inner panels to be welded up at the body assembly stage.

The new car was conceived at a time that Ford-UK was expanding rapidly, and its image was changing considerably. In 1956, when the Mark IIs had appeared, the only other Ford cars on sale were the small side-valve-engined Anglia/Prefect types, and the ancient Popular, a real throwback to the 1930s. Now, for the early 1960s, when the Mark III was expected to be ready, not only would there be a new-generation overhead-valve-engined Anglia and the quirkily styled Consul Classic (and its related Classic Capri coupé), but the mass-market Cortina was due to reach the showrooms just months after the arrival of the Mark III.

What this meant was that the new Mark III could become much more of a 'flagship' than the Mark II had ever been, for it would not have to

try to link up with cars quite so far down the price range as before. In the event, total prices were about 10 per cent higher than they had been for an equivalent Mark II. To make the new car special enough to justify this increase was a challenge to which almost everyone within the company looked forward with relish.

As far as the public was concerned, one very important change was that the famous model name of 'Consul' disappeared from the new range (though it would be back ten years later!). Although Ford's marketing men were seemingly still wedded to the idea of promoting the 'Consul' family pedigree, for the 1960s they had apparently decided to use that name on medium-size cars such as the Cortina and the (still secret) Corsair. The Cortina, in fact, only carried a Consul title until a later stage of its development, when the new 'Cortina' name was finally adopted.

Although the Zephyr versions of the Mark III used much the same body as the top-of-the-range Zodiac III, the lack of a triangular rear quarter window turned the style into a much more conventional offering. Engineers will also note that the rear door pressings, and the alignment of the pillar aft of those doors, was also totally different.

The Consul of the 1950s, and the final 'Consul 375' (as it appeared on the last Mark IIs), were therefore to be put to rest. Instead of Consul/Zephyr/Zodiac, the rather uninspired choice of names for the new range would be Zephyr 4, Zephyr 6 and Zodiac. Zephyr 4, of course, referred to cars with 4-cylinder engines, and was therefore to replace 'Consul'.

Style and Structure

If there was no story to be told about the politics of the shaping of the new cars, this would be quite a compact section. As already noted, much of the Mark III's running gear was merely a developed version of the Mark II type; but apart from its platform, the unit construction of the Mark III was all new. The finalized shape was transatlantic in flavour and extremely appealing, even though at the concept stage it took ages to evolve, and several Ford personalities dabbled with it. Following up the mountains of sketches, doodles and small models always proliferating in a styling/design studios, the very first full-size clay model of what might become a 'Mark III'

'Consul' – What's in a Name?

As everyone surely knows, the 'Consul' model name first appeared on a Ford in 1950 and lasted for two generations, but was then dropped in 1962 to make way for the less-inspired 'Zephyr 4' instead. Not everyone, however, recalls that Ford was so wedded to the 'Consul' name in the 1960s that it tried to add the name, really as a subsidiary title, to various other models of the period. Accordingly, from 1961 Ford called its new Classic the Consul Classic 315, from 1962 called its Cortina the Consul Cortina, and from 1963 called its Corsair the Consul Corsair, too. The problem with this was that the general public simply refused to acknowledge it, and ignored the 'Consul' sub-title of any model. Although Ford's managers were stubborn to the last, they eventually accepted this indifference, and by the mid-1960s all traces of this name had disappeared.

But not permanently, however, because in 1972, when a new generation range took over from the Zephyr/Zodiac Mark IVs, Consul reappeared once again, as the entry-level model among those cars – and by the mid-1970s a 3-litre-engined Consul GT had also made its appearance. Nevertheless, the last Consul-badged Ford of all disappeared at the end of the 1975 Model Year, and has never been revived.

The third-generation Abbott's estate car conversion was even more sleekly engineered that its predecessors. Although the 'square back' version of the Zodiac was not cheap, it was nevertheless an appealing package.

was produced at Dagenham in the winter of 1957/1958.

Unhappily for Ford, its design/styling department was in something of a state of flux at this time, for Colin Neale (who had shaped the Mark II) had been seconded to Ford-USA in Dearborn, and no strong character had emerged at Dagenham to take his place. Seeing this, Ford-UK requested that Neale return from Dearborn, which he did for a short period, bringing with him an American designer, Elwood Engel. Engel had been increasingly influential at Ford-USA since Henry Ford II had begun the revitalization of the company, and had been much involved in shaping late 1950s Lincolns and Thunderbirds, plus inspiring the lines of the original Falcon of 1960; so much was expected of him at Dagenham.

But it didn't quite work out like that. On this, his first secondment out of the United States, Engel was not willing (or able?) to soften his transatlantic tastes, the result being a shape almost instantly rejected by the British management team. Thus rebuffed, Engel soon returned to Dearborn; shortly afterwards he was passed over for the leading job in Ford design in Dearborn, and so left the company to join Chrysler.

The timing of that early Mark III concept, incidentally, is significant. By that time, all styling/design work on the 'reverse slope' rear window style of the new Anglia 105E had been completed, and work on the similarly themed Consul Classic was approaching maturity. As was usual at this stage of such projects, stylists working on one particular car might look at what was being proposed for another, and could always indulge themselves in a little 'why don't we ....?' conjecture. This may explain why, in some ways, there was a tinge of the Classic about the Engel proposal – though it was speedily abandoned when he returned to the USA.

Next to appear was another 1958 study, entitled 'Breakaway', and for which Colin Neale was mainly responsible; and no one should be surprised to know that some of the same details as the Ford-USA 1960 Falcon, including two widely separated crease lines along the flanks, and a similar flat-nosed grille (though with four headlamps on the clay model actually produced) should be present.

When the Neale study did not find favour – and none of Neale's subordinates were then encouraged to do their own thing – Ford broke all its previous habits by commissioning a styling study from an outside concern, in this case Frua of Italy. This, I believe, was the first time that such a step had been taken.

By this time closely linked with Ghia, also of

Although the rear-end sheet metal of the Zodiac Mark III was like that of the closely related Zephyrs, full-width brightwork decoration (and of course, the badge) made its place in the range quite clear.

At this time, Ford-UK was still wedded to locating the spare wheel to one side of the (admittedly very large) luggage boot, for the fuel tank was placed immediately under the floor of the boot.

The Mark III facia/instrument panel was definitely, and obviously, influenced by design trends developing in the USA. In 1962, this was the layout of the Zodiac model, complete with simulated walnut veneer trimmings, and a full horn ring. The 'umbrella handle' handbrake lever is just visible behind the steering wheel, under the gear-change lever.

Italy, Frua was an independent styling house that had never before worked for Ford. Working to a brief that was really little more detailed than 'we want a successor to the Mark IIs', Frua produced an extremely competent-looking four-door saloon, which was the very first to introduce the theme of a big Ford with three side windows, but without a wraparound rear glass. This meant that there was glass in each door, and a small extra triangular-shaped window behind the rear door, this being allied to a slim rear corner pillar.

The Frua design was, by all accounts, an extremely well liked and suitable study, but as far as Ford-USA was concerned, it fell down in one important respect: there was no obvious visual link with the parent company's products. Rightly or wrongly, this was seen as a visual and artistic failure, which soon condemned the concept to oblivion. It was therefore time to start again, and as time was still marching relentlessly on – and the Mark II was becoming progressively over-familiar in the market place – a speedy solution had to be found. On this occasion it came in the shape of a new chief stylist: another transatlantic import known as Roy Brown.

For some years after World War II, Canadian-born Roy Brown had been a rising star at Ford-USA. After starting his working life as a dance-band crooner who later studied industrial design at the Detroit Art Academy, he then became a styling engineer at General Motors before joining Ford in 1953.

After designing the Lincoln Futura concept car, which (years later) was eventually transformed into the original 'Batmobile' used in the very first 1960s television series, he moved on to more mainstream projects. Following this, he took on more and more responsibility at Dearborn; but unhappily he then found himself out of favour after he led the team that produced the unsuccessful Edsel range of the late 1950s – which seems hardly fair, as he was only following marketing instructions. His move to Ford-UK could be seen as banishment to 'Siberia', but he rose above that, and would produce some fine and interesting 1960s products.

This was the totally plain four-door version of the Zephyr 4 (Mark III) which, nevertheless, was a big commercial success. In 1962, when it was announced, such a car cost only £847.

Although Brown would later be the boss of the team that produced the Cortinas and the Corsairs, on arrival in the UK his first and urgent priority was to mastermind an acceptable style for the Mark III. It says much for the Frua design that some of its elements survived a very hectic period. Although Brown takes overall credit for what eventually was chosen, able subordinates, including Charles Thompson (who later worked so successfully on the Cortina which followed), did much of the detail work.

One major 'must have' was handed down by management, which both constrained, and liberated, the stylists. The constraint was that the team was not only obliged to use a single wheelbase for all types, but the same basic platform and 'chassis' layout as had been used on Mark IIs of all types: to some of the designers, this meant that they thought they would be constricted by wheel tracks which were a little narrow.

They were, however, let loose with the freedom to evolve a Zodiac style that could look significantly different from the Zephyr 4/Zephyr 6 types. As happens so often with commissions like this one, in which several 'star' stylists have been involved at the formative stage, the result was at once bland, pleasing, but by no means pure or outstanding.

Zephyr 4 and Zephyr 6 types shared the same basic four-door saloon cabin style, complete with a rather angular roof shape that had been inspired by work being done on contemporary Galaxie styles in Ford-USA, and with curved glass in those doors, which Frua's original style had proposed. Zephyr 4s and Zephyr 6s both had the same basic type of bluff front end, complete with two large-diameter headlamps, though with different grilles and badging.

The Zodiac, on the other hand, looked much more individual, with unique rear door profiles (the profile of the rear edge was more vertical than on other Mark IIIs), and with the extra triangular glass immediately behind those doors. Naturally the roof panel itself was of a unique shape, but the nose was much more flamboyantly styled, with four 5.75in (14.6cm) diameter headlamps.

In both cases, the windscreen was very significantly more raked than before (this must surely have benefited the drag characteristics of the car, and the performance figures confirmed this), and although the roof line had been lowered by 3in (7.5cm), the seats had also been dropped closer to the floor-pan, while the roof and rear of the cabin had been pushed back. The curved side glass in the doors helped the door skins to be re-profiled without increasing the overall width of the shell, and there was up to 3.5in (9cm) more internal body width. Even so, there was no getting round the fact that on the new cars there was a bit less leg room both in the front and the rear.

Once again there was to be an estate car derivative, and once again these 'wagons' were to be provided by Abbott's of Farnham (who made an extremely stylish conversion); but because of the cost and complication of these machines, sales were always limited. The assembly/conversion of estate cars did not begin until the autumn of 1962: the record now shows that no more than 1,453 such cars were built in the peak year, 1963 – and sales were already on the way down before the last Mark III model was built just four years later.

And what about the Carbodies' convertible? Unhappily, not only for Ford but all round the British motor industry, the tide was going out for convertibles; Carbodies was particularly badly hit by this negative trend, and the fact is that no drop-top Mark III ever went on sale. Drawings and renderings were made, but it got no further than that.

In 1960, for sure, Ford and Carbodies were both talking enthusiastically about their future, but after Carbodies had suggested that it might cost £300,000 to tool up for a new model, and that the cost to Ford (which means the wholesale cost – the cost to the retail customer would have been much higher) could be £285 per body, there seemed to be no further progress.

The last Ford-based Carbodies convertibles, therefore, would be Mark IIs, completed in early 1962, after which the assembly line at Coventry was closed down permanently. Times were indeed hard for Carbodies at this time, because Hillman Minx/Singer Gazelle convertibles (also built by Carbodies) were dropped in the same year, and a Hillman Super Minx convertible programme would be short-lived. (From 1965, therefore, Carbodies was very relieved to pick up a major contract from Triumph to produce 2000 estate cars ....)

A quick comparison between Mark II (outgoing) and Mark III (new model) structures, and a look at the specification and dimensions of both, confirmed that the new car had evolved around a lightly modified derivative of the old car's platform, which made a good deal of economic sense, and made the cost accountants purr with pleasure.

Looked at from the outside, few would have realized that this was the case, as the new models looked all the more rakish than before, especially as there was some carefully detailed waist-level creasing along the flanks, and (on the Zodiac at least) a good deal more 'glitzy' detailing around the nose.

The platform itself was made more rigid than before by having five transverse bulkheads welded to it and to the superstructure, the most prominent of these being the passenger bulkhead/firewall at the rear of the engine bay, and the panel across the back of the rear seats. It was

Although the Zephyr 4 was the 'entry level' version of the new Mark III range, it still offered the same basic style as the Zephyr 6, and shared the same capacious cabin. For this and future models, the 'Consul' model name had been abandoned.

very similar to that of the Mark II, though the rear end of the longitudinal 'chassis rails' had also been realigned and reinforced, while the inner wheel-arch/front suspension turret boxes that supported the MacPherson struts had also been beefed up. This meant that pressed-steel 'tie-bars' from there to the front passenger cabin bulkhead were no longer required.

Other details included the relocation of the petrol tank, which was now bolted into the floor of the boot, thus adding to rigidity in that area (on previous models it had lived under the floor), and the realignment of the MacPherson struts – the tops were arranged to lean somewhat further into the engine bay, so that the overall height of the bonnet and front wings could be lowered to suit the new style.

Engines – Major Improvements

Ford's main decision in the late 1950s had been to retain the size of the existing 'in-line' petrol engines – for although more 'meat' could have been found in the cylinder blocks to increase the cylinder bores and to raise the capacities, this would have pushed the cars slightly up the marketing range, thrusting them into more direct competition with more expensive models, something which the planners were reluctant to do.

Accordingly, although the same sizes of engine were maintained from one model to the next – 1703cc 4-cylinder, and 2553cc 6-cylinder derivatives of the same basic design that was still being manufactured at Dagenham – important changes had been made to both types. When one recalls

Very carefully posed under trees in full summer plumage, this Zodiac III showed that Ford styling, and the company's image, had come a long way by the early 1960s.

This side-on shot shows that the Zodiac Mark III estate car (with conversion officially carried out by Abbott) was a very spacious machine. One could, if necessary, fold down the back seats to sleep on the load floor, there being enough space — though somehow the Zodiac's image was a bit too upmarket for that to happen very often.

that the first Consul/Zephyr engines of 1950 had produced 47bhp and 68bhp respectively, the news that they would produce 68bhp and 98bhp/109bhp in 1962 was really quite startling. This meant that in twelve years, peak power outputs had been pushed up by 45 to 60 per cent, for an increase in swept volume of only 13 per cent, and along the way the character of both engines had been quite transformed. Though they were still too bulky and perhaps too heavy to be considered as classics, they were at least capable enough to become successful race engines (Jeff Uren's Zephyr had already won the British Saloon Car Championship in 1959), and sufficiently sporty to be sold to small companies such as AC and Allard for use in their two-seaters.

Although Ford always stubbornly persisted in its unique way of machining the face of the exhaust ports — with hemi-spherical recesses so that a perforated tube or simple manifold could be clamped up to that recess — much work went into improving the manifolds, carburation and breathing of the cylinder heads. When the Mark IIIs were being finalized, this work became very obvious in the latest version of the Zodiac's 2.6-litre power unit. On the out-going Mark II, the peak figures were 85bhp at 4,400rpm/133lb ft at 2,000rpm, whereas with the new Zodiac (which was to be more highly tuned than the Zephyr 6)

they were 109bhp at 4,800rpm/137lb ft at 2,400rpm. Not only that, but the published power/torque curves showed that there had been little improvement at the low end of the range, but that there was a very significant increase all the way up from 2,000rpm to peak revs.

The big and obvious change was that simple exhaust manifolds and twin exhaust down-pipes took the place of the original type, though the major change was inside the head, with a higher compression ratio (8.5:1 instead of 7.8:1), increased inlet and exhaust valve diameters, and gas-flowing attention to port sizes and profiles. All this and a 24bhp increase in peak power, incidentally, was achieved while retaining a single Zenith 42 WIA-2 downdraught carburettor.

On the Zephyr 4 and Zephyr 6 models (which, incidentally, were introduced two weeks after the Mark III Zodiac made its debut), the changes were not quite as radical, for the compression ratio was limited to 8.3:1, the Zenith carburettor was a smaller choke diameter 36 WIA instead of 42 WIA unit, and there were only single exhaust down-pipes.

The result, by the way, was that the latest cars would be faster than any previous Consuls and Zephyrs had ever been, which was exactly in line with the aspirational needs of British customers of the period.

Ford made sure that each of the Mark IIIs had a different front-end style, so that the neighbours would immediately know which car was which. This was the Zephyr 6 (actually a 1964 model, and in estate car form) …

New Four-Speed Gearbox – and a Different Automatic

When the Mark III appeared in 1962, much was made of its new four-speed manual gearbox, but because the performance of the cars, and their widened speed range, had changed so much in a decade, it was in fact high time that Ford adopted such an installation. For years, the reasons given for retention of the old-type three-speed gearbox were tenuous, to say the least – one of them being that the engines produced so much torque that no more intermediate ratios were needed – but the fact was that the use of a three-speed transmission had originally been dictated by Ford-USA on low cost and simplicity grounds, and that for some years no one had been able to advance good financial reasons why it should be changed.

Until, that is, the end of the 1950s, when the projected performance of the Mark III Zephyrs and Zodiacs made it clear that second gear in the existing three-speed gearbox would be given quite a hard time, and that a first gear without synchromesh was no longer acceptable to the sales force. A four-speed gearbox was necessary, it was suggested, and this needed to have synchromesh on all forward gears.

Once again the company's engineers already knew what they wanted to do, for prototypes had been running around for quite a while, though there was a time when thought was given to making the new four-speeder a more expensive option. It was only when further marketing studies showed that the optional 'take' might be limited, that it was decided to make this the only type of manual transmission in the new model. And so it was that a new four-speed box, an entirely different design from anything that had gone before at Dagenham, came on to the scene. As far as the enthusiasts were concerned, the only drawback was that it was still firmly engineered with a steering-column change, and not a central floor-change control.

Nevertheless, the new four-speeder was a complete design generation ahead of the three-speeder, which was totally abandoned in Ford's private cars, and it was typical of Ford's planning that they also intended to find a use for it in other models in due course. Not only did it have synchromesh on all forward gears, but this was of the robust baulk-ring type. However, the new cast-iron casing and the layout of the gear-change mechanism was arranged so that all internal gear selectors were at one side of the casing, and a steering-column change was standard.

At this stage there was no intention to provide a floor change, nor did there seem to be any obvious and easy way of providing one, either. The conversions industry thought otherwise, however, and it wasn't long before Wooler (of Alperton, in Middlesex) had developed a surprisingly precise conversion for which they would charge a mere £17.52p.

There were two sets of internal gearbox ratios in the new four-speeder – one wide ratio set for 4-cylinder-engined Consuls, and a closer ratio set for 6-cylinder-engined cars. For interest, the table below shows how the gearbox internal ratios compared between old three-speed and new four-speed transmissions.

Of the two different sets of internal ratios, the 'wider' set of ratios for the 4-cylinder cars indicated that Ford recognized that this engine would have a demanding job to do in the new and larger body structure of the Mark III.

As before, Borg Warner semi-automatic overdrive was an optional extra, but because it continued to operate on all forward gears (and there were more of them than before), the overdrive ratio had been changed from 0.70:1 (earlier models) to 0.78:1 (Mark III).

Although a third of the transmission options was that of an automatic gearbox, this time round Ford had ditched the bulky old DG unit, and adopted the brand new Borg Warner Type 35 instead. Although engineered in the USA (Borg Warner being an American concern), the new gearbox was to be British built, and was a much smaller, more compact, and purposefully more 'light duty' transmission than the DG had ever been. It was specifically intended to appeal to any

…though the style was, of course, retained on all four-door saloons, too.

and every European manufacturer who wanted to add an automatic option for cars with engines as small as 1.5 litres. Not only that, but it was much cheaper to manufacture than the DG, those cost savings being passed on to the customers.

Announced as recently as September 1961, and manufactured at Letchworth (where Borg Warner had spent £4 million on a new factory extension), the Type 35 was immediately taken up for use in several models built by Britain's 'Big Six', and would soon find favour in Europe, too. Although technically similar to the DG, it was entirely different, smaller, and considerably lighter, for Borg Warner claimed that it was 85lb/38.5kg lighter than the DG (perhaps only 20–25lb/9–11.5kg heavier than a typical manual transmission which it would replace), was virtually the same bulk as a typical four-speed manu-

Ratio	Four-speed gearbox (4-cyl engine)	Four-speed gearbox (6-cyl engine)	Three-speed gearbox (Late model Mk II)
Top gear	1.000:1	1.000:1	1.000:1
Third gear	1.505:1	1.412:1	–
Second gear	2.353:1	2.214:1	1.64:1
First gear	4.412:1	3.163:1	2.84:1
Reverse	4.667:1	3.346:1	3.86:1

Carefully posed Ford 'Z-Cars' night-time study, emphasizing the point that many British police forces used modified Zephyr 6 Mark IIIs as patrol cars.

Z Cars

Amazing, isn't it, that some TV series are forgotten within weeks of their ending, but others seem to live for ever. *Z Cars*, a cops-and-robbers series set in and around Liverpool, was one of those timeless classics which not only made stars of actors like Brian Blessed, but in which a series of police-equipped Zephyrs always figured strongly.

The two Zephyrs, both of them low-line cars painted yellow to make them show up best of all on the rather grainy black-and-white transmissions which the BBC was then transmitting, carried call signs 'Z Victor 1' and 'Z Victor 2', while the base radio station was 'BD'....

Not until the 1970s, when *The Sweeney* would bring fame to Consul GTs of the post-Zodiac vintage, would a big Ford be as famous once again ....

al transmission, and was available with a choice of 9.5in- or 11in-diameter three-element torque converters. Not only that, but both Ford and Borg Warner claimed that in smaller-engined cars it was much more efficient than the previous (and as far as Ford was concerned, now obsolete) DG variety.

It was interesting, however, that though the new Type 35 was an altogether more satisfactory transmission than the DG it replaced, most manufacturers, Ford included, found it very difficult to sell auto-equipped cars. Extra cost, less lively acceleration and significantly heavier fuel consumption were all blamed for this; for many years, in fact, they would find it difficult to convince even one in ten customers that this was what he needed.

True comparative road tests, such as published

Maybe you don't believe this, but we are assured that a specially prepared police-car version of the Zephyr 6 really would swallow all that emergency gear in 1962. But where is this location? Because the picture dates from 1963 and the motorway is not yet open, we guess it is on the about-to-be-completed M6 in Lancashire.

Just for fun, really – with a police-spec. Zephyr 6 Mark III police car supposedly 'catching a criminal' as he dashes away from his tatty old van.

for the Zephyr 4 in *Autocar*, didn't help, because a detailed, measured comparison between manual and automatic transmission cars showed that the automatic transmission reduced the top speed from 84mph (135km/h) to 76mph (122km/h), while the 0–60mph acceleration time rose from 19.6sec (manual) to 23.3sec (automatic).

On the Road

Because many of the 'oily bits' of the new Mark IIIs were all evolved from those of the Mark IIs – except, of course, for the new four-speed manual gearbox, and the Borg Warner Type 35 automatic transmission – much prototype testing and durability proving of the latest running gear could be carried out in public without disguise, under Mark II shells that had been suitably hacked around (the detail of the latest front suspension towers being a good case in point). The first correctly styled Mark III prototype did not take to the road until October 1960, by which time press tooling manufacture was well advanced, and it did not take long for Ford's engineers to confirm that the 109bhp Zodiac, even in standard form, was by far the fastest Ford-UK machine yet designed – and independent road test cars eventually proved that it

had a top speed of no less than 100–101mph (161–162.5km/h).

Even though the development period was, by definition, crammed into rather a short period, Ford claimed they had carried out testing in many extreme-climate territories, and that more than a million miles of testing had been carried out.

During 1961, it seems, the modern PTA (paint, trim and assembly building) at Dagenham was in real turmoil, as preparations for one new model after another got under way. Not only did the planners have to make provision for the new Mark III, but they also had to usher the new Consul Classic saloons and Classic Capri coupés into series production, and to make serious preparations to build the still-secret Cortina range, too.

Much of the upheaval was hidden behind factory walls (or was it merely that in those innocent days, motoring writers did not try too hard to see what was going on?), but we now know that there was actually a short period early in 1962 when both old-type Mark IIs and new-type Mark IIIs were being manufactured – which must have presented a real challenge, especially to the body plant (ex-Briggs) adjacent to the PTA. We now know that the first pilot-build Mark IIIs

The entry-level Zephyr 4, complete with 1.7-litre 4-cylinder engine, had the simplest style of all.

were assembled in December 1961/January 1962, while assembly of old-type Mark IIs carried on until April 1962. However, when the new range was finally launched in April 1962, all derivatives were in series production, and available in most showrooms.

It was typical of Ford's careful product planning that it arranged for a complete spread of models – Zephyr 4, Zephyr 6 and Zodiac – to be available at carefully graded prices and equipment levels. Even so, all were offered with the same basic interior, where a bench front seat and a steering-column gear shift were still standard, and a large, full-width facia/instrument panel included a drop-down glove box and a very prominent hood/cowl over the speedometer; the steering wheel (though somewhat 'transatlantic' in style) was deeply dished, with a full-width horn ring.

Naturally, the ever-loyal British motoring press gave all the new Fords a friendly reception, for every writer made much of the way that the new cars were not only smarter, more powerful and faster than before, but were significantly more expensive, and more subtly upmarket, too. Since this was still a time when cost inflation was very low, it seemed that Ford had definitely moved the Zephyr/Zodiac models considerably up-market – and we now know that this was a deliberate

move, to allow more space in the product range for further new models such as the Cortina (soon) and the Corsair (from late 1963) to find a place, and establish a real pricing ladder on the showroom floors.

In fact it might be easy to become confused between 'new' and 'old' price levels (quite unexpectedly the British government reduced purchase tax just a matter of days before the model changeover), especially as magazine press schedules meant that the description of the new Zodiac was sometimes printed with an earlier, higher price level, at which it would never be sold! Here, therefore, is a direct model-to-model comparison between the British prices (including purchase tax) of new model and old model saloons as they applied in April 1962, on the very day that the new Mark IIIs took over from the Mark IIs:

Mark II		Mark III	
Consul	£796	Zephyr 4	£847
Consul de Luxe	£837		
Zephyr 6	£888	Zephyr 6	£929
Zodiac	£979	Zodiac	£1,071

Although those prices all look incredibly low by early twenty-first-century levels, they were absolutely in the mainstream of what other manufacturers had to ask for their products, and should be related to wages and costs of the period; for instance, a middle manager of this period might be earning £1,500–£2,000 a year, which puts Zephyr/Zodiac prices into perspective. For comparison, too, the current 2.9-litre Austin A110 Westminster cost £1,197, while the top-of-the-range Vauxhall Cresta was priced at £984. Needless to say, Ford-UK was probably quite a lot more worried about the attractively low price levels of the Vauxhall, than the rather inflated ones of the BMC Austin.

What should also be taken into account is that equipment levels were by no means as complete as they would become in following decades. Even though these cars were the flagships of the new Ford range, one still had to pay £20.62p for a fresh-air heater on Zephyrs, and £33.69p for the option of leather upholstery on the Zodiac – though front-wheel disc brakes were now standard throughout the range.

Another measure of the way that it was possible to increase prices in the showroom was that optional Borg Warner overdrive cost £58, while the Borg Warner Type 35 automatic transmission option cost £110. Thus it was not only the automatic transmission's technical limitations, but its high price (about 10 per cent of the normal retail price of one of these Mark IIIs) which kept demand well down.

Nevertheless, all this seemed to be acceptable to the clientèle, who queued up to buy the latest offerings, though their general prosperity and aspirations were such that the purchasing balance had now swung firmly towards the 6-cylinder cars. In 1961, the last full year in which Mark IIs were being built, 48,665 Consuls and 35,621 Zephyr/Zodiac types had been produced, while in 1963 (the first full year of the Mark IIIs) the comparative figures were 30,743 Zephyr 4s, and 52,665 Zephyr 6/Zodiacs. Demand for 6-cylinder cars, therefore, was up, whereas that for 4-cylinder cars was declining – and this was not a one-off effect either, as later trends would show.

Autocar's rather gushing report on the new Zodiac, which was tested in 'basic' form with neither overdrive nor automatic transmission installed, made assumptions that must have caused Ford's PR staff to smile: 'Whenever the assembly lines at Dagenham are geared to the production of a completely new model, one can be sure that several years of intensive thought and searching experiment lie behind it ....' Much thought, perhaps, but as we now know, only a very compressed period of 'searching experiment'!

The test nevertheless confirmed that this was indeed the fastest British Ford so far put on sale (the Lotus-Cortina of 1963 was about to surpass it, but we did not know that at the time), for the top speed was recorded as almost exactly 100mph (160km/h), with 0–60mph recorded in 13.5sec, and the standing-start quarter-mile sprint was reached in 19.2sec. Fuel consumption at 19.1mpg (14.8ltr/100km) was poor, but since in those days fuel cost only about 22p per imperial gallon (4.85p per litre) no one seemed to worry too much about that.

Balancing out all the praise for the car's performance, criticisms centred on the lack of rear seat leg room, on the excessive movement of the steering column gear lever between ratios, and on the generally transatlantic air of all the fixtures and fittings. However, since the engine was thought to remain 'refined and notably unobtrusive at high engine revolutions, and the car can maintain 80–90mph [130–145km/h] on a motorway with most agreeable ease....' the testers forgave every other failing, summarizing that: 'There is every indication that the new Zodiac will attract an even wider public than its predecessor, that it will please them more, and serve them better....'

Perhaps this high overhead front-end study is the most flattering of all angles from which to view the Mark III Zodiac, and it certainly emphasizes the width of the latest big car from Dagenham.

Price Reductions Boost Demand

There was no estate car in the Mark III range at first, for the new Abbott's of Farnham package did not arrive until October 1962, when its launch was almost submerged under the publicity allocated to Ford's all new (and commercially vital) medium-sized Cortina. As with previous Abbott's-plus-Ford enterprises, this was a joint engineering effort, for the estate car was effectively a conversion of the four-door saloon, though this time round the tailgate opened upwards instead of sideways as it had on earlier types. This time, though, Abbott, egged on by Ford's designer/stylists, had made a special effort by providing one long sweep of roof line, so that the 'conversion' aspect had completely vanished.

The new type looked big – and was big – for even though the estate car door leaned rather dramatically forwards, the company still claimed 29cu ft (8cu m) of enclosed luggage space behind the rear seats. As ever, the rear seats were arranged to fold forwards if necessary, in which case no less than 61cu ft (17cu m) of stowage was available. With the seat folded, the flat luggage space was 5ft 10in (1.78m) long, and 4ft 9.5in (1.46m) wide – not double bed size, perhaps, but certainly enough to provide emergency sleeping accommodation.

Amazing, but true – that under the plain looks of the Ford Thames van of the early 1960s period, most of the running gear (engine and gearbox, certainly) was shared with the 1.7-litre Zephyr 4 of the period. In the same way, the Transit of the mid-1960s shared engines with the Mk IV models.

Another change, made at almost the same time, was definitely submerged under all the other product activity. Ford had suffered from a consistent barrage of criticism over the restricted rear leg room in the original Mark III cars, and was looking for some quick solution to the problem. Clearly it was not possible to increase the length of the passenger cabin (or, indeed, to restrict the amount of rear adjustment of the front seats, which was one cause of the trouble), but by making changes to some body panels it was thought possible to make improvements.

This was done by widening the track of the solid rear axle from 52in (132cm) to 53.5in (136cm) (this could be done at little cost, and without altering the shape of the body shell's outer panels), by reshaping the inner rear wheel-arch panel to suit (effectively to push the pressing outboard to follow the movement of the wheel/tyre combination), and then to push the rear seat cushion backwards into the larger gap, reshaping it at the same time. This might appear to be a lot of effort to little advantage, but up to 2in (5cm) was gained, and this seems to have defused the complaints.

It was at the same London Motor Show that the coach-building concern, Hooper's – encouraged by Ford's Walter Hayes, who found money in his PR budget to make it all possible – produced a radically retrimmed Zodiac. Although this was a private enterprise job, in theory there was some clandestine help from Ford engineering behind it all. Naturally there was wood, leather and high-quality carpets in abundance, but perhaps the most promising innovation was the use of separate front seats complete with a Reutter reclining mechanism, for no standard Mark III yet had separate front seats of any type. This, of course, was a very expensive conversion – £575 extra on a Zodiac, which cost just twice that – but it attracted a great deal of publicity, and (if only we had known it) pointed the way to another branch of Ford's future.

But as far as Ford and every other car maker were concerned, the biggest boost of 1962 came immediately after the London Motor Show closed its doors, when Britain's Chancellor

British registration, a Zodiac Mark III – but where was this handsome and evocative picture taken? According to Ford's records, it was shot in Russia, on a privileged trip behind the then Iron Curtain.

reduced purchase tax on the wholesale price of new cars from 45 per cent to 25 per cent. Since it had already been reduced in the spring, this meant that from April to November this much-hated tax had been reduced from 55 per cent to 25 per cent. This was just the sort of boost that Ford and the British motor industry needed, and it was of course inevitable (the government planned it that way, after all!) that demand would soar. After the price reduction, and for the record, this was how the Mark III range of prices looked:

Zephyr 4 saloon	£773
Zephyr 4 estate	£1,051
Zephyr 6 saloon	£837
Zephyr 6 estate	£1,115
Zodiac saloon	£971
Zodiac estate	£1,249

Automatic transmission was now priced at £96

In the next two years, changes to the Mark IIIs were mainly cosmetic, so the launch of a new, though still optional, centre-floor gear change in October 1963 was a welcome innovation. Even so, Ford made so little of this important update that it would have been easy to assume that they were not enthusiastic about it!

Shaped and engineered so that it could be used both with the usual bench seat and with individual front seats, the floor change featured a heavily cranked change-speed lever, whose exterior linkage was close to the right side of the gearbox casing. Because this linkage was so much shorter and more compact than that of the normal steering-column change, it could not help but be more positive. In its road test of a floor-change-equipped Zodiac, *Motor* reported in an article published on New Year's Day 1964:

> The new floor gear change for the four-speed all-synchromesh gearbox is smooth and light. It is bent through a right angle, bringing the substantial knob close to the driver's left knee, and moves through an

Ford always looked on this range – the Vauxhall Cresta types – as their principal competitor in the UK market, and by looking at the style and image of the General Motors product one can see why. This was a late model Viscount, which competed head-on with the Zodiac Executive of the mid-1960s.

unusual plane at a shallow angle to the horizontal. Movements are short against powerful (but not heavy) synchromesh, and they can be made quickly, but working the clutch quickly as well results in slip.

As measured, the latest Zodiac's performance, incidentally, was virtually the same as it had been in 1964, with a top speed of 100mph (160km/h), 0–60mph in 13.4sec, and with overall fuel consumption of just 18.1mpg (15.6ltr/100km). Was it any wonder that *Motor's* testers summarized their findings thus:

> Without offering anything for nothing, the latest development of Ford's luxury car represented outstanding value for money, both to buy and run.... reasonable dimensions, lively acceleration, and a striking appearance make the Mark III Zodiac attractive in traffic and town.

By this time, however, the mechanical specification of the Mark IIIs had settled down, though it was typical of this American-controlled concern that constant attention was given to the detail of colour and trim combinations, and to trim and interior cabin equipment. From the autumn of 1964, the fresh air heater and windscreen washers that had hitherto been optional extras on some models became standard through the range (production planners heaved a sigh of relief, for this was now one detail they no longer had to concern themselves with), and prices edged up accordingly.

The Executive

Before the Mark III gave way to the Mark IV, there was just time for Ford to extend the range even further: taking note of the reaction to the Hooper-transformed Zodiac of 1962, in early 1965 it introduced its own company flagship – the Zodiac Executive. Here was the very first use of the 'Executive' title in a Ford range, and much would be made of this, on all manner of small and medium-sized Fords in the next decade, for it was not until the 'Ghia' badge was adopted in the mid-1970s that 'Executive' took a back seat. Admittedly at the time there was much snobbish comment about this Zodiac derivative – which rather startled Ford, who were really doing no more than BMC had when they introduced 'Princess' or 'Vanden Plas' versions of the Austin A99/A110 Westminster. Business, in any case, is business, and since sales of the type were encouraging, Ford-UK was delighted.

The easy way to describe the original Zodiac Executive was as a Zodiac with all the toys as standard. In almost every case, these items had previously been available on lesser big Fords. Mechanically and functionally, the Executive was based on the Zodiac, though automatic transmission was standard, and manual transmission was a reduced-cost option. Also at this time the earlier twin exhaust system on all Zodiacs was modified to a large bore, single-outlet system; although this may have reduced exhaust noise, it also took the edge off the cars' performance.

Externally there was a choice of four colours, two of them the acrylic metallic hues that had only recently been seen on Fords; there were also two wing mirrors and extra driving lamps as standard.

The bulk of the 'Executive' treatment was concentrated in the cabin, where reclining front seats (as first seen on the Hooper-evolved special of

1962) were standard, with a centre console between them. Seats were trimmed in black leather, deep pile carpets were fitted, and there was extra sound insulation under them.

Other standard items (not found on lesser Zodiacs) were a Motorola push-button radio, Irvin front seat belts (which virtually no one ever wore, they say), and a high-output 30-amp dynamo.

Initially priced at £1,303 (full retail), the Executive was £190 more costly than the normal Zodiac; but at least the customer was not then faced with a long, beguiling and expensive list of possible extras. And if the optional manual transmission was chosen, the price actually came down, to £1,257.

Not everyone liked this car, however. As a young road tester for *Autocar*, I recall the test car that was used in March 1965. The test was published on 9 April, and although I did not actually write the report, I remember contributing opinions – yet it was still a surprise to see the car summarized as having 'Performance and comfort below expectations'. As ever (and this was to persist for many years, on many cars), the

Early in the 1960s, BMC's Vanden Plas Princess 3-Litre might have been well trimmed, and with quite a snobbish image; but it couldn't compete against the Zodiac in the showrooms.

The last Mark III derivative to be announced was the Executive Zodiac, which appeared in January 1965. Mechanically it was identical to the normal Zodiac, but it was trimmed and furnished to a higher standard than any previous Ford. Items such as the extra driving lamps, wing mirrors, and the leather-trimmed interior with separate front seats, were all standard.

Borg Warner Type 35 automatic transmission was not nearly as efficient as a manual transmission, which explains why the top speed of this test car was down to 94mph (151km/h), and the overall fuel consumption was only 17.7mpg (16ltr/100km).

All in all, this was a car with some failings, but a great many virtues, not least its availability from a large and ever-growing list of dealerships, its reliable, trouble-free mechanical specification, and its surprisingly reasonable price levels. Testers who were having a bad day found it easy to sneer about such a car's ambition, yet they had to admit that even if it was large, it was still manageable.

Success in motor sport, in events such as the East African Safari, and in saloon car races – all helped put a little gloss on the show-room, so it was heartening to read that: '…when pushed to the limit there is far more adhesion that one might expect, and the car always remains stable. Braking from high speeds gives every feel of confidence as the large front discs pull the car up with commendably light pedal loads….'

The fact is that the new derivative did its job, and began to lay foundations for many more 'Executives' to follow in future years.

Although sales of all these Mark IIIs – Zephyrs and Zodiacs alike – held up well in the mid-1960s, the world's market place itself was gradually changing in that the public was tending to buy slightly smaller, better equipped new models. It was no coincidence that, at this time, a competing pair of newly launched, well-equipped, 2-litre 'executive' cars – the Rover 2000 and the Triumph 2000 – both went on sale, and proved to be extremely successful. In the UK, in particular, Ford would feel the effects of this market shift.

Among the large car sectors, not only Ford, but Vauxhall, the Rootes Group's Humbers, along with Austins and Wolseleys from BMC, all saw a gradual diminution of their sales. At Dagenham, the drop in overall sales was at least consistent, because Zephyr 4s, Zephyr 6s and Zodiacs all suffered a one-third drop-off between 1963 and 1965.

It was time, once again, to make another change, and in the winter of 1965/1966 the big upheaval followed. Production of the Mark III began to come smoothly towards a close at the end of the calendar year, though a further 2,375 vehicles would be produced in January 1966. But from that date onwards, the face of big Fords would look entirely different.

Ford Zephyr/Zodiac Series III (1962–1966)

Layout

Unit-construction steel body/chassis structure. Front engine/rear drive, sold as four-door five-seater saloon and estate car.

Zephyr 4s had 4-cylinder engines, while Zephyr 6s and Zodiacs had 6-cylinder engines. All shared the same wheelbase.

Engine

Type	In-line 4-cylinder (6-cylinder)
Block material	Cast iron
Head material	Cast iron
Cylinders	4, in-line (6, in-line)
Cooling	Water
Bore and stroke	82.55 x 79.5mm
Capacity	1703cc (2553cc)
Main bearings	Three (four)
Valves	Two per cylinder, overhead, operated by pushrods and rockers from camshaft mounted in side of cylinder block
Compression ratio	8.3:1 (7.0:1 optional)
Fuel supply	One downdraught Zenith carburettor
Max. power	68bhp @ 4,800rpm (Zephyr 6 98bhp @ 4750rpm, Zodiac 109bhp @ 4,800rpm)
Max. torque	93.5lb ft @ 3,000rpm (Zephyr 6 134lb ft @ 2,000rpm, Zodiac 137lb ft at 2,400rpm)

Transmission

Manual transmission : Steering column change: optional floor change from late 1963. Four-speed, synchromesh on all forward gears. Optional Borg Warner overdrive. Optional Borg Warner automatic transmission (standard on Executive Zodiac).

Internal gearbox ratios:

Top	1.000:1
3rd	1.505:1
2nd	2.353:1
1st	4.412:1
Reverse	4.667:1

Final drive ratio   Zephyr 4 3.90:1, Zephyr 6/Zodiac/Executive 3.545:1

Optional Borg Warner overdrive (0.78:1 ratio)

Optional automatic transmission (standard on Executive)

Internal gear ratios:

Top	1.00:1
Intermediate	1.45:1
Low	2.39:1
Reverse	2.09:1

continued overleaf

Ford Zephyr/Zodiac Series III (1962–1966) *continued*

Suspension and steering

Front	Independent coil springs, MacPherson struts, anti-roll bar, telescopic dampers
Rear	Live (beam) axle, half-elliptic leaf springs, lever-arm hydraulic dampers
Steering	Recirculating ball
Tyres	6.40-13in, cross-ply
Wheels	Pressed-steel disc, bolt on
Rim width	4.5in

Brakes

Type	Servo-assisted front wheel discs, rear drums
Size	9.75in diameter front discs, 9.0in diameter rear drums

Dimensions (in/mm)

Track	
Front	53/1,346
Rear	52/1,321 (53.5/1,359 from late 1962)
Wheelbase	107/2,718
Overall length	180.5/4,585 (Zodiac 182.5/4,636)
Overall width	69/1,753
Overall height	57.5/1,461
Unladen weight	Zephyr 4 2,576lb/1,168kg, Zephyr 6 2,744lb/1,244kg, Zodiac 2,828lb/1,283kg

6 Rallies and Races

It should be made quite clear that when the Consul and Zephyr family was being designed and developed in the late 1940s – and indeed, when new generations were also developed in the 1950s – Ford was not at all interested in seeing them in motor sport. As far as Ford's marketing chiefs were concerned, these cars were commercial, potentially profit-making propositions, where high performance and razor-edge road-holding were not even considered.

Yet in the first decade of their careers, the Zephyrs and Zodiacs in particular (Consuls rarely figured) proved to be formidably competent rally cars, and could even acquit themselves well on the race track, too. I only need summarize a career that included outright victories in the Monte Carlo, the East African Safari and the RAC Rally of Great Britain, along with mention of Jeff Uren's amazing victory in the BRSCC British Saloon Car Championship, to make

that point. Yet the way it happened was almost haphazard and unplanned, with no long-term strategic vision, merely the intention of trading on two of the cars' remarkable assets: reliability and sheer strength.

Before that remarkable character Walter Hayes joined Ford in 1961/1962 in order to revitalize its public affairs image, Ford had never really been serious about motor sport. Victories had come along almost by chance, mainly because a few drivers – many of them Ford dealers – had been clever enough to pick the most suitable events, in the best available Ford cars. The programme, such as it was, was rather casually organized, in a part-time fashion, and arranged in the most informal way. Under the overall control of 'Edgy' Fabris, but with that outstanding organizer Bill Barnett tackling all the day-to-day work, the job always got done. Barnett had become Ford's legendary rally manager at Boreham in the 1960s and early

Throughout the life of the 'works' Consul/Zephyr/ Zodiac rally team, the cars were prepared at the Lincoln Cars building, on the A4 main road close to where the elevated section of the M4 motorway now stands.

1970s, and when he came to leave his post in 1973 (for another job within the Ford empire), Ford vice president Walter Hayes organized a presentation dinner in his honour, and told this story:

> Lincoln Cars, in Brentford, was one of my responsibilities – that was where the Press fleet was located. When I joined Ford I had to ask 'Edgy' Fabris what he did, and he replied:
>
> 'Publications and Competitions.'
>
> 'And what does Competitions consist of?'
>
> 'Rallying. Around the end of the year we finish Publications early and go off on the Monte Carlo rally.'
>
> 'And who organizes it all? I mean, surely it takes a lot of planning, all this rallying?'
>
> 'Oh,' said Fabris, 'Bill Barnett does that. Bill does everything!'

That summed up Bill's pre-Boreham job exactly. From the late 1950s to 1973, he was Motorsport's top planner, the one man who knew every car's programme, every service schedule, every driver's private phone number – and he also knew where the best restaurants and hotels in rallying really were. In the beginning, though, he could not even have imagined ever working in motor sport: 'I started work at Ford in the advertising department,' Bill told me, 'I had no motor sport ambitions, and there were no connections, none at all.'

The motor sport connection finally 'clicked' with Bill in the 1950s. At that time Edgell ('Edgy') Fabris ran the 'works' rally team, where the cars were always prepared in the Lincoln Cars building, on the A4 Great West Road on the way out to Heathrow Airport, alongside other Ford cars that were being maintained as Press demonstrators. This was a massive, white-distempered building in the Art Deco style, which had earlier been occupied by the importers of French Delage cars and, from the later 1930s, had been set up to handle the importation of Lincoln motor cars from Canada. By the 1950s, that import operation was still small, and the Press fleet was relocated into the echoing workshops. Its only real advantage was that it was there, and that space was available. For Motorsport, any move to more specialized premises would be an advance.

In later years, Bill sat down and, with remarkable recall, gave me every detail about the way the 'works' team at Lincoln Cars developed:

> When I got to know him, 'Edgy' had a triple role. He was head of administration at Public Relations, head of Publications, and he was also competitions manager. He had built up a team around people like Ken Wharton in V8 Pilots, then with Gatsonides in the Zephyr, and dealers like the Harrison family. One day, quite simply, he called me in and said:
>
> 'Bill, I've got to go on the Alpine rally, will

Before the first Zephyrs were prepared for rallying, works-supported Fords either had to be two-door Anglias or ....

.... Four-door Prefects, neither of which had enough performance, handling or character to make any sort of mark in motor sport.

In 1952, trials driver and motor trader Ken Wharton amazed everyone by winning the Dutch Tulip rally outright, in his own Ford Consul. Maybe a favourable performance handicap helped, but his achievement can never be underestimated, for it was the first significant win by this family of cars.

you please start organizing some travel and hotels for me?' It was as casual as that. The next year, 1959, 'Edgy' asked me to do the same thing again – I recall Anne Hall, Gerry Burgess, the Harrison family, Vic Preston and Denis Scott were all in the team, and on that occasion I actually travelled with them. It was fascinating, because apart from my wartime service, I hadn't been out of Britain before – yet here I was, driving 'Edgy' around in France and Italy!

From that day on, there was more sport and less 'Publications' in Barnett's life, and it wasn't long before the entire 'works' effort relied on his method, his knowledge and his planning. Rally car specifications were settled by Jack Welch, and team tactics were usually dictated by 'Cuth', the senior of the Harrison family. Technical support and some sponsorship came from Castrol.

> I wasn't really interested in rallying, not at first, but I was bitten by the bug on the 1959 Alpine, and I came

to love it. I organized entries for other events after that, including the RAC and the Monte, before Jeff Uren came in as team manager for about a year.

Changes then came thick and fast. Uren moved out, Walter Hayes arrived to replace Colonel Buckmaster as the head of public affairs, and Syd Henson was hired as competitions manager:

> But it wasn't a happy time. Syd was always threatening to resign, thumping on the table until he got his way. Walter Hayes didn't like that, so one day he called Syd in, with me listening, smiled sweetly, and told him: 'Syd, I've decided to accept one of your resignations!' – and that was that.

At about this time Hayes realized he needed to put the entire operation on a more professional footing, and so the Boreham project was born. At almost the same time, Hayes elected to concentrate on racing and rallying new high-

Ken Wharton (in the dark suit) astonished all the officials by his 1952 Tulip rally victory, and from this view it seems that the Consul was very standard indeed.

performance Cortina GTs and Lotus-Cortinas; when Motorsport finally moved to Boreham in 1963, the last 'works' Zephyrs and Zodiacs had already been sold off.

Simple Beginnings

Although V8-engined Fords had already won the Monte Carlo rally twice in the 1930s, at the time there was no such thing as a 'works' team at Dagenham to support them. Even in the late 1940s it was individuals such as Jackie Reece and Ken Wharton (both of them in the motor trade, as Ford dealers) who started to bring home the victories. Their simple approach was that of the scrounging motor trader. When the most glamorous rallies came around – notably the Monte Carlo rally, of course – they usually had enough influence to borrow suitable cars from Ford's Press fleet (which explains why their competition cars often had Essex-based registration numbers), though in preparation terms those cars were not at all special.

Even before the Consul/Zephyr range was properly established, Ken Wharton (not only a motor trader, but a sporting trials specialist and a budding race driver) won the Tulip rally in a massive V8 Pilot, while Jackie Reece (who ran a Ford main dealership, Blakes of Liverpool) achieved brave but inconsequential Monte Carlo rally results in a side-valve Ford Anglia.

It was not until 1952, after Wharton had once again won the Tulip rally (an event where driving-test skills counted for more than high performance), this time in a Consul of his very own, that Ford's publicity chief (and ex-SOE hero during World War II), Colonel Maurice Buckmaster, persuaded Sir Patrick Hennessy to back a limited motor sport programme.

Perhaps it was Wharton's spirited showing that tipped the balance, for in that Tulip rally there had been circuit tests, special stages in the French mountains, autotests, and hour after hour of grinding endurance in a three-day event that featured a dozen starting points, a common route from Brussels to France's Central Massif, through Luxembourg and back to Noorwijk-aan-Zee, where there was a final circuit test around the Zandvoort F1 race circuit. Not only did Wharton's Consul win outright, using a favourable handicap to make that possible, but he defeated Ian Appleyard's Jaguar Mark VII into second place. Other cars that could not beat Wharton in the capacity class included Jowett Javelins, Volvo PV444s and Riley RMA types.

1953

Accordingly, for the 1953 season, what was effectively Ford-UK's first-ever 'works' Competitions Department was set up, and operated on a strictly part-time basis. 'Edgy' Fabris devoted some of his time to administration, Jack Welch, Alf Belson and Norman Masters were the principal mechanics who maintained the cars, but it was the team of drivers, usually led by Ford main dealer T.C. ('Cuth') Harrison of Sheffield, who carried out much of the organization, and set the strategy, such as it was.

At this time every single personality – manager, mechanics and drivers – had other full-time jobs to do, so there was very little time for the development and improving of the cars, while strategy and forward planning were both extremely sketchy.

First time out, in January 1953, Ford could have been forgiven for finding rallying quite easy, because Fabris persuaded the Dutch rally ace Maurice Gatsonides to drive one of the new Zephyrs, and he rewarded them by winning the Monte Carlo rally outright. This, incidentally, was without paying him a fee, with a co-driver, Peter Worledge, whose principal job was with the brake lining company Cape Asbestos (one of Ford's important suppliers), and with a car to which most attention went into adding

more comfort for long distance driving and a display of instruments, than of improving the performance.

Gatsonides, however, was a wily character: he had very nearly won the Monte on a previous occasion (he was second in 1950 in a Humber Super Snipe), and he spent weeks practising on the regularity sections, which included a 47-mile (76km) circuit in the mountains, taking in the Col de Braus behind Monte Carlo itself. The organizers could, and did, mount secret checks to see how close to a steady average every rally car was being driven, and for the drivers the trick was to know which sectors were easy, and which were difficult.

Although the Gatsonides/Worledge/Zephyr 6 partnership could not be accurate to the last second at every point, they only incurred two penalties for being two seconds away from the ideal schedule. But as *Autocar* told us after the event, this phenomenal performance in VHK 194 was enabled because of Gatsonides' preparation:

> On Gatsonides's winning Zephyr no fewer than eight stop-watches reinforced the information provided by the Monastere average speed indicator, which is made by Van Munster, and developed by Gatsonides. This is a mechanically driven clock which, by comparison with an ordinary clock, indicates whether the car is ahead of, or behind, a given scheduled speed....

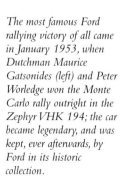

The most famous Ford rallying victory of all came in January 1953, when Dutchman Maurice Gatsonides (left) and Peter Worledge won the Monte Carlo rally outright in the Zephyr VHK 194; the car became legendary, and was kept, ever afterwards, by Ford in its historic collection.

This was the facia layout of Gatsonides' 1953 'works' Zephyr, complete with all the detritus that seemed to infest the inside of rally cars at this time. The auxiliary panel in front of co-driver Peter Worledge included (top right) an average-speed computing device which Gatsonides had personally developed over a period of years.

Not only was the Gatsonides car well equipped for navigation, but the passenger seat was arranged to be reclinable so that the off-duty occupant could get some rest.

Incidentally, rudimentary brake cooling was provided on the tightest hairpins by Ford mechanics throwing buckets of water over the hard-pressed front-wheels as Gatsonides arrived at one particular corner – and if you don't believe it, there are photographs to prove it – the most remarkable achievement being that the water wielders actually hit their target!

In the pandemonium that followed this stunning victory, most people missed another fine Jaguar performance by Ian Appleyard (second), Stirling Moss (sixth), Sydney Allard (ninth) – and by 'Cuth' Harrison whose 'works' Zephyr took twelfth place. Ford, incidentally, would not win the Monte Carlo rally again until 1994....

Just in case this made 'works' rallying feel easy,

What the best-dressed rally drivers of 1953 were wearing.... Flying suits to keep Gatsonides and Worledge warm.

Gatsonides and Worledge started the 1953 Monte from Monte Carlo itself, having spent many days practising the regularity section in the mountains behind the principality.

En route, and making haste on the final section in the 1953 event, where on the final day all cars carried a colour wash panel on the nose to allow officials to identify them at secret checks.

The fruits of success – with the winning 1953 crew about to land again on British soil, nosing out of a Silver City Airways Bristol Freighter. The huge cowl was fitted over the extra driving lamps to stop their rays spilling upwards to dazzle Gatso in the night sections.

No sooner had VHK 194 got back to London after winning the 1953 Monte than it was put on display in a Ford showroom to celebrate that success.

Above *Three months after winning the Monte, Lincoln Cars re-prepared VHK 194 to compete in the RAC rally of March 1953, but it finished well down the lists: here it is seen tackling a driving test at Hastings at the end of the event.*

Left *On its third event in four months, Maurice Gatsonides used VHK 194 to tackle the Tulip rally. After a fine show, the Ford team might have won the Manufacturers' Team Prize, only to be disqualified at the end due to an eligibility dispute.*

Above *VHK 195 was a sister to Gatsonides's Monte winning legend. 'Cuth' Harrison took twelfth overall in the 1953 Monte....*

Left *....And, along with co-driver Reg Phillips was also well placed in the 1953 Tulip until disqualification robbed him of success.*

the fates then played against Ford, for none of them performed well on the RAC rally, or on the Tulip rally. Even at this stage, Ford was discovering that it could not merely buy success by building special cars, and providing great on-event service.

On the other hand, the Norwegian private owner C. Johansson won the International Viking rally outright, which made the Scandinavians sit up and take notice.

1954

Looking back, it's difficult to realize that there were no serious saloon car races in Britain before 1952, and that no coherent British Saloon Car Championship was promoted until 1958. Before then, it seems, saloon car racing was not thought to be credible, and was not seriously tried before the 1950s. Soon after World War II there was a serious shortage of competitive single-seaters,

VHK 196 was the third of the new-for-1953 'works' cars – driven on the Tulip rally by Jack Reece (disqualified)....

.... and most bravely in the gruelling Liege-Rome-Liege rally of August 1954 by Nancy Mitchell (left) and Joy Leavens, where the gallant ladies finished twenty-eighth overall.

so racing for 'production' cars was introduced, but in the first few years these events made no attempt to separate open two-seaters from other types, the XK120s from the Zephyrs. Early events therefore attracted only out-and-out sports cars, and although all sorts of odd, sometimes handicap, events were held at club level, it was not until May 1952 that the first international saloon-car-only race was held, at Silverstone in the *Daily Express* meeting. Furthermore, for a time this was merely a once-in-a-year event that was not originally copied by any other promoter.

Massive, tyre-squealing, 'works' Jaguar Mark VIIs dominated that first event, just as they would always do for the first five years. Naturally there was keen competition in the smaller-engined capacity classes, but since much of the opposition came from more expensive sports saloons – such as the Riley 2.5-litre, Jowett Javelin and MG models – there was no interest from Ford, whose cars were not yet in the same league; although the new Consuls and Zephyrs had surprisingly tunable overhead-valve engines, they were too heavy, and their nose-heavy chassis layout did not look promising. For competition purposes, too, the engine sizes were all wrong: because the original Consul had a 1508cc engine it had to compete in the 2-litre class, while the Zephyr's

2262cc 'six' meant that it had to run in the 3-litre category – which was most unfavourable in either case.

Perhaps this explains why there were no Fords in the entry for the *Daily Express* races in 1952 and 1953 – but for the 1954 race, to everyone's surprise, Basil De Mattos entered a privately prepared Consul. Although this car sounded most unpromising at first, knowledgeable ears were pricked when it was realized that the event regulations were quite flexible, and a great deal of free-for-all engine tuning was allowed – and that De Mattos had business connections with Laystall, the tuning concern. This was a time when Laystall's advertising claimed that Consul engines with twin SU carburettors and a full tune-up job developed 70.5bhp at 5,200rpm – a 54 per cent improvement on Ford's own production line figures.

Although seventeen different makes took the start in 1954, and none of them was ever likely to beat the Mark VII Jaguars, De Mattos' Consul was always favourite to win the 1.5–2-litre class, as its only rival was a diesel-engined Borgward Isabella! This performance, by the way, was achieved without the use of racing tyres. Nevertheless, the Consul finished strongly, at 65.91mph (106.05km/h), which was no disgrace, as the 200bhp/3.4-litre Jaguars averaged only

75.55mph (121.56km/h) to win the race outright. So although the opposition had been thin, this was a credible start for the marque; but no one was really impressed – these days, of course, clever advertising would have made such a modest beginning seem as important as a successful moon shot!

All in all there wasn't a great deal of rallying success in 1954, even though the well used 'VHK…' fleet of 1953 had now been joined by new 'XNO…' cars. For the Monte Carlo rally there were major changes for Ford, as the 'modified class' regulations allowed significant alterations to the specification of cars. Lincoln Cars therefore fitted the 'works' Zephyrs with high compression heads and triple carburettors – the power output being perhaps 90bhp – while inside the cabin there were big, squashily comfortable, separate front seats, and navigational panels containing a mass of instruments, controls and speed-keeping devices.

Ford's strong team was led by Gatsonides, this time partnered by 1950 Monte victor Marcel Becquart, backed by 'Cuth' Harrison, Jack Reece, Nancy Mitchell and Denis Scott – a formidable line-up by any standards. This year, however, the rallying accent was more on performance than on accurate time-keeping; there was to be a strict regularity run from Gap to Monte Carlo itself, no less than 165 miles (265km) of it, and the final challenge was to be a five-lap race around the legendary Monaco GP street circuit itself. The regularity run included the serpentine Col des Lecques, near Castellane, and this was where most of the cars were having to be driven flat out. And according to magazine reports, the 'works' Ford drivers enjoyed themselves:

> …The Zephyrs, particularly, travelled faster than any motorist would dare to attempt. T.C. Harrison was typical of this Zephyr contingent…. Marcel Becquart tore by, driving the Ford in stage one…. Gatsonides took it up the col on stage two in a furious series of slides….

In motor racing, Consuls were rarely prominent (their 1508cc engine capacity put them into the 2-litre capacity class, which didn't help), but Basil de Mattos won that class in the Touring Car Race at Silverstone in 1954: a year later, as can be seen, he is about to be swallowed up by a much faster 2-litre Bristol 403.

Above *Different 'works' cars, different registration number sequences, and different events – showing that Lincoln Cars were very busy in the mid-1950s. VVW 458 was competing in the Portuguese Lisbon rally of 1954….*

Below *….VHK 196 (driven by Jack Reece) tackles a driving test at Llandrindod Wells in the 1953 RAC rally, where he finished twelfth, while….*

Clearly the 'works' Zephyr was very driver-friendly, and somehow these heroes had all worked out a way of killing the understeer with which those cars were usually afflicted. Although they were fast on the GP circuit, clearly they could not keep up with Louis Chiron's winning Lancia Aurelia GT, which won the event outright, or with some of the 'works' Sunbeam-Talbots, which were in the same class. On this occasion, if Gatsonides had not made an unfortunate timing error on the regularity section he might have finished higher up – so as it was, Ford had to be satisfied with 'Cuth' Harrison's thirteenth place, and fourth in its capacity class.

Shortly after this, Maurice Gatsonides was 'head hunted' to drive for Triumph, where he stayed for the next five years; subsequently the 'works' Ford team gradually began to settle down, with the same dealer-dominated crews – the Harrison family (father and sons), Syd Allard, Jackie Reece, Dennis Scott – usually making up the entry, and with Anne Hall, and guest drivers

....XNO 497 (Denis Scott driving Reg Phillips's entry) tackles the final race circuit test of the 1954 Tulip rally, on the way to a fine class victory.

such as Gerry Burgess putting in appearances. Slowly but steadily the cars became more competitive, but because of their weight, their lack of disc brakes (until 1960, that is, though in 'prototype' events these appeared from 1958), and their relatively agricultural engines, they could rarely do more than win classes, or finish well up the placings in rough, tough, endurance events. Just occasionally, where the rally handicaps and class structures favoured an entry, a Consul or two would be entered; but in almost every case it was the 2.2-litre (later 2.6-litre) Zephyrs that flew the Ford flag. Occasionally, too, there would be an outstanding individual performance, which bears analysis.

Thus in the RAC rally of 1954, a four-day extravaganza including round-the-country navigation, driving tests, hill climbs and circuit tests, 'Cuth' Harrison (driving XNO 496) astonished everyone by taking third place overall behind two of the new Triumph TR2 sports cars, annihilating the 'works' Sunbeam Talbot team along the way, and finishing way ahead of any other Ford. For 'Cuth', it helped that he managed to 'clean' the tight road navigation sections: he was one of only eight drivers to achieve that.

Two months later, there were class wins in the Dutch Tulip rally, with Jack Reece winning his group in a Consul (totally unexpected), and Dennis Scott (driving Reg Philips' Zephyr) pipping Sheila Van Damm's Sunbeam Talbot 90 on the last corner of the last lap at the Zandvoort race circuit.

For 1954, that was the height of it. 'Cuth' Harrison borrowed a Zephyr to tackle the French Alpine rally, and converted it to centre-lock wire wheels, they say to aid the cooling of the drum brakes – but it was the wheels that let him down when several spokes broke, thereby rendering the car unsafe. Nancy Mitchell tackled the gruelling Liege-Rome-Liege in another borrowed Zephyr, but could finish no higher than twenty-eighth in an event where sheer brute strength and endurance was asked of the crews.

1955

In the Monte Carlo rally, furniture maker Gerry Burgess used his own personal Zephyr (TPG 825), in standard condition, and almost repeated Gatsonides' fine Zephyr victory of 1953, defeating all four of the much-modified 'works' cars. Choosing to start from Monte Carlo itself, Burgess battled through very changeable winter weather in France, and completed the lengthy regularity run from Gap to Monte Carlo in ninth place overall. After a short accelerating-and-braking test on the Promenade, the top hundred cars were then faced with a final, absolute regularity test in the mountains behind the principality. This was no longer a mere 47 miles (76km) as in Gatsonides' event, but no less than 180 miles (290km), and the route took in the Col de

'Cuth' Harrison (left, with pipe) and his son Edward (far right) at the end of the 1955 RAC rally in Hastings, where they had won their class, running in the GT category with a highly modified engine.

Ford's first outright victory in the Coronation Safari (eventually renamed East African Safari in future years) came in 1955 when Vic Preston (left) and D.P. Marwaha won the event in fine style. This was an event for standard-specification cars, where reliability and sheer brute car strength counted for more than performance and handling. The Zephyr was ideal for this task.

Valberg, the later legendary Col du Turini, and the Col de Braus. Burgess fought his way up to fourth place, and after a series of five-lap races around the Monaco GP circuit, the gallant privately owned Zephyr confirmed its fourth place, beaten only by a Sunbeam Mark III, a front-wheel-drive Dyna Panhard, and a Mercedes-Benz 220.

If it was any consolation, 'Cuth' Harrison's works car (913 AVX) later won its class on both the RAC and the Tulip rallies (where his car ran with an overdrive, which made it admittedly non-standard, and pushed it up a class). But there was then another amazing victory to celebrate – in the Coronation Safari.

Rallying? To Ford's publicity chiefs it must all have been looking very straightforward. In an event where class and category were settled by selling price, rather than by engine size, the value-for-money Zephyr performed extremely well. As shown in the panel on page 141, the very experienced and well proven partnership of Vic Preston and D.P. Marwaha won the East African Safari of 1955, using a privately owned and privately prepared car.

On this 3,490-mile (5,615km) marathon, this was an amazing performance (it helped that the drivers were locals, and knew every inch of their native East African lands), and it proved the sheer brute strength that the engineers had built in to this model when it was being designed. It was also, if truth be told, something of a one-off, as no Zephyr would ever win the Safari again – the next Ford victory was with Cortina GTs in 1964.

This was the season in motor racing when there was an important consequence to Basil De Mattos's 1954 performance. Having seen the way that the Consul performed (for De Mattos was

One of the sensations of the 1955 Touring Car Race at Silverstone was the performance of Ken Wharton's privately prepared Zephyr Six, which was fitted with a highly tuned, 100bhp-plus, Raymond Mays power unit. Not only did it win the 3-litre class (it beat that 'works' Riley Pathfinder, incidentally), but it took fourth overall behind three twin-cam-engined Jaguar Mark VIIs.

not even a regular club racer), one-time Ford 'works' rally driver and Ford dealer Ken Wharton, who had already turned to single-seater racing with great success, read the rules for the Silverstone race very carefully, and entered a remarkably rapid 2.3-litre Zephyr for the 1955 *Daily Express* event. Once again it was built without reference to the factory.

This time the 6-cylinder Zephyr was in the 2–3-litre class, and faced much more formidable opposition than the Consul had done, including a trio of newly developed 2.5-litre Riley Pathfinders. Once the race began, however, it was clear that Wharton was not just looking to beat them, but to pulling clear, and making a challenge to the race-winning Jaguars, too! On this occasion it was Raymond Mays (of ERA and BRM race car fame) whose tuning business had worked wonders on the 6-cylinder engine, and with Wharton behind the wheel, the car, registered

JCT 17, really flew. With more than 100bhp from the engine (that doesn't sound much today, but in 1955 it was a creditable output), and with stiffened-up suspension, this had all the makings of a formidable saloon racer.

In fact the Zephyr's chase was in vain, for no one could catch the big Jaguars; but the big Ford tangled successfully with the Rileys (which, as road tests proved, were really much faster in normal road-car form), taking a class lead on the fifth of twenty-five laps, and swept home in fourth place overall. Mike Hawthorn's winning Jaguar Mark VII averaged 78.95mph (127.03km/h), while Wharton's Zephyr averaged 76.18mph (122.57km/h) – a remarkable achievement.

Two Consuls, one with Laystall and one with Derrington modifications, also started, but one burst a water hose and the other finished well behind the much faster 2-litre Bristol 403s. There was no future, clearly, for this car in motor sport.

1956

Because the new-generation Mark II models were launched early in 1956, and the big workshops at Lincoln Cars spent much time building up, fettling and maintaining a new fleet of Press and appraisal cars, there was neither the time nor the finances to run a big motor-sport programme, especially as some effort had to be put behind the small Anglias, too.

There was still no 'works' input to saloon racing – though in fairness, Lincoln Cars had absolutely no knowledge of this sport, so was not about to humiliate itself for the time being! Thus there were no 'works' Zephyrs in Monte Carlo, none on the snow-bound RAC, and none on the Tulip (where, in any case, a handicap favoured small-engined cars) – but then an impressive team of brand-new Mark IIs appeared in the French Alpine.

This was brave, because the Alpine, held on public roads in July, used every high mountain pass between Geneva and the Riviera coast, plus a trip across northern Italy to the badlands of Jugoslavia; it also had an incredibly demanding time schedule, and was quite closely related to a flat-out road race. Three cars – 511 GHK, 512 GHK and 513 GHK – all used much-modified engines fitted with triple Zenith carburettors.

Although the schedule was demanding, two of the cars – driven by 'Cuth' Harrison and Denis Scott – kept clean sheets; moreover 'Cuth' not only won his class and finished sixth, but was also the best placed saloon car in the entire entry, beaten only by Alfa Romeos, Porsches, a Denzel and a Ferrari!

1957

For rallying, 1957 was a rather difficult year: in the aftermath of the Suez crisis of November 1956 there had been petrol shortages all over Europe, the British government had imposed petrol rationing until the spring of the year, and for a time the political climate was definitely anti motor sport. The Monte Carlo and RAC rallies were both cancelled (as was the French Alpine later in the year, for non-fuel-related reasons), so Ford had to wait until May to enter the Dutch Tulip rally, which on this occasion wound its route down from Holland into France, then through West Germany to Austria and back: no Riviera hill climbing this time round.

As ever with the Tulip, there was a long and often turgid road section, several speed hill climbs to be tackled, a final speed test on the Zandvoort race circuit – and a handicap system to encourage small-engined cars to excel if they could. Gerry Burgess joined the 'works' team for the first time, as did Irishman Ronnie Adams (who had won the 1956 Monte in a Jaguar Mk VIIM); but of the five cars entered it was Denis Scott who won his class, Anne Hall who won the Ladies Cup, and the three cars of Scott, Harrison and Adams that won the team prize. Burgess's car let him down with fuel starvation, otherwise this was an impressive team performance.

As far as the 'works' team was concerned, that was virtually all they did for 1957, for in the second half of the season only the Liege-Rome-Liege marathon was of a sufficiently high standard, and since Lincoln Cars had no experience of this four-days-and-four-nights nightmare, they kept well clear of it.

Anne Hall borrowed a 'works' Zephyr for the event, but suffered a succession of setbacks: a front wheel bearing failure, a crash with an oncoming Army truck in Italy (not her fault), and brake failure going down the fearsome 9,000ft (2,750m) Stelvio Pass later in the event. Anne was not best pleased, for she had no factory support on the event, while the car (629 HVX) was quite badly crumpled as a result.

Gerry Burgess's effort failed for entirely predictable reasons. He was running his own car with a very high-tuned 'Raymond Mays' engine that needed 100-octane fuel to survive; but in Jugoslavia petrol supplies were of abysmal quality, and within hours of filling up, several pistons in the engine had failed – he was lucky to get the car to the finish of the event at all, many hours off the pace. Of course it was his own car, and to build it in this way had been his idea, but since the fuel supply situation in Jugoslavia was well known, he could not have been more misguided.

Nor was there much success on the track in 1957. Ken Wharton's 1956 racing success, it seemed, had been no more than a flash in the pan, for saloon car races were still only being held at Silverstone, and there would be no more Ford successes until 1958. In 1956, in any case, Wharton had dropped the Zephyr in favour of a highly tuned 2.6-litre Austin A90 Westminster, while Vic Derrington's Consul could only finish third in its class, well beaten by two Alfa Romeo 1900TIs.

Nor was there any success for the larger-engined, 2.6-litre Zephyr Mark IIs in 1957, for although no fewer than six cars started the race, they really could not compete with other, more highly developed cars such as the Austin A105s (which carried a lot of BMC 'works' assistance), or the Riley Pathfinders that had replaced the early post-war Riley RM types. There was much 'works' support for some of the Zephyrs on this occasion, and the line-up of drivers, at least, was noteworthy: Peter Riley, 'Cuth' Harrison, Edward Harrison, Denis Scott, Jeff Uren and Ian Walker. All were either current Ford 'works' rally drivers, would eventually rise to that level, or were much respected private owners.

All these cars were so-called private entries – none carried the obvious 'registered-in-Essex' identities that we came to recognize so easily – but there is no doubt that Ford was already beginning to take a limited interest in this new type of motor sport. The racing Zephyrs prepared by the factory, though, merely took the latest 'works' rally specifications, improved on what they could for Silverstone circuit racing, bolted on Michelin-X radial-ply tyres, and did the best they could.

The Zephyrs had a good and flamboyant tilt at the 3-litre class. It wasn't enough, for although the big Fords looked spectacular, they were still no match for 'Gib' Grace's Riley Pathfinder, Ron Flockhart's Jaguar 2.4 or Jack Sears' Austin A105.

1958

By this time, racing and rallying had evolved so much that increasingly specialized cars were needed to be capable of winning. Slowly but inexorably, on the race track competitors needed cars that were lighter, which handled better, and which had engines capable of being power-tuned to an incredible degree. In rallying, not only did a car need all those virtues, it also needed to be physically strong, too.

Ford, while producing amazingly reliable and strong 'works' Zephyrs, could never even dream of approaching the straight-line performance of some of their rivals. Not only that, but the cars still did not have disc brakes, and on rallies the lack of these was becoming a major problem. Further (and Ford was just about to admit this to themselves), the 'works' team still lacked the guidance of a professional team manager who knew all about his sport, about the 'wrinkles' that could go into making the cars better, and the ways of 'bending' the regulations to suit his team's products.

In rallying at this time luck often seemed to be against the big Fords. In the 1958 Monte, for instance, no fewer than seven 'works' cars started, three of them with triple-carburettor engines; but the awful wintry weather was against them, and blockages by other rally cars or non-competing machines didn't help. The result was that all of them finished well out of the running, and the capacity class was won by a privately entered Zodiac driven by R. Nellemann.

Now we come to the latest edition of the Safari (still called Coronation Safari, by the way), where we can celebrate a 'phantom' victory for the Zephyr Mark II. The reason is that although the Kopperud brothers set the equal best performance of all (alongside a valiant little two-stroke Auto Union 1000) – they lost just three minutes on a demanding schedule – the organizers had stated, well in advance of the start of the event, that there would be no outright winner, only class and team winners.

Although this was still, in theory, an event dominated by locally domiciled private owners, clearly there was much interest from Lincoln Cars in the four Zephyrs that started at the head of the field. One needed only to see the names of the first drivers – Vic Preston, A. T. Kopperud, Bill Young and Mrs Mary Wright, to appreciate a strong Ford connection from the past.

As before, the Safari was run for cars in absolutely showroom condition, as sold in East Africa; but although the engines and transmissions were strictly standard, a great deal of attention had gone into making the heavy duty bodies as sturdy as possible. Those were the days, of course, before roll cages were fitted, the only evidence of rallying really being the extra lamps fitted at the front.

Although the Kopperuds were eventually proclaimed class winners, this was not confirmed for

some months because at first they were heavily penalized when post-event scrutineering revealed that a front shock absorber seal was broken (that seal had been placed there by the scrutineers themselves to make sure the unit was not changed during the event). Protest and counter protest was made, before the organizers agreed that this seal had broken because it was inherently too weak, and that the crew could not possibly be blamed. Even so, it rather took the gloss off a fine performance by the team of Zephyrs. They may have had the advantage of running at the front of the field where the dust was not all-pervasive, but this was still a gruelling 3,000-mile (4,800km) event – and in the end the Kopperuds' car (KFN 235) was reinstated at the head of its class, a long way ahead of John Manussis' Mercedes-Benz 219.

For once the 'works' team had little luck in the Tulip rally; their class was won by a previously unknown pair of twins – Donald and Erle Morley, in a Jaguar 2.4-litre – who would go on to achieve world-wide fame in 'works' Austin-Healey 3000s. However, they made up for this in the French Alpine rally, where no fewer than six Zephyrs took the start, with three of them taking

In the RAC rally of March 1958, the wintry weather all but disrupted the entire event, as this shot makes clear. Carrying one of Lincoln Cars' easily identifiable sequences of registration plate, on this occasion, 628 HVX, this Zephyr is being very carefully eased downhill on the braking test at Ulpha in the Lake District, with Denis Scott at the wheel. Driving this highly modified machine, they eventually won their capacity class, beating exotica like Lyndon Sims' Aston Martin DB2 and Brian Mitton's Jaguar XK150 along the way.

advantage of regulations by running with front-wheel disc brakes and triple-carburettor engines. This, of course, was still more than a year before front discs even became optional on road cars – and was the toughest possible test that prototype installations could have.

In fact it was one of the toughest Alpines so far held, where every car lost time on the road sections, and which included some of the highest passes in France and the Italian Dolomites. It is also one that has been recorded, for all time, on an excellent Shell-financed film of the event, and it shows just how rapidly rally cars were being driven, even in the late 1950s. Outright victory on a tightly timed event eventually went to a Zagato-bodied Alfa Romeo, effectively a lightweight racing car set up for this sort of going.

Just twenty-five of the original fifty-eight starters made it to the finish. Two of the unmodified, drum-braked Zephyrs took class honours, with Edward Harrison (son) beating 'Cuth' Harrison (father). Edward Harrison took fifth overall in a startling display, and was headed only by four out-and-out sports cars. Incidentally, BMC team captain John Gott, writing after the event, suggested that disc brakes were definitely the future

for rallying and that '…the drum-braked Rapiers and Fords were forever changing linings, at which the crews became remarkably expert.'

This was the year in which the British Racing & Sports Car Club (BRSCC) realized the attractions of saloon car racing, and ran an eleven-round Saloon Car Championship, with six of the events at Brands Hatch (the home of the BRSCC). This was the forerunner of every other saloon series in this country, and as far as Ford is concerned it was certainly the point at which they began to make progress, and when the results began to mount up.

There was no regular 'works' presence in this pioneering series; however, private owner Jeff Uren, who had beaten all the 'works' cars at Silverstone in 1957, astonished everyone by preparing his own Zephyr (it was also the car he used on the road between races!), and fighting head-to-head throughout the year with Jack Sears'

Above *Jeff Uren came to fame in 1958 when he drove his own Zephyr into contention in the British Saloon Car Championship; in 1959 he won the Saloon Car Championship in a new and more powerful car. He went on to become Ford's team manager for 1960 and 1961.*

BMC-backed Austin A105. These two drivers easily outscored all their rivals, ending the season as the class act in the new championship.

Well before this drama unfolded, however, there was one moment of show business (some would call it farce), when Ford entered three 'works' Zephyrs at the *Daily Express* meeting in May 1958, all of them fitted with automatic transmission! As motor sport it was a waste of time because the cars were totally uncompetitive, but as a publicity spectacle it certainly paid off. Borg Warner automatic transmission (with three forward speeds) had been introduced at the end of 1956, but sales had been slow, and petrol rationing that followed the first Suez crisis didn't help; so for 1958 Borg Warner and Ford's marketing chiefs needed a boost: 'The initiative mainly came from Desmond Scannell at Borg Warner,' Ford's long-time PR man Harry Calton recalls, 'and it was purely to give impetus to the Borg Warner automatic transmission installation.'

As a publicity exercise it worked, for everyone remembered that these cars had automatic transmission – and all of them finished. Incidentally, was this the only time that cars with automatic transmission ever started a touring car race in the UK? It was certainly a gimmick, and by most sporting standards it was rather pointless – but both Ford and Borg Warner got their share of publicity. Prepared by 'Edgy' Fabris' 'works' rally team at Lincoln Cars, these machines were driven by rally team members 'Cuth' Harrison, his son Edward, and Denis Scott. According to Ford handouts, these automatic-transmission cars were otherwise standard.

That was almost the end of the news, however, for the cars were not even remotely competitive. In a race where the 3-litre class was won by Jeff Uren's privately prepared Zephyr (he beat Sears' A105, too), the best of the 'automatics' was Denis Scott's car, which finished 65sec behind in eighteen laps – or 3.6sec every lap. Ford never considered that sort of gimmick again...

Jeff Uren's privately financed attack was much more serious, and more successful. Uren had been racing an Anglia 100E, and then a Willment-converted Prefect for some time. Then,

thinking that he could do even better in a big car, he had entered a Zephyr in the 1957 *Daily Express* event; he was not highly placed, though he beat all the other Zephyrs. Then in Jeff's own words:

> I wrote to 'Edgy' Fabris, and told him I was the greatest thing since sliced bread, and that I could win the championship for Ford. He told me to come back when I'd actually done something.
>
> So I went out and bought a Zephyr, did really very little to it, and at the *Daily Express* at Silverstone I blew off all three of the 'works' Zephyrs. Immediately after the race I ran into 'Edgy' in the paddock and said 'There, I told you I could do it!'. He said 'Get out of my sight – you've probably got me the sack, and I never want to see you again....'

Accordingly, Uren tackled the series on his own. In 1957 he had the engine totally rebuilt, lightened, balanced, and fitted with an SU instead of a downdraught Zenith carburettor, and did the best possible with revised suspension settings; and in 1958 the car was little more special.

Although Jaguars won most of the races outright, the highlight was usually the running battle between Jeff Uren's privately prepared Zephyr, and 'Gentleman Jack' Sears' BMC-backed Austin A105 Westminster. Both cars were big, nose-heavy and ungainly saloons with 2.6-litre 6-cylinder engines. Neither car, and certainly neither engine, was race bred or even meant to be a race unit, but both were driven by real racers.

It was almost level-pegging throughout the year, and across the eleven events. Although Uren only started in eight of the races, the Zephyr won its class three times; Sears won six times, however, so in the end it was the BMC car that just won the category (and Sears went on to win the championship outright).

David Haynes (the enthusiastic Ford dealer from Maidstone) drove his own Zephyr in several races, and was closest to the A105 at Brands in April, but in May (the race where the automatic-transmission Zephyrs appeared), Uren's Zephyr (247 MMY) defeated the A105 by 4sec in front of a huge crowd, to win the class and finish fourth overall, at a stirring average speed of 75.77mph (121.91km/h). The Zephyr was at its best on longer, faster, tracks – though this was little consolation to Uren, for many of the BRSCC races were on the short kidney-profiled Brands Hatch track!

Only a week later Uren repeated the trick at Mallory Park (a fast track apart from the one, bottom-gear hairpin), while Sears took the honours at Brands Hatch. Sears won again at Brands Hatch in June (Uren did not appear), but Uren triumphed at Crystal Palace in July. Then it all went wrong for Ford, as in the Grand Prix meeting at Silverstone, in front of a huge crowd, the Zephyr spun off on the very first lap, and was badly damaged. If 'starring role' is the correct description, then it described the Zephyr in Castrol's film record of this event...

A month later, at the Bank Holiday Monday event at Brands Hatch, the A105 beat Uren's second Zephyr – just – and repeated the achievement at the end of the same month. With no chance of catching Sears in the standings, Uren did not appear in the last round in October, preferring to save his money for an assault on the following season.

1959

In the new season a Zephyr became dominant in saloon car racing for the first time, its successes quite overshadowing anything achieved on rallies. Uren told me:

For 1959 the BRSCC announced a much more open set of regulations, which was promising. I wrote another letter to Ford, and to Raymond Mays at BRM, at Bourne. I told them I could win the Saloon Car Championship, but that I needed their assistance. Would they help me? Fortunately they both said 'Yes'.

Although neither provided money, Mays built and supplied two engines, both with aluminium cylinder heads, triple Weber carburettors, and a claimed 168bhp at 5,800rpm, while Ford allowed Jeff to base his car at their Lincoln Cars premises

'...where I would have to pay for work done, but at a "special rate". Mine was the only race car they supported.'

The engineers – Jack Welch, Alf Belson and George Cheeseman among them – helped enormously, while some of the rally team's expertise and kit (including the latest in prototype front-wheel Girling disc brakes) was applied to the car. Although the Zephyr wasn't quite fast enough to win races outright, Jeff won his class six times and finished second once. Jeff then received a summons from Ford: 'Colonel Buckmaster called me to lunch with him. He told me how grateful Ford was for the way I had raced successfully in the last couple of years – and then invited me to become competition manager!'

No one had ever officially held a competition manager's post before; even so, the canny Uren turned down a staff job, and accepted a one-year consultancy contract instead. It was a demanding job, for he had to look after his own racing programme as well as the 'works' rally team.

For the Monte Carlo rally, not only did Uren somehow find the funds to prepare eight 'works' Zephyrs, but he also drove one of the cars himself. Even so, it was not an event Ford would recall with pride, as every team car fell foul of penalties incurred at 'secret checks' on the route. (It was widely rumoured that these were by no means secret to some favoured French crews in French cars....) In the event the best-placed 'works' car (that of the Harrisons, father and son) finished way down the lists in thirty-fourth place.

This, though, was a season in which Ford and Lincoln Cars decided to invest heavily in an attack on the Safari, which had quite suddenly turned into an international event. Although they were under pressure from the world of motor sport, the organizers had still not abandoned their classification by selling price – though this didn't really trouble Ford, as their competition was always likely to come from the Mercedes-Benz cars that were in the same 'Over £825' price category.

Did Ford (and Jeff Uren) ever think they could win? It seems that they did – not only did they know that the Zephyrs were good and strong

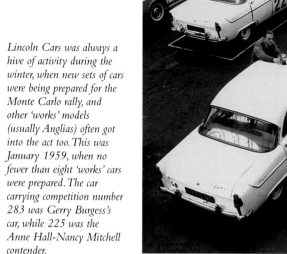

Lincoln Cars was always a hive of activity during the winter, when new sets of cars were being prepared for the Monte Carlo rally, and other 'works' models (usually Anglias) often got into the act too. This was January 1959, when no fewer than eight 'works' cars were prepared. The car carrying competition number 283 was Gerry Burgess's car, while 225 was the Anne Hall-Nancy Mitchell contender.

(and had proved their worth in East Africa in previous years), but they were able to draw on Vic Preston's invaluable 'man-in-the-bush' experience. For the very first time, this became an official Ford Motor Co. Ltd entry.

'Edgy' Fabris' engineers and mechanics, led by Jack Welch, prepared three brand-new Zephyrs (and three Anglias, too!); these were nominally driven by Edward Harrison, Kenyan resident Vic Preston, and Denis Scott, though in each case they had experienced local men alongside them. Though the team cars started as favourites, Safari luck hit hard, the result being that there were breakages where none were expected.

Even so, Denis Scott (in KGD 691) lay third at half distance (12min off the pace), and even took over second place in the second leg, though he ended up 16min behind the winning Mercedes-Benz saloon. Ford, though, also took the Manufacturers' Team Prize, which made very good copy for the advertising agencies.

On the Tulip rally, too, there was a quite unexpected bonus, for although Ford did not officially enter any cars, most of the team's regular drivers turned up in cars that had demonstrably been prepared at Lincoln Cars – make of that what you wish. After a thoroughly testing run –

from Paris down to Avignon, then back to Holland, on an increasingly tight schedule – new recruit Peter Riley, with Dickie Bensted-Smith of *Motor* as his co-driver, took a rousing third place overall, beaten only by the Jaguar 3.4 of the Morley Twins, and Keith Ballisat's 'works' Triumph TR3A. As an added bonus, Ford won the team prize, too ....

In a later edition of *Motor*, Bensted-Smith wrote up his adventures in 155 LVX in an entertaining way, headlining the feature 'Dutch Treat'. Describing Riley's driving as heroic, and of the difficulties of servicing a big Ford without factory help, he also wrote about the horrors of keeping a schedule in thick fog, and complained of the Zephyr's hard-pressed drum brakes:

> Peter had the hang of the brakes by now, having discovered that the normal sequence of squeal-grab-lock which occurred on any prolonged descent, was not only reversed as they cooled off again on the way up the other side, but could be interrupted in the middle by pushing a little harder. Nothing much happened except that the squealing stopped.....

There was no question that the braking capabilities of the Zephyrs was hard pressed on any event with a tight schedule, but Uren and his drivers could only wait impatiently for disc brakes to be added to road car specifications.

But Ford's fortunes were clearly on the way up again, for in the picturesque French Alpine rally no fewer that nine Coupes des Alpes were awarded to crews without penalties on the road sections, and three of them went to Zephyr drivers. Compared with the 1958 event, which had left everyone breathless, the schedule was slightly eased – but this did not make it a walkover for the serious crews. Even so, as *Autosport's* correspondent, John Gott, wrote in his report: 'Ford Zephyrs went brilliantly to win three Coupes, every team prize open to non-French cars, and, of course, their class ….'

On this event, for once, the Zephyr's construction also helped, rather than hindered, for Gott later wrote that: 'The timed climb of the Turracherhohe…was appalling, rough and steep….Here the Zephyrs, with their fine ground clearance and magnificent torque, were outstanding….'

In fact, Ford's party was only spoiled near the end, when on the descent of the Mont Ventoux test: '…the hard-pressed Anne Hall/Nancy Mitchell Zephyr dropped its propeller shaft into the road….A similar fate had earlier overtaken the Walker/Patten Zephyr…'

All in all, for Ford's Zephyrs this had been a fascinating and high-profile season of motor sport, and it ended in a suitably flamboyant way, when Gerry Burgess' car quite unexpectedly won the RAC rally.

This was the first of the 'new-look' RAC rallies, which put more emphasis on fast open-road motoring and high performance, than previous rather milk-and-water events that relied on driving tests to achieve a result. Because of this new approach, Ford was not expecting to win any major awards, though a phalanx of Zephyrs took the start from Blackpool. In an event that meandered on for four days without any overnight rest halts, the route took in the far north-west of Scotland, the Welsh mountains, and would finish at London's Crystal Palace race circuit. Driver endurance was at least as important as that of the cars, and fatigue became a big factor later on.

As well as the constant pressure to keep up with the time schedule, performance would be crucial, in manoeuvring tests, speed hill-climbs, and on race circuits (but no special stages – that would follow in future years) – until, that is, the event was hit by a blizzard in the Scottish Highlands, where the route between Nairn and Braemar became snow-bound. Many crews, including most factory team cars, tried to bulldoze their way over what is known as the Lecht Road, but found it impassable. In the end, thirty-one crews elected to detour many miles out of their way to Braemar, just fifteen of them arriving within their one hour lateness limit (the author was in one of those cars).

Finding an alternative route on that snowy November night was a lottery, but Gerry Burgess (driving the self-same Zephyr, 155 LVX, which had performed so well in the Tulip) hurtled round the blockage through Dufftown, and eventually arrived at Braemar no less than 29min late (the author, co-driving 'Codger' Malkin's Sunbeam Rapier, was 39min late). Normally speaking this would have put him out of contention, but no other car approached that figure, and if Burgess could keep it all together for the rest of the event, he was bound to win.

Two days later, and on his way into the Brands Hatch circuit for one of the final tests, Burgess almost lost everything when he met Lyndon Sims' Aston Martin on a narrow approach road, and hit it! Fortunately the damage was only slight, and the car made it to the finish at Crystal Palace.

And so it was that Gerry Burgess and the Ford Zephyr won their only RAC rally – one that it still memorable to all those who survived that icy night in Scotland.

1960

After such a season, where good fortune played a part in Ford's success, there was no likelihood of it happening again – and nor did it. Apart from setting another fine performance in the East African Safari, the works' Zephyrs did not win

Above *Gerry Burgess (right) and Sam Croft-Pearson drove this Zephyr to win the 1959 RAC rally; here they are seen at the Crystal Palace circuit on the last afternoon. The front end of 155 LVX was damaged after it hit another rally car close to the gates of the Brands Hatch circuit!*

Right *This was the interior of 155 LVX on the 1959 RAC Rally.*

anything significant during the 1960 season. In the Monte Carlo rally, for instance, where victory went to the big-spending Mercedes-Benz team (who spend week after boring week practising the regularity sections), two of the three 'works' cars went out with a breakage (Edward Harrison) or a crash (Denis Scott), while 'Cuth' Harrison's car could not keep up to the immac-

ulate time-keeping of the Germans, and finished way down in twentieth place.

Amazingly, years of experience in British rallies, where strict timekeeping was essential, enabled private entrants Mike Sutcliffe and Phil Crabtree to finish sixth overall, beaten only by four big Mercedes-Benz cars and one 'works' Sunbeam Rapier (driven by Peter Harper and

As expected, there was a full team entry of 'works' Zephyrs, for 'Cuth' Harrison, his son Edward Harrison and for journalist Tommy Wisdom, along with a team of the new-type Anglia 105Es. That distinguished 'local', Vic Preston, entered his own Zephyr (John Harrison shared the car with him), thus making up a formidable attack from Ford. Much of Tanganyika was flooded in the days leading up to the start, so sweeping route changes had to be made. Even so, much

Raymond Baxter). In addition, the Handley/Harvey Zodiac won its class, though in general classification it was well down the lists. Even so, the Zephyr's record on the Safari was now so good that the 'works' Zephyr team was almost expected to do well, if not to take outright victory, on every occasion. For 1960, and for the very first time, the old classification by selling price was abandoned in favour of conventional engine size limits, so Ford put in a really big effort.

Above *Four of the new 'SNO' cars being readied for the 1960 Monte, complete with the swivelling roof-mounted spot lights that were fashionable in rallying at this time.*

Below *This was one of the fleet of new Low-Line Zephyrs prepared to compete in the 1960 Monte Carlo, and other events during the season.*

Denis Scott drove a 'works' Zephyr II in the 3,200 mile (5,150km) East African Safari of 1960, and along with 'Cuth' Harrison and Vic Preston in sister cars, helped to win the Manufacturers' Team Prize.

Safari Myth

Way back in the 1950s a long-distance rally called the Coronation Safari was set up, for strictly standard cars that ran in selling price classes, rather than against engine capacity; from these beginnings the 'Safari myth' rapidly evolved. Simply and some might say arrogantly, this reputation suggested that road conditions were so unique, and driving demands so specialized, that this rally could only ever be won by an East African driver. Held on sometimes awful roads in three adjoining nations – Kenya, Uganda and Tanganyika – it required reliability from the car, experience from the drivers, and endurance from the entire crew. Until 1957 it did not carry an international permit, which meant that no foreign driver could even try his luck.

And the Safari myth persisted until 1972: but in that year the Scandinavians, Hannu Mikkola and Gunnar Palm, finally buried that myth in their 'works' Ford Escort RS1600. In the meantime, however, Ford had set up several fine performances, including an outright win by a locally driven Zephyr 6 in 1955.

In the first year, 1953, no outright winner was nominated, but local Zephyrs took second and third in their price class. Another class was won by a Tatra, of all things, crewed by D.P. Marwaha and Kenyan motor-trader Vic Preston: their names would become important to Ford in the future. The same crew won again in 1954, this time in a VW Beetle, so when they elected to drive a Ford Zephyr in 1955, everyone sat up and took notice: at the close of that Easter weekend, not only did this duo win the event outright, but by the healthy margin of seventeen clear points. They certainly deserved this success; at one point the Zephyr's windscreen was shattered when it was struck by an unfortunate vulture! Sadly only one picture of this epic adventure seems to have survived, showing a perfectly standard-looking Zephyr, even with its wheel hub-caps in place!

There would be other epic Ford performances in the future – the 'works' Cortina GTs would sweep the board in 1964, for instance – but this one was something special.

Bill Young (who would later crew a winning Cortina in the 1960s) drove this privately entered Zodiac II in the 1960 East African Safari. That's a novel way of cleaning mud away from the radiator!

of the event was wet, and the entire route seemed to be as car-breaking as ever. Not unexpectedly, it was 'privateer' Vic Preston who finished third, but all the 'works' team Zephyrs kept going, to win the much prized Manufacturers' Team award yet again.

Back in Europe, and with marketing reasons partly behind the decision, the 'works' team began to use more and more of the newly launched overhead-valve Anglia 105Es. This undoubtedly explains why only one 'works' Zephyr figured prominently in the Tulip rally, where tight road sections and speed hill-climbs made up much of the route; Anne Hall/Valerie Domleo took third place in their capacity class.

Nor was there much to play for in the French Alpine rally where, as team boss Jeff Uren once told me: 'We couldn't win anything on the Alpine because the time schedule was impossible for the Zephyrs, and the regulations were totally anomalous.'

Indeed the Alpine was even more of a summer 'road race' than ever before. Starting from Mar-

seilles and finishing at Cannes, but taking in all the usual high passes in the French Alpes Mar-itimes, and in the Italian Dolomites, the timing seemed to get tougher as the event wore on. All four 'works' Zephyrs finished the event, but all found the schedules impossible to achieve, par-ticularly on the last day. Pure horsepower, in the form of 3.8-litre-engined Jaguars and fuel-inject-ed Mercedes-Benz cars, proved too much for the standard-production Zephyrs.

At the end of the season, in the long and gru-elling RAC rally, special stages were used for the very first time, and it was a similar story. Three 'works' Zephyrs were also joined by a team of 'works' Anglias, but once again this was an event that favoured high performance cars, and the Zephyrs were no match for a 3.8-litre Jaguar, dri-ven by Jeff Uren's old adversity, Jack Sears; the best they could do was to take second and third places in their capacity class.

In the meantime, and after completing his year as a motor-sport consultant, Jeff Uren presented his own ideal for Ford's motor-sport strategy: a twenty-seven-page paper that included a recommendation to set up a separate department, with its own budget, and a separate ability to sell parts; it also forecast the need for a Boreham, and for an Advanced Vehicle Operation. But these recommendations were not accepted at the time, and this discouraged Jeff so much that he returned to his plant hire business for the next two years, and had little more to do with motor sport.

1961 and 1962

By the early 1960s, Ford's 'works' team of Zephyrs and Anglias was beginning to look increasingly more professional, though the whole operation was still clearly motivated by publicity, rather than engineering concerns; furthermore the Zephyrs were beginning to look outpaced by their lighter and more nimble opposition. Some things, however, did not change, for although Fabris once again became titular competitions manager, he still relied heavily on 'Cuth' Harrison's advice, and this was still a period when the drivers were 'good chaps' rather than thrusting young heroes.

Although the Zephyrs were still the backbone of the team, they had now been joined by the much more promising Anglia 105E, complete with its enormously robust and tunable overhead-valve engine. Keith Duckworth's Cosworth concern produced a great deal of horsepower, Lotus produced amazingly agile Formula Junior cars – and suddenly Ford began to look like a modern company.

In 1961 there still seemed to be one last opportunity for the Mark II Zephyr to win the Safari, but as in previous years, local conditions, brilliant driving by the opposition in Mercedes-Benz models, and the usual dollop of bad 'Safari luck' against non-African drivers meant that the best Zephyr could only take third place. That

In Africa, Ford's finest hour with the Mark II Zephyr came in 1961, when Anne Hall and Lucille Cardwell took third place overall in this 'works' car.

third place, though, was taken by the redoubtable Anne Hall, who had been promoted from her more usual Ford Anglia on this occasion.

This was the longest Safari so far – all of 3,350 miles (5,360km) – and it was run in mainly dry conditions; otherwise the event evolved much as usual. No fewer than five 'works' Zephyrs – driven by Anne Hall, Gerry Burgess, Tommy Wisdom, Vic Preston and 'Cuth' Harrison – took the start, while three of them – Anne Hall, Wisdom and 'Cuth' Harrison – took third, sixth and seventh places overall, and also lifted the Manufacturers' Team Prize. It was a great way to bring the Zephyr's African career to a close.

Even so, as a rally car, the 'writing was on the wall' for the Mark II Zephyr as it passed its fifth birthday. Even though the 'works' cars were now using front-wheel disc brakes, they were simply not fast enough to beat other cars with a similar size engine. Perhaps the final insult came in the

1961 RAC rally – the first RAC to use special stages throughout its route – when Raymond Baxter's 'works' 3-litre Humber Super Snipe defeated every Zephyr in the field.

Soon after this, Ford's chairman, Sir Patrick Hennessy, decided that Ford-UK's image needed to be revitalized, and – as already noted in an earlier chapter – hired Walter Hayes, a successful Fleet Street newspaper editor, to do that for him. It was an outstanding appointment, and Hayes would be the guiding genius behind almost every Ford sporting initiative of the next thirty years. Yet it was not inevitable: 'I knew nothing about motor sport when I joined Ford,' Walter Hayes once told me. 'Except that I'd hired Colin Chapman to write about cars for one of my newspapers, I was a complete novice.'

This was maybe, but he certainly learned – and fast. Who but Hayes could have transformed Ford's public and sporting images, could have

In 1961, and by Kenyan standards, this counted as a main road in East Africa. Apart from having beefed-up suspension, cars competing in the East African Safari had to be absolutely standard. The 'works' Zephyrs were strong enough to win the Team Prize and the Ladies' Prize (Anne Hall, this car) on that occasion.

Ford had no chance of winning the Monte Carlo in 1961, as the organizers imposed a weight and engine size handicap formula that favoured small, under-powered cars. Here that celebrated 'works' mechanic Norman Masters (later he would become Roger Clark's favoured car-builder at Boreham) prepares the only 'works' Zephyr to be entered, driven by Gerry Burgess, Ian Walker and Sam Croft-Pearson. Even with a triple-SU carburetted engine, it was not competitive for outright victory, but took second place in its class behind the privately entered Zephyr of Handley and Harvey.

A colossal fleet of 'works' Fords being prepared for the 1962 Monte – eight Anglias and four Zephyrs …

persuaded its management to back the Lotus-Cortina project, could have eased the company into Formula 1, got the entire Rally Sport programme approved, and made the Escort into the world's most successful rally car? If not Walter Hayes, you might say, wouldn't someone else have done the same? Absolutely not: not according to Sir Terence Beckett (who became chairman and managing director in that period), nor to Stuart Turner (Ford's most famous director of motor sport), and not according to Henry Ford II himself, who made Hayes his closest British confidante.

We must remember just how different a company Ford-UK actually was before Hayes arrived. A big company, certainly, and a profitable company, definitely – but with a sporting image, certainly not. Although the Zephyr had won the Monte, the RAC and the Safari rallies by that time, even in 1960 Ford-UK's image was still very mundane. Yet by 1970, after a decade, there would be glamour all around. In 1960 Ford was barely involved in motor sport, but by 1970 Ford was winning everywhere. The last side-valve-engined British Fords were made in 1962, yet the first 16-valve twin-cams were on sale by 1970.

In, around, and behind this transformation was the small, dynamic, dapper and utterly persuasive character of Walter Hayes. These days we would call him a fixer, a wheeler-dealer, or a spin-doctor – and he was vital to what followed. Hayes arrived at Ford in the winter of 1961/1962, at the same time as Ford-USA embraced its new Total Performance philosophy. Although Ford, along with other car makers in Detroit, had tacitly agreed to ignore motor sport in the late 1950s, Henry Ford II soon found that his rivals were finding underhand ways to get round that agreement. By the early 1960s, therefore, he was ready to tear up the agreement, and in May 1962, at a stroke, he abandoned the old AMA (Automobile Manufacturers' Association) and set out on a high-performance strategy aimed at attracting the mass of young drivers – the 'baby Boomers' who had grown up in recent years.

All of his subsidiary companies, and especially those in Europe, were encouraged to embrace a philosophy of 'Total Performance'. Bright ideas

... the Zephyrs running with three-SU-carburetted engines.

Rally engineer Jack Welch, who led the team which developed the three-SU engines, inspecting such an installation in one of the 1962 team cars.

and a new approach to performance motoring were needed, and it came at exactly the right time to inspire Walter Hayes, who recognized a great publicity challenge when he saw one. Hayes already knew some of the right sort of people, in racing, if not in rallying. Having employed the brilliant engineer Colin Chapman, of Lotus, on the *Sunday Dispatch* ('but he was hopeless at meeting deadlines...'), he soon turned to Chapman with an exciting proposal, and dined out for years on the way that the Lotus-Cortina was invented.

Before this, however, Hayes had to keep the pot boiling. Knowing that the Anglia was too slow to make a difference, and that fast Cortinas would not be ready until 1963, for 1962 he had to carry on with the latest Zephyrs and Zodiacs. In a bitty programme that encompassed only the Safari, the French Alpine and a bit of racing, it kept Ford's sporting name in the public eye, if not in the winner's circle.

For the Safari, no fewer than six 'works' Zodiac Mark IIIs were prepared (the money seemed

to go further in those days...), to be driven by Gerry Burgess, Edward Harrison, Vic Preston, Eric Jackson, Anne Hall and journalist Tommy Wisdom. This was a very serious assault by the 'works' team, and although they were not expected to win (the new car had only been launched a week before the start, and its structure was totally unproven in these rough, hot and dusty conditions) they were expected to win their class, and perhaps even win the team prize.

Gerry Burgess and local co-driver Beau Younghusband duly delivered the class win, but were a long way off the pace, while two cars retired with damaged radiators after hitting the same patch of uncivilized Kenya, one fell into a very large hole from which it could not be recovered, while a fourth broke its clutch. Good, but not good enough – and a result which really proved that rallying in big standard Fords was no longer going to be a guaranteed success.

Later in the year, 'works' Zodiacs tackled the French Alpine rally (high speeds and high passes)

Although 'works' Zodiac Mark IIIs were prepared at Lincoln Cars for motor sport in 1962 and 1963, they had a very short life. Looking rather travel-stained after it returned from a very arduous RAC rally, KOO 50 was already looking forward to...

and the Liege-Sofia-Liege marathon (endurance, awful roads, tricky route-finding) with commendable success. Driving 'KOO 50', a very memorable registration number for a big car, the Frenchman Jean Vinatier won his class in the Alpine, losing only one minute on a tight schedule and finishing second in the entire Touring Car category; while in the Liege the Harrison brothers (Edward and John) finished an exhausted 13th in 'KOO 48', in an event where all but eighteen cars were eliminated, and all the Zodiacs suffered from front suspension strut failures.

Having given the special-stages-only RAC rally a miss, Ford then prepared three of the 'works' 'KOO' Zodiacs for the high profile Monte Carlo rally of 1963. This was mere bravado, and very much a final fling, for without front-wheel-drive these cars were never likely to succeed. In an event run in blizzard/white-out conditions, only 102 of the 296 starters actually slithered to the finish; for Ford, there was no success against the might of the Mercedes-Benz team, so the Zodiac programme was immediate-ly wound down in favour of the new Cortinas, which were just arriving on the scene.

Zodiac Mark III in Racing

Before the end of this period, however, there was one more chance for Ford's big cars to race, and to make a statement. In 1962 there was a real opportunity, because the BRSCC decided to hold a Six-Hour saloon car race at Brands Hatch.

Although the Six-Hour race got most attention from the press that year, the Mark III also appeared in the saloon car race at the *Daily Express* meeting in May. Amazingly, the class structure and the wet weather favoured the unproven Zodiacs, which took 1-2-3 in their class, with F1 driver Innes Ireland taking the honours at 76.19mph (122.59km/h). We must not get too excited by this, though, for in general classification the Zodiacs were beaten not only by the 1.6-litre Sunbeam Rapiers, but also by the 1-litre Mini-Coopers.

In October, *Motor* sponsored the Six-Hour race, which like the BRSCC Championship, was being run to Group 2 ('Improved Touring Car') regulations, and was run on the new, lengthened, 2.65-mile (4.26km) Brands Hatch international circuit. Although Ford entered two 'works' Zodiacs – KOO 48 (an ex-'works' rally car, totally refreshed after the Liege-Sofia-Liege) for Jeff Uren and David Haynes, and COO 10 (ex-Safari rally car!) for Paul Hawkins and Brian Johnstone – both were prepared outside Lincoln Cars, by the Ian Walker racing team.

Although the result was creditable, it was not a triumph, for although the Zodiacs could seemingly match the pace of a sophisticated Italian-prepared Lancia Flaminia Coupé, during the six hours they needed to make more pit stops to replace worn tyres, and lost a lot of time. Even so, the Uren/Haynes car finished eighth overall, and

...the 1963 Monte Carlo, where Gerry Burgess and Ian Walker took the start. When this picture was taken, close to the Mediterranean, Gerry needed sunglasses, and there was no snow; only hours later the big car would be swallowed up in a blizzard. This was the last 'works' appearance by a Zodiac III.

second in its capacity class, averaging 70.06mph (112.73km/h), which compared very well with the 75.37mph (121.27km/h) of the winning Jaguar 3.8 Mark II. The other Zodiac finished seventeenth.

Swansong

Even so, the 'works' Zephyr/Zodiac story was still not quite over. Fast forward to late 1969 when, soon after his appointment as Ford-of-Britain's competition manager, Stuart Turner had to begin preparing for the World Cup rally of 1970.

After four decades, the sheer scale of the *Daily Mirror*-sponsored World Cup rally of 1970 has not faded. Inspired by the success of the London-Sydney Marathon of 1968, it was scheduled to take place in April and May 1970. It would take six weeks out of everyone's lives – six exhausting, but eventually exhilarating, weeks. For publicity purposes it was loosely linked to the forthcoming football World Cup, due to take place in Mexico, and was designed to link Lon-

Above *Only days after the new model had been announced, Ford entered a team of Zodiac Mark IIIs in the East African Safari of 1962. This was the Vic Preston/Baillon entry that took second place in its capacity class, close behind the sister car, driven by Gerry Burgess and 'Beau' Younghusband.*

Below *By the 1960s the Ford rally team was turning away from the Zephyrs and Zodiacs, to smaller, more nimble 'works' cars such as this Anglia 105E. The face of rallying was changing rapidly, with high performance now of more importance that sheer strength and reliability.*

don with Mexico City via a seven-day section in Europe, and a full circuit of South America along the way. In the end it was the *Daily Mirror* that agreed to provide blanket sponsorship.

This 16,000-mile (25,745km) event attracted the attention of all of rallying's 'big hitters'. Both Ford and British Leyland (who had failed to win the London–Sydney Marathon in 1968) were determined to win in 1970, while Citroen, with DS21s, were sure to be there, too. Almost from the moment that Turner arrived at Boreham in June 1969, to the end of May in 1970, never a day passed when the event, and the cars to be used, were not discussed. Even before the practice sessions and the route surveys began, there was one 'Big Question' being raised: there were to be no homologation/eligibility restrictions, so as this was a free-for-all, what cars should be used? Large or small? Fast or slower, more reliable? Two-man

Old rally cars (and drivers) never die, they just return for classic events. This was the Pirelli Classic Marathon of 1988 (London – Cortina in Italy, and return) where the Harrison family, main Ford dealers from Sheffield, entered this immaculate Mark II model.

or three-man crews? The Taunus 20MRS (it had just won the Safari for Ford-Germany), the Escort but fitted with larger capacity, non-standard engines, or even the massive Zodiac Mark IV (lots of space for a three-man crew) were all considered.

To convince themselves, Turner, rally engineer Bill Meade and engine builder Peter Ashcroft decided to build different test cars to see how they performed. First of all, in September, Roger Clark tackled the French Alpine rally in a new Escort fitted out with a Ford-Germany 2.3-litre V6 engine, which produced 165bhp, and with the new-fangled ZF five-speed gearbox. That was a disaster, for the engine was under-cooled, and boiled persistently, while the gearbox also gave endless trouble.

A few weeks later, Roger (poor Roger!) was lumbered with driving a vast Zodiac Mark IV on the Three Cities (Munich–Vienna–Budapest) rally, though the car had been prepared for Boreham by British Vita Racing (of Lancashire). Boreham's workshop was at the time totally swamped with the building, maintenance and

Would a Mark IV Zodiac be suitable for entry in the London – Mexico World Cup Rally of 1970? To find out, Ford's motor sport department entered this car in the European Three Cities Rally, for Roger Clark to assess. Although Roger won his class, he concluded that this machine was too large and too heavy, and it was not used again.

development of 'works' Escort twin-cams. Of the many outside concerns that might have been approached, Turner chose British Vita because in his previous life as BMC's competitions manager he had worked with this company on a series of very fast racing Mini-Coopers. But on an event that was a European Championship qualifier involving eight high-speed special stages (some on tarmac, some on smooth gravel), there was no way that a Zodiac Mark IV could have been competitive on performance, especially as a team of ultra-light and nimble 'works' Alpine-Renaults were expected to set the pace.

And so it proved. The Zodiac was way behind the pace of the Alpine-Renaults, though Roger tried his very best to beat the fleet of privately entered BMW saloons in his class. In the end it worked, but although 'business is business' for a 'works' driver, he must have felt this to be an insult to his talents.

In the end, Roger and Jim Porter won their class (on one 27-minute stage, the Zodiac was

more than four minutes faster than anything else in its class!), but in fairness this massive saloon was totally outclassed by the 'real' rally cars. Because the Zodiac was showing signs of overheating in the early stages, at one point it was necessary to change the car's radiator, but otherwise it seemed to be reliable enough, if slow. As Roger later wrote in his autobiography *Sideways to Victory*:

> Someone once said that driving a Zodiac was like driving an aircraft carrier, but I could throw it at the corners... It was a safe and interesting car. It had a lot of character, but not a lot of performance. It also proved to me that it wasn't the right car for the World Cup....

Nor was it apparently the right competition for any other type of event, for this was the very last time that a 'works' Zodiac ever took part in a timed event. Once back in the UK, this example – ETW 690G – was swiftly decommissioned, and returned to a more mundane life. I doubt very much if it has survived.

7 V-engines for the Mark IVs

In the twenty-two years that cover the life of this family of big Fords, the biggest change of all from one model range to the next – both visual and technical – came in 1966 with the launch of the Mark IV range. Although some of the same old names were retained – Zephyr and Zodiac, this time with Zephyrs available in V4 and V6 varieties – there was to be no other mechanical carryover from the Mark III range. Almost everything in the Mark IV was to be new: platform, body style, rear suspension and, above all, engines.

Although a big financial investment was involved, it is important to recall just what huge changes and modernization Ford-UK was making to its business at the beginning of the 1960s, and how it was always tending to develop new 'corporate' components that could be used on many more different models than hitherto. As I

have already noted, although there was now a thoroughly modern PTA (paint, trim, assembly) building in place at Dagenham, Anglia and Corsair assembly had recently been relocated to the brand new Halewood plant, trucks had gone to the ex-Hurricane fighter assembly factory at Langley (near Heathrow Airport), and tractors were on their way to Basildon. This meant that, from 1963, manufacturing and assembly at Dagenham could be concentrated on the best-selling Cortina range, and on the 'Big Fords'.

First Thoughts

Because every aspect of the Mark IV range was to be new, it took a very long time to bring it forward to production. We now know that original work on 'Project Panda' was first suggested in

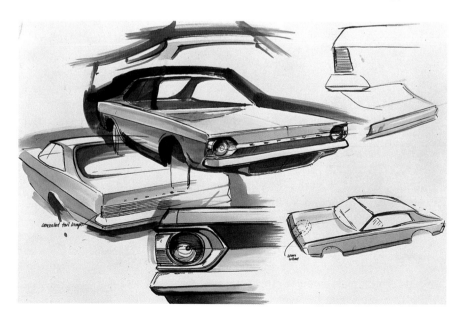

Early in the 1960s, design sketches for a new big Ford began to come together at Dagenham. Even at that point, the chiselled rear end, and the front-end spare wheel position, were becoming evident.

February 1961, and the new project confirmed in May 1961 – and in fact this was well before the previous Mark III range had even been announced, which rather proves the point that Ford saw the Mark III as no more than the final flowering of the original Consul/Zephyr line, which had made its debut in 1950.

Although it then took five years to bring 'Project Panda' to market, this was not the fault of the design, nor of the engineers developing it, or of the management team behind it. These new models, in fact, had to take their place in the queue (for attention, financial investment and facilities) behind all other new Ford-UK projects of the period. For proof, just take a look at this time line:

1961:   Launch of the new Classic/Classic Capri saloons and coupés.

1962:   Launch of the Zephyr/Zodiac Mark III range of saloons, estates and convertibles.
Launch of the Cortina range of saloons and estates.

1963:   Opening of the new Halewood assembly plant, near Liverpool, on Merseyside.
Launch of the Corsair range of saloons and estate cars.

1964:   Opening of a new tractor factory at Basildon in Essex.
Opening of a new HQ building complex at Warley, near Brentwood, in Essex.

1965:   Launch of the all-new Transit van range, to be assembled at Langley.
Opening of a new axle-manufacturing plant in Swansea, South Wales.

The miracle was that the Mark IV retained its place in this queue – for attention, for loving care, and subsequently for introduction to the public.

In engineering and design, Ford-USA's North American influence was still very strongly felt at Ford-UK, and the engineering director's post was almost inevitably filled by an American on sec-

ondment. There was no doubt that the Mark IV was always going to be a larger, heavier, and even more flamboyantly styled range than the Mark III it was to replace. Not only that, but the directors were ready to authorize a big investment in a new body platform, a new range of engines, and (for the very first time on any Ford-UK product) the introduction of independent rear suspension.

Before discussing what appeared to be a radically new type of styling, attention must be given to the mechanical layout, and the rationale behind it all. Technically this was a project that would feature several 'firsts' – it was the first British Ford to use modern V-layout engines, the first to use all-independent suspension, and the first to use an all-disc-brake installation. By any standards, in other words, this was a big gamble for Ford-UK to make – and with the benefit of hindsight one can now suggest that it was only partially successful.

When the new range finally made its debut in April 1966, Fred Hart (chief engineer, passenger cars, Ford-UK) gave a fascinating interview to Ronald Barker of *Autocar* magazine, providing a real insight into the way that such projects make their way to the public. Fred had worked under the guidance of executive engineer George Halford (who had, of course, been involved, way back, in the original Consul/Zephyr project), the technical director of the day being the flamboyant American Harley Copp.

Among the information that Fred provided was that full 'programme approval' came in December 1963, which gave the planners rather more than two years to get the car into series production. Much of the closed track testing, he confirmed, was not only done at Boreham airfield, in Essex (Ford Motorsport had recently moved into new workshops on that site, by the way....) but at a still-developing new facility at Lommel in Belgium:

We tested the cars... mainly in Belgium, on circuits combining pavé, rough going and hilly country, totalling about 60,000 miles in that area alone. Another 10,000 miles in Belgium, Austria, Germany and Italy on ride and handling and mountain circuits.

We did 15,000 miles in Scandinavia, mostly north of the Arctic Circle. For extended durability trials in a hot climate we ran up about 5,000 miles over the dusty mountain roads of Spain. Add some 10,000 miles hammering up and down autobahnen, and you have some 100,000 miles overseas.

Although such a mileage would be dismissed, these days, as skimping the job, Ford was obvious proud of what had been achieved and:

Of twenty prototypes, nine were mechanical ones disguised by [Ford-USA] Fairlane bodies, but with correct underbodies so that we could get the suspension and other mechanicals correctly related. The first of the nine Phase 1 prototypes was ready by October 1963, whereas the eleven Phase 2 and 3 prototypes, complete to the correct body form, were progressive from the beginning of January 1965....

It cost about £28 million to produce the first car off on the Mark IV, which is the total figure including the engines. £2 million was spent on engineering the car excluding engines, which were developed as a separate project....

No matter how much one might argue over the chosen style, packaging and general layout of the Mark IVs – and there were certainly protagonists for and against this car before it appeared – there was no doubt that the design was thoroughly developed before it was launched in April 1966. Not only were the very first 'pilot-build' models – just three cars – built on the Dagenham assembly lines before the Christmas break in 1965, but nearly 50,000 of all types would follow in 1966.

Independent rear suspension was a novelty for Ford in the 1960s, so when it was chosen for use in the Mark IVs, a great deal of rig-testing was needed. Wheels and tyres (still cross-ply, please note) were still normal in those days.

The changeover from Mark III to Mark IV types might have been complete and radical – quite startling in some areas, indeed – but it was achieved very smoothly.

Style and Structure

Although the style was completed in the ex-Briggs (now Ford) design studios at Dagenham, there was much Detroit influence in it. Undoubtedly, too, the Detroit influence of Ford-UK's then engineering chief, Harley Copp, a high-profile and flamboyant American who had been

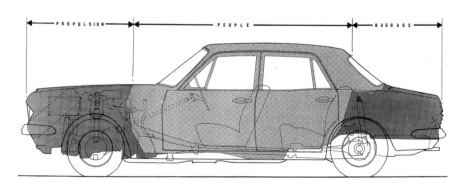

This is how the Mark IV models were packaged. In the case of the Zephyr V4, which had an even shorter engine, there was even more spare space up front. Note that although the luggage boot looked quite short when viewed from outside, there was a sizable volume under the rear parcel shelf.

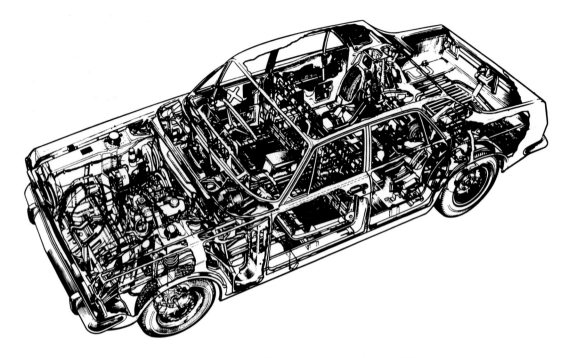

It is immediately obvious from this excellent cutaway drawing of the Zodiac Mark IV that it could have been significantly shorter and lighter. The V6 engine is placed almost entirely behind the line of the front wheels, there being a cooling radiator, an angled spare wheel and a great deal of fresh air up front.

appointed in late 1962, and the Canadian Roy Brown (who was running the styling studios at the time), had much to do with this.

Much of the detail style was carried out for Brown and Copp by Ron Bradshaw, and by Charles Thompson, who had already made his name at Ford with his work on the original 'Archbishop' (Cortina) style. After the usual viewings, modifications, re-viewings, and the rather tortuous approvals process had been completed, original clay models with Mark III-type side window profiles, and short bonnets, were rejected, and it was a Charles Thompson theme that was finally selected.

It was at Copp's insistence that the Mark IV was made considerably larger than the out-going Mark III, in all respects, though little of the increase in wheelbase was given over to a spacious front end; this had a massively long bonnet with more front-end overhang than before, under which the spare wheel was mounted ahead of the engine and on top of the water radiator. The

cabin was more spacious than ever, particularly in the rear seat, and though the boot appeared to be smaller it was just as big as before: the fact that the bulky spare wheel was now stowed up front helped enormously.

Details such as the concave rear style (called a 'bow back' by some) were credited to Charles Thompson, but in later years he admitted to being heavily influenced from above, and to be guided by the size and bulk of the contemporary, early 1960s, Ford-USA Fairlane range. It was also made clear that if the then-new Mustang's long-bonnet/short-rear-deck style was such a success, then the new Mark IVs might just benefit by using similar proportions.

As explained in the next section, because management had taken a different view on this range's potential place in the motoring firmament, as compared with the Mark III, the 'footprint' of the new Mark IV was significantly larger than before. The platform and of course the body shell itself were to be totally new, with no panels, sections or structures – nothing – carried over from the platform of the Mark III (even though that component, therefore, had a life of only four years, which was very short by developing modern standards).

Compared with the Mark III, on the new car the wheelbase had been increased by no less than 8in (20cm), the whole car was 4in (10cm) longer and 1.5in (4cm) wider and (this being a measure of the way the cabin had been made more spacious – it was almost 5in (13cm) wider at the front, across the shoulders, for instance) the rear track had been pushed out by no less than 4.5in (11.5cm).

On the other hand, because Ford was now building up a remarkable portfolio of experience

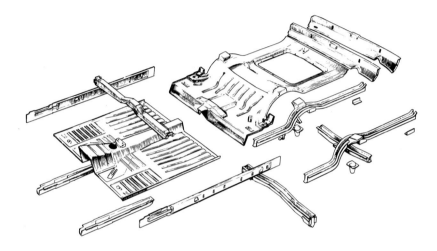

Details of the intricate presswork that went into the make-up of the platform of the Mark IV…

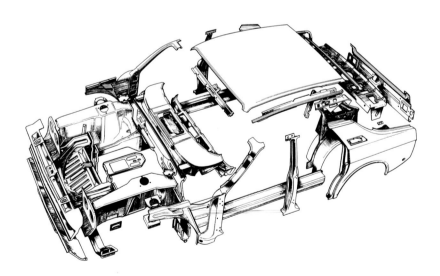

…and of the body shell that was built up on that platform. No immediate provision was made for an estate car type, so a considerable amount of new engineering would be needed when that derivative came along.

with the engineering of unit-construction body shells, the Mark IV assembly was conventional in every way. Based on a solid floor platform, cross-braced with rails of triangular cross-section which ran right through to the tail, there were also substantial box-section members running 3ft (90cm) forward of the passenger bulkhead, which tied up to a welded in front suspension cross member, this being of a sturdy top-hat section. In addition, there was a sturdy pressing welded across the front of the car (at the front of the engine bay), which not only added to the torsional strength, but also supported wheel-arches, radiator mountings, and fixings for the spare wheel itself.

As ever with a Ford of this type and period, the front inner wings that surrounded the engine bay also incorporated stiffened sections to support the towers of the MacPherson struts, and although tests were certainly carried out at the prototype stage, on production cars there were no cross-bracing members from the top of the strut towers to the passenger bulkhead itself. Not only did this cut costs, but it also made access to the engine bay, for service and maintenance, that much easier.

The rear-end structure was conventional too, though on this design the fuel tank also doubled as the boot floor for much of the width, and the transverse rear body panel behind the boot lid was made particularly high to aid overall rigidity. Even at the design/prototype stage, Ford learned much from what had obviously just been achieved on newly launched BMWs and Triumph 2000s, both of which had been launched before Mark IV design was frozen. To help in the search for refinement, the massive final drive unit/torque tube was not bolted up direct to the floor, but to two separate sub-frames that were themselves fixed to the floor through insulating mounts, one supporting the outer pivots of the semi-trailing arms, the other supporting the axle casing itself.

Once again, Ford had no plans to produce an estate car version of their own, but at least their favoured contractor, E.D. Abbott of Farnham, was given a privileged early look at the saloon as it was being engineered, and knew just what, and how, they would have to move to produce the estate car for which there was a firm, but limited demand.

Fred Hart, in that seminal *Autocar* interview, was obviously a great fan of what was produced, or was at least very well briefed, because he stated that: 'The styling is exclusively Dagenham, but influenced by world-wide requirements... America feels that, as we have to sell the car, the shape must be exclusively ours.' However, when interviewer 'Steady' Barker commented about the long nose/short tail theme, Hart retorted that: 'We say here the big car man has power under the bonnet, and the longer bonnet the stronger this image!'

That had echoes of 'mine is bigger than yours...' about it, but perhaps we had better leave the comparison at that point.

As ever, Ford decided to use just one basic four-door saloon style, but they made sure that different front- and rear-end treatments delineated each model from its closest relatives. On this occasion there were to be Zephyr V4, Zephyr V6, Zodiac and Executive types, with the Zodiac and Executive models having a bluff four-headlamp nose, the others using just two headlamps.

Although it was difficult to believe this by looking at the chosen, rather craggy styles, Ford actually took the trouble to put the cars through wind-tunnel assessment before finally signing them off. The Cd factor of all scale models tested was apparently between 0.41 and 0.51 (which is, of course, quite appalling by modern, early-2000s standards), and the definitive car returned a figure of 0.47. That was claimed to be 8 per cent better than the drag factor of the Mark III, which gave Hart's team some quiet satisfaction.

Suspension and Brakes

Compared with the out-going Mark III, of course, the suspension and chassis of the Mark IV was completely different. Because the monocoque of the Mark IV was itself quite new, almost every important dimension and feature had been changed, as the table opposite makes clear.

Feature	Mark III	Mark IV
Wheelbase (in)	107.0	115.0
Track, front (in)	53.0	57.0
Track, rear (in) (later models)	53.5	58.0
Front suspension	Independent, coil springs, MacPherson struts	Independent, coil springs, MacPherson struts
Rear suspension	Beam axle, half-elliptic leaf springs	Independent, coil springs, semi-trailing arms, fixed-length drive shafts

It was the cost accountants, not the engineers, who would have resisted this progressive enlargement. Designers always wanted longer wheelbase and wider track dimensions, as this can help give an improved ride and an increased passenger cabin package, while the cost accountants would respond that every extra inch had costs in sheet metal, costs which should be eliminated wherever possible.

In some ways it was odd that the new car should have shorter (V-layout) engines than the old, but a much longer front end to cover them. To utilize that extra, yawning space, Ford chose to mount the spare wheel up front, on a cradle ahead of the engine, under the bonnet; this also –

possibly quite coincidentally – acted as extra crash resistance in the unfortunate instance of a head-on collision.

The front suspension was conventional by Ford standards, for it had the latest refinement of the well-proven MacPherson strut layout, and there was optional power assistance for the recirculating ball steering, though in unassisted form this was very low geared, with nearly five turns needed to swing the front wheels from lock to lock.

This was the very first British Ford to have even the option of power-assisted steering and, once again, Ford-UK drew on all the accumulated experience of their American parent

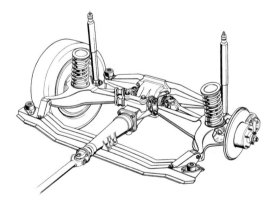

This was the layout of the independent rear suspension fitted to the Mark IV range. Because fixed-length drive shafts were fitted, the swinging links fixed to the inner joints of the semi-trailing arm were essential to allow the system to articulate properly. Ford-UK engineers insisted that much prototype testing had taken place, but the fact was that this was not a satisfactory layout. When the time came to launch the Granada – see page 185 – it would be abandoned.

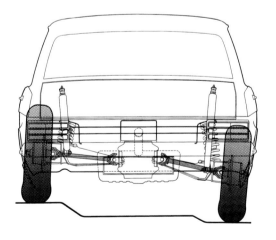

This was how the independent rear suspension, as fitted to the Mark IV range, was packaged under the rear of the body shell.

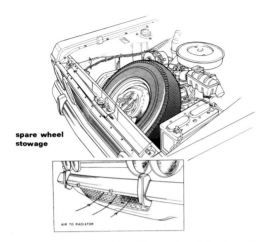

Even at the concept stage, Mark IVs were intended to have short tails and long noses, so the spare wheel was located in that long nose. Cooling air for the cooling radiator was ducted under the wheel from a low-mounted grille.

company. In the end, they chose to use a Hydrosteer mechanism, by Thompson, with a Mustang-type pump.

In later years it was the layout and performance of the novel type of independent rear suspension that would cause all the controversy, for in normal, soft conditions there was a great deal of wheel movement, some of it not nearly ideally controlled for road-holding purposes. When Ford-UK was developing the Mark IV cars, the engineers eventually chose independent suspension for the very first time on a British Ford, the main components featuring semi-trailing arms and coil springs. Unlike many other cars, the coil springs were mounted ahead of the line of the rear drive shafts, and the telescopic dampers were separately mounted behind that line.

Certainly there was nothing novel in such a basic layout – it had been seen on small Fiats since the mid-1950s, on small and medium-sized BMWs since the late 1950s, and of course on the Triumph 2000 from late 1963, though, in fairness, that car appeared when the Mark IV layout was almost ready to be finalized; however, it had never before been tackled in the way that Ford's cost-conscious engineers chose to do it (or perhaps were obliged to).

Unlike their main rivals, instead of using fixed-

pivot semi-trailing arms allied to drive shafts that would have had to include a plunging joint to make the geometry viable, Ford chose to use fixed-length drive shafts (that were much cheaper to manufacture), along with semi-trailing arms in which the inner joints, close to the final drive unit itself, were shackled around diff-mounted pivots. Fred Hart's rationale was sound, even if the result was not always satisfactory:

> We evaluated just about every type we could find before settling for the semi-trailing-link type as used on the Mark IV. It was to overcome the main problem of this layout – friction in the drive-shaft sliding splines restricting the value of the i.r.s. – that led us to fixed-length shafts and swinging links or shackles. This allowed the axle to move in the plane we wanted on a free basis – that is, the inner part of the wishbone moves quite freely without restricting the changes of camber and toe-in. In fact, it helps these....
>
> Packaging advantages have to be taken into account. But, again, we haven't found a better i.r.s. than the one we've chosen to employ. It certainly gives us advantages in cost and sheer simplicity. And its durability has been well proven.

Added to the fact that the chosen spring and damper settings were relatively soft – this car was certainly more 'boulevard' than 'sporting' – and a great deal of up-and-down road wheel movement was provided – up to 9in (23cm) at the front, and 8.6in (21cm) at the rear – the sum total of all this enterprise was a very soft-riding car that rolled considerably when hard pressed. Because of its heavy front/rear weight distribution bias (57.5 per cent front, 42.5 per cent rear on V6-engined cars), this was a car that understeered strongly in all normal circumstances, and in which it was all too easy to upset the composure of the rear wheels.

The other big chassis-orientated change was to the braking system. To recap, Mark IIIs had always used a conventional Girling installation with front discs and rear drums. For the Mark IV, however, Ford decided to leap further ahead – effectively to compete in a higher technical class than before – by using disc brakes at front and rear. Both front and rear discs/rotors were solid (the era of ventilated discs had not yet arrived), and at the rear the mechanical handbrake operated on the same pair of disc pads as the servo-assisted foot-operated hydraulic circuitry. This was the first recorded use, by Ford or any other manufacturer, of Girling's latest swinging-caliper layout.

New Engines

At this time Dagenham was the centre of all Ford-UK's engine and transmission manufacturing departments, and by the early 1960s, management began to consider replacing the ageing Consul (4-cylinder) and Zephyr (6-cylinder) engines, which would certainly reach their fifteenth birthday (in 1965) before they reached the end of their continuous lives. Even if Ford had wanted to prolong that career (which it did not), the tooling would have needed much attention, and also capital reinvestment, to cope.

One major engine-building upheaval had just been completed at Dagenham, when the old-type small side-valve engines had been phased

New V4 and V6 Engines

Years before the Mark IV Zephyrs and Zodiacs went on sale, Ford laid down a compact new family of engines for use in its cars and light/medium commercial vehicles such as the Transit van. Although Ford-USA controlled both companies and laid down general strategy – which, in this case, was to insist on the evolution of new families of V-formation engines – Ford-of-Britain and Ford-Germany were allowed to develop competing ranges. Both concerns set to, and designed, new overhead-valve 60-degree V4 and V6 engines, which in each case were machined and assembled on carefully integrated transfer line equipment.

Over the years Ford-of-Britain's new range, coded 'Essex', would span 1.7-litre (V4) to 3.1-litre (V6), while the entirely different Ford-Germany 'Cologne' engine range would span 1.2-litre (V4) to 2.9-litre (V6). Before the commercial rationalizations made under Ford-of-Europe were established, British-built cars (which included the Capri coupé and the Corsair range) only used Ford-UK 'Essex' V4s and V6s. In the UK the last of those would be phased out in 1977, though manufacture was then transferred to Ford-South Africa, where it continued into the 1990s.

First used in the Ford Mark IV models, but later adopted for other Ford cars and commercial vehicles, the 'Essex' V6 engine was brand new in 1966. This display engine shows a sectioned 3-litre type, complete with high-mounted alternator and a twin-choke Weber carburettor.

Looking amazingly stubby – which they were – the first of the 60-degree V4 'Essex' engines were seen in the Transit van in 1965, then in the Corsair V4, before being fitted to Zephyr V4 (Mark IVs) in the spring of 1966. Manufactured on the same facilities as the 'Essex' V6 power units, these engines needed an extra 'Lanchester' balancer shaft to make them acceptablys smooth.

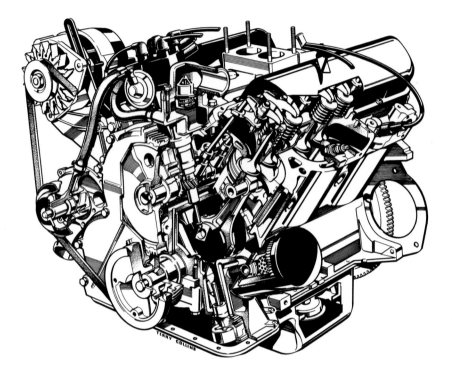

Not even ace technical artist Terry Collins could make the 'Essex' V6 engine look simple. 3-litre engines (as fitted to the Zodiac Mark IV) had twin-choke Weber carburettors, and a high-mounted alternator.

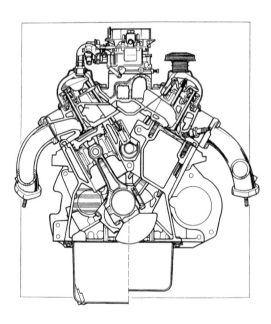

This was the cross-section drawing of the new V4/V6 family of engines fitted to all Zephyr and Zodiac Mark IVs. This particular drawing is of a 3-litre V6. On V4s, the 'Lanchester' balancer shaft was located to the left of the crankcase, as shown in a 'hatched' section of this drawing.

out, and a completely new range of overhead-valve engines spanning 997cc to 1498cc – Anglia 105E to Corsair 1500 – had been put on to the market: now it was time to do it all again, at the bigger/heavier end of the market. This project, the 'Essex' as it was soon coded within Ford, was vital to the company's modernization.

As the panel on page 161 confirms, Ford would not merely be laying down a new engine for Zephyrs and Zodiacs, but for a whole range of its car and truck products. Previewed in 1965, with many versions in production by 1969, this new range came to full maturity in the early 1970s; by this time one or other derivatives had found their way into Cortinas, Capris, Zephyr-Zodiacs, the brand new Granadas, and the Transit and A-Series trucks, while engines were also supplied to a long list of specialist manufacturers, including Reliant and TVR.

A long time previously – and this means just that, because it takes a very long time for such an

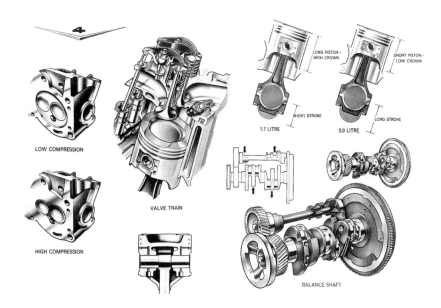

Ford-UK was proud of the technical innovation which it had included in the layout of the new range of 'Essex' engines, first seen in 1965. All cars had 'bowl-in-piston' ('heron') combustion chambers, while V4 engines needed a 'Lanchester' balancer shaft geared to the crankshaft of the engine.

engine to mature from the 'Why don't we…?' stage to series production – in the early 1960s Ford's long-term planners settled down to rethink the future of their large car engine plans. Well before a single line was drawn on paper (there were no small viable computers in those days, which meant that every innovation was schemed up with pencils, cartridge paper and much animated discussion around drawing boards), the general layout had to be agreed. This time, with different 'must haves' laid down by the product planners, the engineers were told that the new engine family should span 1.6 litres to 3 litres, that every version should be able to go into the same engine bay of a particular product, and that under no circumstances was the idea of having two wheelbases on one platform even to be considered.

Ford's major rivals in Europe – Opel-Vauxhall (General Motors-controlled) and Fiat being perfect examples – faced similar challenges, but came to different conclusions, whereas both of Ford's major businesses came to the same conclusions: that in each case they should settle on a more compact solution, involving V4 and V6 engines to be machined and manufactured on the same production lines. As I am sure every reader must be aware, a great deal of influence, and even some pressure, came across the Atlantic from Ford-USA

while this process was going ahead. It can be no coincidence that both Ford-UK and Ford-Germany ended up choosing the same basic layouts. Amazingly, Ford-USA had absolutely no experience of building engines of this type – their list of engines included straight 4, straight 6, V8 and V12 types – but the financial and manufacturing logic

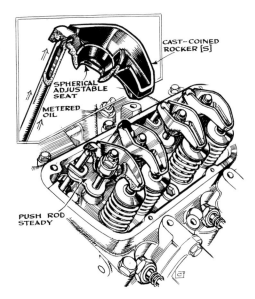

Detail of the 'Essex' valve gear and its lubrication, which would become very familiar to Ford mechanics over the years.

was such that they readily gave their approval to the 'compact' V-layouts.

The logic centred around a decision to use a 60-degree V-layout for the V4 and V6 engines, which could share all manner of common components such as valve gear, pistons, connecting rods and drive details at the front of the cylinder blocks. Accordingly, Ford-UK could lay down the same machining facilities for the cylinder heads and cylinder blocks – and the engines could eventually be screwed together on the same assembly lines. Ford pointed out that the decision to choose a V6 instead of an in-line 6 saved almost 10in (25cm) in the overall length of the power unit. The 3-litre V6, too, weighed just 377lb (171kg), compared with no less than 401lb (182kg) for the last of the straight sixes. Even so, later competitions (especially motor racing) experience showed that the cast-iron cylinder blocks were by no means as rigid as they looked, though for all production purposes they were totally serviceable.

All such major decisions involve compromises, and in this case Ford had to come to terms with the fact that it would prove difficult to balance a 60-degree V4 engine (as opposed to a 60-degree V6). In the end, the only way that this could be done was by fitting the V4 with what engineers know as a 'Lanchester' balancing shaft – a counter-rotating shaft, geared to the crankshaft and rotating at twice the speed of that crank – which was placed in the cylinder block. Although there was space in the cylinder block, no such balancer shaft was needed on the V6.

Other details included the choice of the 'Heron', or what became known as a B-I-P combustion chamber (bowl-in-piston), a distributor mounted high between cylinder banks, and a direct current electric generator positioned high above the off-side cylinder bank/head. Not only that, but in stark contrast to the long-running Consul/Zephyr/Zodiac straight 4 and straight 6 engines, on the 3-litre V6 there was a downdraught dual-choke Weber carburettor – Ford had already had much satisfactory experience with the Webers, these being used on the latest Cortina GT engine. Not only that, but on the outside of these new engines there were logically shaped exhaust ports, and conventional cast-iron exhaust manifolds instead of the pierced tubes used on the old type. The Zodiac power plant, incidentally, had an alternator, rather than a direct-current dynamo, as standard equipment – this being yet another technical innovation that Ford had finalized at this time.

Ford-UK insisted they had designed every detail of these engines themselves, but it must surely have helped that Ford-Germany's similar V-formation engine range was well established by the time the detail work was done; said Fred Hart:

> Naturally we did co-operate with Dearborn and Cologne, because we couldn't ignore the many design requirements of V-engines of which they have experience, but the designs themselves are entirely British. We looked over the shoulders of Cologne and America to see what to do, as well as what not to do....

To show just how universal this engine was to be, the V4 derivative made its bow in the all-new Transit van in mid-1965, and in the latest Corsair V4 saloon model in October 1965 when, to Ford's embarrassment, a photograph was issued showing the engines being assembled. Although the V4 was the star of that shot, several V6s were also to be seen in the background!

Both V4 and V6 types then figured in the launch of the Mark IVs in April 1966, and the V6 would also be used in the Capri 3-litre of 1969, and in well regarded independent cars such as the Reliant Scimitar and Scimitar GTE of the late 1960s. For the Mark IVs, too, there were to be two different-sized V6s – a 2495cc and a 2994cc unit – which replaced the old Mark III method of sharing the same engine size, but boosting the power of the Zodiac version.

In this application, the V4 and 3-litre V6 engines shared the same 93.7mm cylinder bore and 72.4mm stroke, while the 2.5-litre V6 also retained the same cylinder bore (the cylinder block, in fact, was just the same as the 3-litre), with a shorter, 60.3mm, stroke.

Although these new engines were, in many ways, meant only to be workhorses for a whole range of Ford products in the 1960s and 1970s,

Engine	Capacity (cc)	Peak power (bhp/rpm)	bhp per litre
Mark III '4'	1703	68/4,800	40.0
Mark IV V4	1996	88/4,750	44.0
Mark III '6'	2553	98/4750	38.4
	2553	109/4800	42.7
Mark IV 2.5-litre	2495	112/4,750	44.9
Mark IV 3-litre	2994	136/4,750	45.4

they were both competitive in power, and of course in first cost to Ford. For interest, the table above gives a quick comparison between the new (Mark IV) and the old (Mark III) engines.

Even at this stage the new V-layout engines were more power-efficient than the last of the straight-4/straight-6 types, though we were not to know that there would be very little improvement in the next decade: even Ford-UK engineers, it seemed, were dismayed to see how these heavy but robust engines were somewhat resistant to serious power tuning.

Transmissions

Not only was the four-speed manual transmission a much-modified design (it had been engineered with other products in mind, such as the new Transit commercial vehicle, and the still-to-come Capri 3-litre coupé), but there had been yet another change of mind over the automatic transmission and the overdrive options.

For the Mark IVs, Ford tried to convince the media that it had developed a new type of four-speed all-synchromesh manual transmission – but

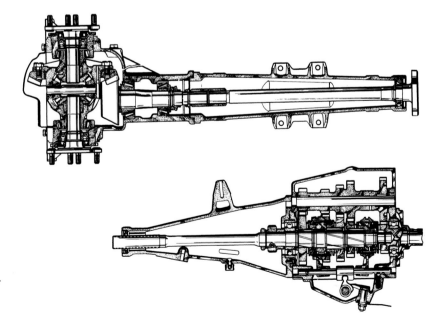

Engineering detail of the new final drive unit (lower section) and the latest four-speed manual transmission (upper section) shows just how much investment Ford-UK was putting into the Mark IV range. One reason for having such a long extension casing behind the main gearbox was that the optional Laycock overdrive unit could occupy the same place, and still use the original propeller shaft.

in fact this was no more than a thoroughly (and logically) re-engineered version of the Mark III's transmission, which had been new, of course.

Although the launch press release mentioned that 'the general dimensions have been increased to take care of the extra torque of the 3-litre' this was not as technically important as the use, for the first time in the Zephyr/Zodiac, of a centrally mounted, remote-control change speed lever as standard, though a steering column change remained available, too. Just to reinforce the fact that the post-war (and export-led) fashion for using steering-column gear changes at all times had well and truly gone, this featured a brand new cast-iron casing where there was a detachable top plate for access to the selectors. The remote control linkage protruded from the tail of the main casing, and was located over the tail-shaft extension: this extension was lengthy, not because of any unique reason, but so that the optional overdrive could fit into the same space, while keeping a common length of propeller shaft.

So, how do we know that there was a close relationship between Mark III and Mark IV transmissions? By comparing the internal gear ratios of new and old types. Taking the Zodiacs as an example, this is the comparison of internal ratios, which were the same:

Mark IV (1966 onwards)	1.00, 1.41, 2.21, 3.16, reverse 3.35
Mark III (1962 – 1966)	1.00, 1.41, 2.21, 3.16, reverse 3.35

There was a similar, telling comparison between Zephyr 4 (Mark III) and Zephyr V4 (Mark IV) types, which had wider ratios but were similarly identical when compared. Internally, and essentially, therefore, the transmissions were the same. Once again, this had been done with wider issues of product planning in mind. The same (Mark IV) type of gearbox was already to be found in the new Transit van – where there was a direct-acting change speed lever, and where a top opening to the casing was essential – and it would also be used from 1969 in the Capri 3-litre coupé, where a remote-control centre change was also needed.

Quite without fuss, incidentally, this was the point at which Ford abandoned the optional Borg Warner overdrive installation in favour of the Laycock overdrive system adopted by so many other car makers in the UK and in Europe. Not only was this a more robust overdrive, but it was more sophisticated than the old-type B-W component. Because it had a simple 'in' or 'out'

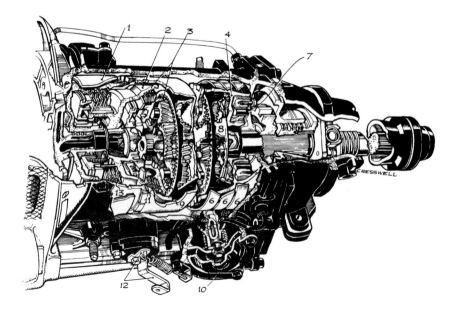

For the Mark IVs, Ford-UK chose yet another type of automatic transmission, this time opting for a Ford-USA C4 installation to replace the Borg Warner Type 35 fitted to the Mark III.

Launched in April 1966, the Zephyr/Zodiac Mark IV was a complete and bold departure from the style of any previous Ford. This was the Zodiac type.

operation on a stalk, and changes could be made without the driver lifting his throttle foot or dipping the clutch, this was a great advance on the old Borg Warner installation.

For this new range, the optional automatic transmission was now to be Ford-US's own C4 model, a conventional installation that featured a torque converter, epicyclic gearing, and three forward ratios. Not only was this equally modern, indeed 'state of the art', compared with the Borg Warner transmission that had been optional on Mark IIIs, but it was also considerably cheaper to buy, even though it had to be imported from North America where it was manufactured. Although by no means as sophisticated as the 1990s/2000s 'Tiptronic' changes, it was also arranged to have D1 and D2 manual holds in the selector quadrant – manual low hold, for instance, locking the transmission

in low gear, and being very useful in extreme circumstances.

Launching a Complete Range

Those were the days when Ford-UK launched a new saloon car and had examples to sell straightaway, when cars were in showrooms on the very day that they were revealed in motoring magazines and daily newspapers. (How standards have slipped since then....) Accordingly, when the Mark IVs made their bow on 20 April 1966, all except the Executive model were available for immediate delivery. Series production had already begun, slowly at first, in January 1966, and several thousands had already reached Ford dealerships by mid-April.

The table below shows the immediate line-up, and the UK prices that applied.

Model	Drive line (bhp/capacity)	Retail price (incl. purchase tax)
Zephyr V4	88/1,996	£932.83
Zephyr V6	112/2,495	£1,005.33
Zodiac	136/2,994	£1,228.20
Optional extras:		
Laycock overdrive		£54.37
Automatic transmission		£102.71
Fixed bucket seats plus		
steering-column change (Zephyr only)		£24.17
Radio		£27.79
Front seat belts (pair)		£ 6.32

At this time it was only the basic range of four-door saloons that were revealed and put on sale. Six months later, as described below, the Abbott-engineered estate cars and the top-of-the-range Executive would be there too.

All three cars were based on the same 115in (292cm) wheelbase, four-door hull, and Ford, whose product planners were already known as the sharpest of all such operators in the British motor industry, also made sure that all had carefully graded levels of trim, decoration and interior cabin fitments. In addition, each of the models had specific, and easily understood, features:

Zephyr V4: This was the 2-litre-engined 'entry level' car, first of all with a model title that clearly indicated the use of a new engine. It was fitted with just two 7in (18cm) headlamps, it had a bench front seat as standard (not even the option of separate seats), automatic transmission was optional, but overdrive transmission was not available, nor was optional power-assisted steering, and the tyres were normally 6.40-13in. Nine exterior colours were immediately available.

Zephyr V6: This was the lowest-priced V6-engined example, with 2.5-litres, and was also given a suitable title ('Zephyr V6') to emphasize the use of the new power unit. Although it shared the same two-headlamp nose as the Zephyr V4, separate front seats were optional, it could be had with automatic or overdrive transmission, and also with power-assisted steering; tyres were 6.70-13in. Nine exterior colours were immediately available.

Zodiac: For the first few months at least, this was the flagship of the range. Not only did it have a 136bhp 3-litre V6 engine, but this featured a twin-choke carburettor and an alternator. Both overdrive and automatic transmission were available, and expected to be very popular, as was the option of power-assisted steering. The nose of this derivative had four 7in (18cm) headlamps (a 'first' on British cars), there was full-width red glazing across the tail (and reversing lamps were standard – they were optional on other types),

lots of special exterior decoration, separate front seats were standard, and it ran on 6.70-13in tyres. Twelve exterior colours were available.

The world's press naturally tried the latest cars and offered a very wide range of comments, but perhaps it is best simply to note what *Autocar* thought of the Zephyr V4, and what *Motor* thought of the Zodiac in the first few days after launch, both these tests being carried out on very early production cars before they were even announced to the public.

Of the Zephyr V4, *Autocar* immediately noted vagaries in the rear suspension behaviour, and the very heavy steering at parking speeds. When fully loaded, the handling was acceptable, but:

> With only two in the front there is a big difference. As the car goes into the turn, it feels just the same until the lateral forces reach the tail, which rolls appreciably and causes very definite oversteer.
>
> During fast laps of a closed test circuit [this, in fact, was the MIRA proving grounds, near Nuneaton], we lifted the inside rear wheel at this point, and rather than be caught out by sudden breakaway, we preferred to flick the tail round in stages by sawing at the steering wheel.
>
> On ordinary roads, of course, one never reaches this point....

Even so, the overall summary was that:

> Most features of the new Ford show considerable improvements over the Mark III models. It is a bigger car overall, with much more room inside and considerably better and more comfortable furniture. There is a substantial performance increase, better braking, less heavy fuel consumption, and the roadholding (especially with the car laden) has been made safer ....

The 'substantial performance increase' of the Zephyr V4, incidentally, included a top speed of 96mph (154km/h), 0-60mph in 14.6sec, but with overall fuel consumption of a rather startling 19.4mpg (14.6ltr/100km).

Motor's opinion of the Zodiac (as a manual transmission car without overdrive) emphasized many of the same features, though the significantly higher performance (a top speed of 102.5mph (164.9km/h), 0–60mph in 11.0sec, and overall fuel consumption of 18.4mpg (15.4ltr/100km)) coloured their overall impressions:

> …the 3-litre engine endows the car with acceleration which is striking by any standards, as well as with a maximum speed comfortably over 100mph. And all this with no appreciable increase in fuel consumption…. Overall fuel consumption (18.4 mpg) was very similar to that of the last Zodiac Mark III we tested.

Clearly the centre-floor gear change was a great improvement on that of previous cars: 'Some experience of the new Zephyr with a steering column change makes us believe that that anyone who does not need a bench seat will be a great deal happier with the [gear] lever on the floor….'

Unhappily, there were the same reservations over the handling characteristics conferred by the new suspension system:

> Let us say right away that in comparison with the previous Zodiac, the extra cost of this arrangement is justified in every way in terms of roadholding, handling and ride – but by comparison with the best all-independent saloons from some other manufacturers we found it a little disappointing …

This was the detail, which came to almost precisely the same conclusion as *Autocar* did in the same week:

> If you are in the habit of entering corners extremely fast, either deliberately, or by misjudgement; if you are the sort of person to whom high speed emergencies happen; if you drive on wet and slippery roads, the picture is less satisfactory.
>
> It is possible on a dry corner to list the inner rear wheel right off the ground, but even before this stage the onset of wheelspin can give a reduction in cornering power which brings the tail round quite sharply.
>
> Some of this may be blamed on a weight distribution which puts only 41½ per cent of the unladen load on the driving wheels, but most of it, we thought, could be put on a roll centre too high at the back, giving excessive weight transfer from the inner rear wheel on corners…

Was Ford dismayed by this criticism which, by 1966, was stark, brutal and to the point? It seems that top management – whose priorities were really to sell huge numbers of these new Mark IVs to businesses all around Britain, and indeed, the world – still believed that a combination of choice, low prices, high specifications and ready availability would do the trick – and so, for the time being, it did.

Ford engineers, on the other hand, were taken aback, and (according to some long-serving characters who remember those days) went into denial for a short period. As another distinguished

Just for fun, it seems, Ford sent a near-standard Zodiac Mark IV to the banked circuit at Monza in May 1966, to attack and set new endurance speed records for cars in the 3-litre class. Succeeding almost beyond their wildest dreams, the team of drivers kept the car going for seven days and nights, averaging no less than 103.04mph (165.79km/h) throughout, and covering more than 17,000 miles (27,353km) in the process.

Ford historian has written: 'But Dagenham were not convinced at this stage that they had got it wrong....'

It could be that few of their test drivers were used to driving prototypes in such an extrovert fashion, but there is no doubt that, for a time, there was a refusal to believe what independent testers were saying. A rogue specification of Goodyear tyres was found to be one culprit (of low grip, that is, for there could be no excuse for wheel waving in tight corners), and there is no doubt that radial ply tyres, which Ford did not yet fit, was another way to make amends: with a 185-14in section, these became optionally available on all types from late 1966.

Then, in that practical way that always characterized Ford's engineering approach, they settled down to see what could be done, and how quickly. In the meantime, there was a performance demonstration that just might have helped things a little....

Record Run at Monza

Just for fun, as it were, Ford then celebrated the arrival of the new Mark IV Zodiac by sending a standard example to the banked circuit at Monza in May, intent on achieving more than 100mph (160km/h) over seven continuous days and nights, by driving round and round in a clockwise direction. Castrol, incidentally, sponsored this attempt, which coincided with the launch of a new type of 'liquid tungsten oil', so the potential publicity benefits were obvious.

Drivers included Ford's renowned 'Marathon Men', Eric Jackson and Ken Chambers (both of whom were the owners of Ford dealerships in the UK), race driver John Bekaert, product planner Jon Maclay of Ford, and *Motor* journalist Michael Bowler. Except for running with a special 40gal (180ltr) fuel tank in what had been the rear seat area, a high, 3.09:1, rear axle ratio, rather special Goodyear radial ply tyres, and an engine with cleaned up cylinder heads, the car was virtually standard.

In a pre-record run practice the car suffered an engine failure (a carburettor needle valve came loose, starving the engine and causing a piston to burn), which necessitated a major rebuild including using parts from the spare engine that Ford had brought along with them; the run itself, however, proved to be amazingly incident free. As Bowler later wrote:

[John Bekaert started slowly, gradually easing the speeds up over three hours to the 1min 30sec (106mph) which was our original target speed. After that it was fairly plain sailing: five drivers – three hours

No rush, it seemed from this picture; but this was a pit stop for the seven-days-and-seven-nights Zodiac run at Monza in May 1966. Castrol supported the team effort, the car averaging 103.04mph (165.79km/h) throughout, including all stops.

Executive versions of the new Zodiac Mark IV range were mechanically like those cars, but had many extra features, including whitewall tyres, extra driving lamps, wing mirrors and a sunshine roof. Also fitted, but not obvious in this view, were the power-assisted steering, and the automatic transmission.

on, twelve hours off; driving just consisted of pounding monotonously round the banking .... During the run we had both heavy rain and fog to contend with....

It wasn't all trouble free, however, for there were four cases of tyres chunking and throwing off treads (most of these on the left side front wheel), and late in the run the team also discovered that a rear coil spring had broken, but they kept on going. Nonetheless, at the end of seven days and nights, the Zodiac had averaged 103.04mph (165,79km/h), and had covered more than 17,000 miles (27,353km). Later calculations showed that it had recorded between 11mpg and 12mpg (26 and 24ltr/100km), for it was being driven virtually flat out all the time.

Executive and Estate Cars – Filling out the Range

In October 1966, and immediately before the opening of the London Motor Show, the Mark IV range was completed by the addition of two new derivatives: the estate car types, and the top-of-the-range Executive Zodiac. The latter, incidentally, was to cost £1,567, which put Ford pricing into a hitherto untapped area of the market place.

As ever, the estate car was a neatly engineered conversion – still definitely and obviously a conversion, but nonetheless smart for all that – of the four-door saloon into a five-door estate car – carried out by E.D. Abbott of Farnham, who would build the cars themselves. This very neatly retained most of the sheet metal of the saloon, including all four passenger doors, and the new roof line swept straight to the top of the upward-opening tailgate. A vinyl roof covering was standard, which brought two blessings, one being to visually enhance the style, the other meaning that Abbott could cut a few corners in the body-shell modification process where the joins could henceforth be concealed! The same conversion was available on all three types – Zephyr V4, Zephyr V6 and Zodiac.

Above *On the Executive Zodiac Mark IV, leather trim and individual reclining front seats were standard.*

Below *Ford-UK clearly intended the Executive Zodiac for use as a top-of-the-range model, and went out of their way to photograph the cars in suitably 'business' or 'executive' locations.*

*When photographed from this angle, the length of the bonnet and the stubbiness of the tail are apparent.
On this and all other Mark IVs, the front grille was for decorative purposes only, as cooling air was
drawn in through mesh mounted under the bumper.*

*This was the general layout of the facia/instrument panel of the
Mark IV range, showing a full array of instruments. Because the
original type of V6 engine was by no means free-revving, the red
lining of the rev-counter at 5,500rpm looks distinctly optimistic!
The minor instruments had frustratingly little detail on them, and
that radio was standard on top-of-the-range models.*

*The scope and standard of Big Ford fittings had come a long way
since the original Zodiac was introduced in 1953. This was the
1966 version of Executive Zodiac, complete with leather trim,
individual reclining seats, and automatic transmission, plus safety
belts for front seat passengers.*

For structural and practical reasons, Ford insisted that existing tail-lamp clusters should be retained, which meant that access to the rear load space was a little restricted; but with the rear seat folded flat, the claim was that up to 70cu ft (19.8cu m) of material could be stowed between the front seats and the tailgate. With the rear seat folded forwards, there was almost 6ft (2m) of flat floor, though its width was restricted by the retention of the rear wheel-arch pressings, and fixings for the rear seat squab.

As might have been expected, the new Mark IV Executive followed the same lines as the short-lived Mark III Executive: it was based on the Zodiac, automatic transmission was standard (manual transmission with overdrive was available to special order), and the technical specification of the Zodiac was carried over complete,

Above *On Zodiac and Executive versions of the Mark IV, full width decorated brightwork linked tail lamps on each side of the car, complete with appropriate boot-lid badges. This, clearly, was the 'Executive'…*

Left *…and this was the 'Zodiac'.*

Above *Wherever Mark IVs were discussed, it was always the Zodiac that received most of the attention. Even so, most sales went to the cheaper, less powerful versions of this range. This particular car, complete with only two headlamps, was the Zephyr V6 De Luxe, a 2.5-litre motor car with rather more up-market trim than the ordinary V6, radial-ply tyres as standard, and this distinctive, positively discreet, radiator grille.*

Below *Although the addition of an estate car derivative was always in Ford's product plan for the Mark IV range, it did not actually break cover until October 1966.*

with almost all the extras from that car made standard on the Executive. Every Executive, therefore, normally came with the same 136bhp/3-litre engine as the Zodiac, together with the latest Ford (USA) C4 automatic transmission, and Hydrosteer power-assisted steering as standard. In addition, there was a rake-adjustable steering column, separate reclining front seats, inertia reel safety belts (years before they were even compulsory fitments), a push-button radio, a wind-back sunshine roof and auxiliary driving lamps.

The sunshine roof was making a welcome reappearance to any car in the Ford range, and Ford insisted that the fit, finish, and weatherproofing would be a quantum leap better than it had ever been on cheaper saloon bodies of the 1930s and 1940s.

However, it was in the visual detail that the latest Executive was laid out to appeal to status seekers. Externally, of course, the low-mounted driving lamps (they were under the outer corners of the front bumper) were joined by special 'Executive' badging, by white-wall tyres, wheel trims like those of the Zodiac, and twin wing mirrors. No fewer than twelve different colours were available, four of them being special acrylic metal finishes.

Inside the car, the facia panel was now faced in burr walnut, two-speed windscreen wipers were standard, the radio had two speakers (front and rear, considered to be advanced by mid-1960s standards), and the Aeroflow ventilation system of the Zodiac was carried forward as expected.

Separate reclinable front seats were covered either in crushed leather, or in nylon cloth (to choice), with a small separate console/stowage compartment between them, and there was deep pile carpeting to add to the luxury effect. Perhaps this was not enough to bring the Executive up to true coach-built standards, but Ford could always plead (and, privately, did so) that they had done everything possible within cost constraints.

For the record, at this time Zodiac prices started at £1,241 (or £1,346 with automatic transmission), whereas the Executive cost just £1,567, which meant that the effective premium was only

£221, or 16 per cent. A bargain? Many customers apparently thought so.

With Abbott-built estate and Ford-built Executive types now added to the range, no fewer than seven Mark IVs were listed. At the end of 1966, with all types in production, the line-up of prices was as follows:

Model	UK Retail Price
Zephyr V4	£949
Zephyr V4 Estate	£1,379
Zephyr V6	£1,023
Zephyr V6 Estate	£1,453
Zodiac	£1,241
Zodiac Estate	£1,672
Executive	£1,567

Automatic transmission was standard on the Executive, while on other models it was an optional extra costing £105.

A Rethink for 1968

Although Ford worked hard to make the Mark IV a better car as time passed, some of these cars tended to hang about in showrooms, or worse, in storage compounds where they were open to attack from the weather. The result was that production plummeted, from 49,773 in 1966 to a mere 18,406, and although this was clawed back to 24,744 in 1968, it was clear that the huge sales enjoyed by previous Marks could never again be matched.

Even so, from October 1967 – and this was actually announced at the London Motor Show – Ford brought in an entire package of changes and improvements, which by their standards had been brought forward at breakneck speed. Not only were some prices cut, but 'De Luxe' versions of Zephyrs were introduced, and rear suspension changes were made, though the problem could not be entirely eliminated.

As a result of the marketing re-jig, 'standard' Zephyr V4 and V6 models were given substantial price cuts (to £906 and £980 respectively), and at the same time lost their options of separate front seats and centre-floor gear changes. The new De Luxe Zephyrs (costing £961 and £1,035) had fixed-back individual front seats, a floor gear change, and more upmarket trim, plus a special front grille to make them obvious.

Revised rear-end suspension geometry gave the cars a slight touch of negative wheel camber in the static unladen condition, which boded well for the future – though independent road tests soon showed that this had not really been enough. On the other hand, radial-ply tyres and power-assisted steering became standard in the Zodiac, but manual-steering Zephyrs were given an even lower steering ratio to cope with radials – the result being more than six turns from lock to lock, which was not really acceptable.

In the winter of 1967, the older type Borg Warner Model 35 automatic transmission option took over from Ford's own C4, though rather confusingly the C4 was then reinstated on 3-litre Zodiac models for a time in 1986/1969.

Figures show that just 16,758 Zephyr/Zodiac types were built in 1971, and that the assembly of all types ran out just before Christmas of that year. It was the end of a technically fascinating, and commercially successful twenty-two-year career for the British big Fords.

Maturity – the Final Years

By 1969, within Ford-UK the impetus to go on making improvements to the Mark IV range was ebbing way. Because it was now known (internally, that is – the general public did not know what was going on within Ford of Europe) that this would be the last of a long-running Consul-Zephyr-Zodiac family of cars, more and more attention was being turned to a successor, the 'MH' (Ford-of-Europe's secret code), later to be badged Granada range.

Accordingly, there were few important innovations in those final years, and production, which had bounced back to 24,744 in 1968, slowly began to ebb away again. Padded 'safety' steering wheels were standardized from October 1968, UK prices rose slightly because of an increase in Purchase Tax, and by the end of 1969 yet more slight changes were made to the suspension settings to improve on ride quality, heated rear windows became an optional extra, and the Zodiac inherited the walnut facia originally confined only to the Executive.

Much later and (if only we had realized it) as a 'run-out special', Ford also announced the

Some Zodiacs were longer than others! This was a 'stretch limo' version of the car, privately constructed by Coleman Milne of Bolton in Lancashire, and was in great demand for ceremonial or taxi use. How many bridal processions, for instance, did you see, with a car like this at the head?

limited-edition Zephyr Special in November 1971. Just 1,000 such cars were built: was this, I wonder, the first ever, truly limited-edition car to be produced at Dagenham? Based on the Zephyr V6 De Luxe, it was mechanically unchanged, but the spec. featured a radio, heated rear screen, fabric upholstery, over-riders, exterior wing mirrors, and a special uranium blue paint job, with a parchment-coloured vinyl roof covering, and Zodiac-style wheel covers.

By now it was really all over. At the end of 1971, preparations were in full swing for the launch of a new generation of big Fords – the Consul and Granada series – which would be assembled on two sites, at Dagenham, and at Ford-Germany's massive plant in Cologne.

This picture shows just how versatile Ford engineers could be, for the V4 engine fitted to the Zephyr V4 made its original debut in mid-1965 in the first of the world-famous Transit vans.

Although the big 'Essex' V6 engine was originally intended for use in the Zephyr V6 and Zodiac Mark IV models, from 1969 it was also used in the sleek Capri 3000GT and 3000E coupés, which sold themselves under the slogan of 'The Car You Always Promised Yourself'.

Ford Zephyr V4/Zephyr V6/Zodiac/Executive Series IV (1966–1972)

Layout

Unit-construction steel body/chassis structure. Front engine/rear drive, sold as four-door five-seater saloon and estate car.

Zephyr 4s had V4-cylinder engines, while Zephyr V6s and Zodiacs had V6-cylinder engines. All shared the same wheelbase.

Engine

Type	4-cylinder (6-cylinder), in 60-deg V-formation
Block material	Cast iron
Head material	Cast iron
Cylinders	4, in 60 deg.V (6, in 60-deg.V)
Cooling	Water
Bore and stroke	93.7 x 72.4mm (Zephyr V6 93.7 x 60.3mm, Zodiac 93.7 x 72.4mm)
Capacity	1996cc (2495cc, 2994cc)
Main bearings	Three (four)
Valves	Two per cylinder, overhead, operated by pushrods and rockers from camshaft mounted in centre of cylinder block 'V'
Compression ratio	8.9:1 (9.1:1/8.9:1)
Fuel supply	One downdraught Zenith carburettor (downdraught dual-choke Weber carburettor on 3-litre engines)
Max. power	88bhp @ 4,750rpm (Zephyr V6 112bhp @ 4750rpm, Zodiac and Executive 136bhp @ 4,750rpm
Max. torque	116lb ft @ 2,750rpm (Zephyr V6 137lb ft @ 3,000rpm, Zodiac and Executive 181lb ft at 3,000rpm)

Transmission

Manual transmission: Centre floor, or steering column change. Four-speed, synchromesh on all forward gears. Optional, Laycock overdrive. Optional, Ford C4 automatic transmission (standard on Executive model).

Internal gearbox ratios:

[V4-engined cars]		[V6-engined cars]	
Top	1.000:1	Top	1.00:1
3rd	1.505:1	3rd	1.41:1
2nd	2.353:1	2nd	2.21:1
1st	4.412:1	1st	3.16:1
Reverse	4.667:1	Reverse	3.35:1
Final drive ratio	Zephyr 4 3.70:1	Final drive	Zephyr V6 3.90:1, Zodiac 3.70:1

Optional Laycock overdrive (0.82:1 ratio)

Optional C4 automatic transmission. Internal gear ratios:

Top	1.00:1
Intermediate	1.46:1
Low	2.46:1
Reverse	2.20:1

continued overleaf

Ford Zephyr V4/Zephyr V6/Zodiac/Executive Series IV (1966–1972) *continued*

Suspension and steering

Front	Independent, coil springs, MacPherson struts, anti-roll bar, telescopic dampers
Rear	Independent, coil springs, semi-trailing arms, telescopic dampers
Steering	Recirculating ball, optional power assistance (standard on Executive, standard on Zodiac from late 1967)
Tyres	6.40-13in, cross-ply (6.70-13in). Later cars had 185-14in radial ply tyres
Wheels	Pressed-steel disc, bolt-on
Rim width	4.5in

Brakes

Type	Servo-assisted front wheel discs, rear discs
Size	9.6in diameter front discs, 9.9in diameter rear discs

Dimensions (in/mm)

Track	
Front	57/1,448
Rear	58/1,473
Wheelbase	115/2,920
Overall length	185/4,700
Overall width	71.3/1,810
Overall height	58.5/1,490
Unladen weight	Zephyr V4 2,708lb/1,229kg, Zephyr V6 2,820lb/1,279kg, Zodiac 2,884lb/1,308kg

8 After the Mark IVs

By the late 1960s Ford knew it was high time that the Mark IV range was replaced – but they also knew that demand for this type and size of Ford model had already peaked. In marketing terms the Mark IV was looking tired, and its styling was now out of line with other Fords in the company's European product range. Not only that, but economically it was no longer a profitmaker for the burgeoning Ford-of-Europe concern, and that was a serious worry.

Sales statistics speak for themselves. A long time before, and at the height of its popularity (1959), no fewer than 132,492 saloons of the Consul/Zephyr/Zodiac family – Mark IIs in those days – had been produced at Dagenham in a single year. Even the Mark III had not approached that figure – 84,851 had been built in calendar year 1963 – and by comparison the Mark IV had been a real disappointment. As already noted in the previous chapter, 49,773 Mark IVs were built in 1966, the very first year in which that range was on sale – but within months of that new model appearing on the streets, and after its reputation for handling badly got around, demand began to slump alarmingly. By 1969, only 19,828 such cars were sold in an entire year – just over 400 every week, on average, which was not good for factory economics – and the balance sheets were looking very sad in consequence.

Ford did actually consider abandoning its presence in this market sector – for large saloon and

When Ford came to replace the Zephyr/Zodiac range, it produced a totally new platform and cabin, the result being the original Granada.

Although the Granada of 1972 was a direct replacement for the Zodiac Mark IV, it had a different platform, structure and style.

estate cars – at this time, but the product planning staff still weren't ready to recommend such a drastic decision. Even so, it was interesting to realize that it wasn't just Ford whose big car sales were suffering: the equivalent (and rival) Vauxhall models, the Cresta and Viscount, would also be dropped in 1972, while the last of the big British Leyland cars, the Austin 3-litre, would die in 1971. Maybe Ford was wise not to have killed off its big cars, for suddenly it had two fewer rivals in the market place.

Although financially pragmatic, Ford was always proud, and stubborn. Once it had picked up the vibrations that its rivals were likely to drop out of the race for sales in a shrinking sector, it elected to keep going. However, there is no doubt that the rapid evolution of Ford-of-Europe was a factor that made that still economically possible. Even so, Ford decided that it had to take big decisions, and to make a new approach. Although times and customer fashions seemed to have changed, the company was willing to react to

This doors-off study of the 1972 Granada shows the interior packaging, which was very similar to the car it replaced – the Mark IV Zodiac.

that, and this was overdue. Not only had there been customer resistance to the style of the Mark IV (what the Ford-US-orientated top management had judged appropriate had not lined up with what British customers actually preferred), but innovations in the chassis engineering – specifically the independent rear suspension – had not worked as well as expected.

In fact, even more than the desire of engineers and product planners to make a fresh start, it was the still-young Ford-of-Europe's ambitions that gave the impetus to develop a new model, and to replace the Mark IV. In fact what happened next came at exactly the right time.

As part of its rationalization strategy (which did not always happen in text-book fashion) in the late 1960s, F-o-E took a very big and brave decision: to replace both the large cars in their still-sprawling range of cars – not just one of them, but both the large cars, British and German, with one commonized new design. Out would go the British Mark IVs, and at the same time, out would go the Ford-of-Germany Taunus 17M/20M/26M range, which had been running in parallel (and in competition – in some markets British and German Fords were sold, side by side, in the same showrooms!) for some years. In addition, for marketing reasons, and to put clear blue water between the company's past and its future, the British subsidiary of Ford-of-Europe also decided to abandon the old names – Zephyr and Zodiac – after two decades of familiar success.

Even so, at this stage there were still many massive egos within Ford-UK and Ford-Germany at top management level, who fought hard to retain their independence, which meant that the obvious process of rationalisation was somewhat delayed. Accordingly, what happened from early 1972, when the range of new cars was announced, was not entirely logical. Ideally (and to make financial sense), Ford-of-Europe should have chosen to concentrate on one factory and just one production line, to assemble cars that used just one range of engines, and which should be sold in the UK, in Europe, and all round the world. Ideally, and according to all business models, this made sense – but it wasn't adopted at first.

This was the facia/instrument display of the Granada, as launched in 1972 – totally different from the Zodiac Mark IV, but clearly a lineal descendant from that car.

What actually happened for the first five years satisfied the national companies but not, if they were honest, Ford's cost accountants. In the end, the decision was made that the new cars would be built on two geographically different assembly lines – one of them in the modern PTA building at Dagenham, and the other one some hundreds of miles away in Cologne: although they would share the same style and unit-construction body shells, each would have their own rather eclectic mix of British-made or German-made engines.

Britain's new cars would use developed versions of the 60-degree V-engines that had powered all the Mark IVs, while the new German types would use a mixture of German V4s and V6s (as previously noted, these were different in every detail from the British 'Essex' units), the new Ford Pinto 'four', and the 'Essex' V6. In that illogical way which typified Ford-of-Europe's antics in the 1970s, there would also be some shuffling, to and from one factory to the other, of some engines, and some major components.

New Compared with Old....

Accordingly, and to bring this story tidily to a close, I should now summarize how far Ford had gone to update the old Zephyr/Zodiac layout; this emphasizes why what became known as the new Consul/Granada types have no part in my main story. My main conclusion is that Ford's engineers had learned a lot from the Mark IVs, and were determined to extract only the good features for what became known, internally, as the new 'MH' cars:

- The platform, and the proportions of the cabin in the new car, had changed completely. Whereas the Mark IV had run on a 115in (2,920mm) wheelbase with a very long bonnet, the new Granada's wheelbase was only 107in (2,718mm), but with a larger cabin and

a much shorter nose. It was much more of a 'European' than an 'American' car, more efficiently packaged and dynamically balanced – and, of course, the spare wheel was now mounted in a conventional place at the side of the boot compartment.

- Strangely, MacPherson strut front suspension was not used on the new car, which instead ran on double wishbone front suspension – called an SLA (short and long arm) installation by Ford's publicists. This was a development of the latest Cortina Mark III installation (and used some common components), imposed by the

Two different artists' approach to showing the anatomy of the new-generation Granada in 1972. This Executive version is by Terry Collins of Ford…

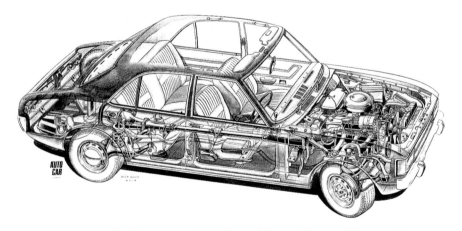

…while this, by Dick Ellis of Autocar, is a less highly specified type, with many differences of trim, and engine packaging in evidence. Both cars have manual transmission.

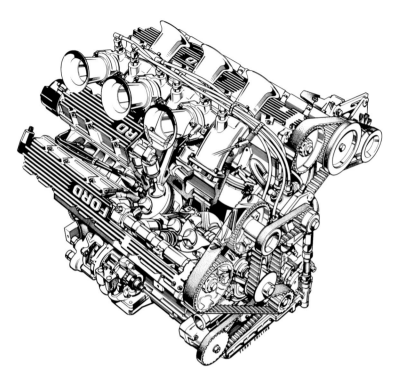

When the time came to explore the limits of the 'Essex' V6 engine's capabilities, Ford consulted Cosworth. By the time the Northamptonshire concern had finished, not much of the original engine remained, though the cylinder block, bored out to provide 3.4 litres, was retained. Otherwise, twin-cam cylinder heads, four valves per cylinder and fuel injection all helped to produce 440bhp! This engine, when fitted to 'works' Capri RS3100s, helped to make that car the fastest in European touring-car racing in the mid-1970s.

American, Harley Copp, technical chief of the mid-1960s – and frankly, went against all the accepted standards of performance and packaging that other Fords had enjoyed for so long.

• The new car used a different type of coil spring/semi-trailing link rear suspension, which proved to be a great improvement on that of the Mark IV. Whereas the Mark IV

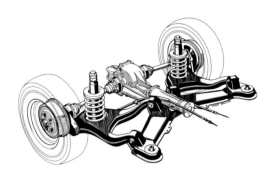

Although the Granada of 1972 retained independent rear suspension with semi-trailing arms and coil springs, there were major differences compared with the Zodiac Mark IV. Ford engineers had learned from the Zodiac, and were now ready to fit drive shafts with plunging C/V joints, which allowed them to have fixed-pivot semi-trailing arms. The Granada, incidentally, reverted to drum rear brakes.

had used a fixed-length drive shaft with an articulated semi-trailing arm joint to allow it to operate, the new Granada used a more conventional type of semi-trailing link layout with no articulated trailing link joint, but with drive shafts incorporating plunging shaft joints. Although it was considerably more expensive to build (the complex drive shafts made that certain), it was an altogether more efficient installation, and quite transformed the handling.

• The new Granada used a Cortina-Mark III-related rack-and-pinion steering system (much more accurate than the recirculating ball layout of old), and used drum brakes at the rear instead of discs; both of these chassis installations were completely different from the old Zephyr/Zodiac installations.

This, then, was the way that Ford saw its future for large cars. The Consul/Zephyr/Zodiac family had served the company well for more than twenty years, yet from 1972 it was laid neatly to rest. Many cars have survived, some of them in better-than-original condition, and are well thought of by old-Ford enthusiasts.

Appendix I
Consul and Zephyr Performance

Over the years − cars in this family were on sale for twenty-two years − not only did each model get more powerful and faster, but heavier too.

This summary chart, quoting figures extracted from *Autocar* and *Motor* road tests, shows just how things developed in a full generation:

Model	Year	Top speed (mph)	0–60mph (sec)	Typical fuel consumption (MPG)	Weight (unladen) lb
4-cylinder cars − Consuls and Zephyr V4s					
Consul I	1951	75	31.1	24–28	2,415
Consul II	1956	75	25.0	27–34	2,464
Zephyr 4 (Mark III)	1962	84	19.6	20–30	2,547
Zephyr V4 (Mark IV)	1968	95	17.7	25	2,844
6-cylinder cars − Zephyrs and Zodiacs					
Zephyr I	1951	81	21.1	23–25	2,697
Zephyr II (o/d)	1956	84	17.9	18–32	2,709
Zephyr 6 (automatic) ★★	1964	93	16.5	19	2,758
Zodiac III	1962	100	13.5	18–25	2,814
Zephyr 6 (Mark IV)	1966	96	14.6	17–25	2,896
Executive (Mark IV Zodiac-based)	1967	100	13.1	18	3,054

★★ Neither *Autocar* nor *Motor* ever published a road test of a Zephyr 6 fitted with manual transmission.

Appendix II
Production Figures

Calendar year	Production	Grand total

Dagenham-built cars

Mark I range

Consul

1951	35,667	
1952	36,292	
1953	48,225	
1954	49,893	
1955	55,226	
1956	6,178	231,481

Zephyr/Zodiac

1951	3,463	
1952	24,326	
1953	44,130	
1954	49,294	
1955	50,950	
1956	3,148	175,311

(Of this total, 22,634 were Zephyr/Zodiac, 152,677 were Zephyr Six)

Mark II range

Consul

1956	40,044	
1957	54,928	
1958	67,268	
1959	68,406	
1960	64,014	
1961	48,665	
1962	6,919	350,244

Calendar year	Production	Grand total

Zephyr/Zodiac

1956	38,255	
1957	49,346	
1958	53,156	
1959	64,086	
1960	56,015	
1961	35,621	
1962	4,938	301,417

(Of this total, approx. 80,000 were Zodiacs)

Mark III range

Annual figures by model are not available for 1966 calendar year, when 2,375 vehicles, all types, were produced.

Zephyr 4

1962	29,984	
1963	31,011	
1964	25,876	
1965	21,365	105,236

Zephyr V6

1962	24,725	
1963	32,533	
1964	29,365	
1965	20,743	107,006

Zodiac

1961	41	
1962	20,660	
1963	21,667	
1964	20,234	
1965	14,721	77,323

Mark IV range

Zephyr V4/Zephyr V6/Zodiac figures combined (accurate individual builds not available).

1965	3	
1966	49,773	
1967	18,406	
1968	24,744	
1969	19,828	
1970	18,925	
1971	16,758	148,347

(Production of each model was approximately: Zephyr V4 45,000, Zephyr V6 57,000, Zodiac/Executive 46,000)

Other assembly sources

Consul/Zephyr/Zodiac estate cars (Mark II)	5,643
Pick-up/utility (Mark II)	17,580
Australian station wagon (Mark II)	7,470

Appendix III
Race and Rally Successes

(Unless marked by ★★, all were by 'works' or 'works-sponsored' cars)

Year	Event	Model (First driver)	Success
1952	Tulip rally	Consul (K. Wharton)	1st
1953	Monte Carlo rally	Zephyr (M. Gatsonides)	1st
	Norwegian Viking rally	Zephyr (C. Johansson) ★★	1st
1954	RAC rally	Zephyr (T.C. Harrison)	1st Saloon Category
	Tulip rally	Consul (J.G. Reece)	Class 1st
		Zephyr (R.W. Phillips)	Class 1st
1955	RAC rally	Zephyr (T.C. Harrison)	Class 1st
	Tulip rally	Zephyr (T.C. Harrison)	Class 1st
	Coronation Safari	Zephyr (V. Preston)★★	1st
1956	French Alpine rally	Zephyr Mk II (T.C. Harrison)	Class 1st
1958	Monte Carlo rally	Zodiac Mk II (R. Nellerman) ★★	Class 1st
	RAC rally	Zephyr Mk II (D.G. Scott)	Class 1st
	East African Safari	Zephyr Mk II (A.T. Kopperud) ★★	Class 1st
	French Alpine rally	Zephyr Mk II (E. Harrison)	Class 1st
1959	East African Safari	Zephyr Mk II (D.G. Scott)	2nd Overall
		Zephyr Mk II (E. Harrison)	3rd Overall
	Tulip rally	Zephyr Mk II (P. Riley)	Class 1st
	French Alpine rally	Zephyr Mk II (P. Riley)	Class 1st
	RAC rally	Zephyr Mk II (G. Burgess)	1st
	BRSCC Saloon Car Championship	Zephyr Mk II (J. Uren)	1st
1960	Monte Carlo rally	Zodiac Mk II (L. Handley)	Class 1st
	East African Safari	Zephyr Mk II (V. Preston)	3rd Overall
1961	Monte Carlo rally	Zodiac Mk II (L. Handley)	Class 1st
	East African Safari	Zephyr Mk 2 (Mrs A. Hall)	3rd Overall
1962	East African Safari	Zodiac Mk III (G. Burgess)	Class 1st
	French Alpine rally	Zodiac Mk III (J. Vinatier)	Class 1st
1969	Three Cities rally	Zodiac Mk IV (R. Clark)	Class 1st

Index